Voices

of

Democracy

To

DAVID MATHEWS

*for the good years
and all I have learned
from him*

Voices
of
Democracy

by

BERNARD MURCHLAND

CONVERSATIONS WITH

Benjamin Barber	*William Connolly*
Jean Bethke Elshtain	*Elmer Johnson*
Daniel Kemmis	*Mark Kingwell*
Erazim Kohák	*Arthur Kroker*
Christopher Lasch	*Merab Mamardashvili*
Martin Matustik	*Daniel Yankelovich*

University of Notre Dame Press

Notre Dame, Indiana

Manufactured in the United States of America

The editor and publisher are grateful for permission to quote from W. H. Auden's "September 1, 1939," *W. H. Auden: Collected Poems*, edited by Edward Mendelson. Copyright © 1940 and renewed 1968 by W. H. Auden. Reprinted by permission of Random House, Inc.

Library of Congress Cataloging-in-Publication Data
Murchland, Bernard.
Voices of democracy / by Bernard Murchland.
p. cm.
Includes bibliographical references and index.
ISBN 0-268-04354-X (cloth)
1. Democracy. I. Title.
JC423.M82 2000
321.8—dc21
00-008863

∞ *The paper used in this publication meets the minimum requirements of the American National Standard for Information Sciences—Permanence of Paper for Printed Library Materials, ANSI Z39.48-1984*

Democracy is the name for what we cannot have yet cannot cease to want.

—John Dunn

When we cannot communicate our thoughts to one because of difference of language, all similarity of our common nature is of no avail to unite us in fellowship.
—Saint Augustine

*May I, composed like them
of Eros and dust,
Beleaguered by the same
Negation and despair,
Show an affirming flame.*

—W. H. Auden

We may think of the components of culture as voices, each the expression of a distinct condition and understanding of the world and a distinct idiom of human self-understanding.

—Michael Oakeshott

Contents

Acknowledgments

This kind of book cannot come to be without the collaboration of many people.

I want to acknowledge the support of the Kettering Foundation over a number of years. I also acknowledge several grants and leaves from Ohio Wesleyan University. Academic institutions, however grievous the problems that beset them, remain the great incubators of ideas in our society and the freest of our institutions.

I want to thank James Langford, Barbara Hanrahan, Ann Rice, and all those at the University of Notre Dame Press who encouraged and guided this project.

Rebecca Murchland provided invaluable editorial assistance.

My greatest debt of all is to my co-conversationalists for their generosity and insights and for their unfailing courtesy not only in the interviews themselves but as well in responding to my follow-up questions and commenting on the various drafts of these conversations which I submitted to them.

Most of these conversations were first published in *The Civic Arts Review*. "Making Democracy Strong" and "How the Public Learns the Public's Business" appeared in somewhat different form in my *Voices of America*. The interview with Merab Mamardashvili was first published as a Kettering Foundation occasional paper. They are reprinted with permission.

My thanks to all.

The Future of Democracy

We know now that democracy is a minimalist idea. It does not change human nature; it does not deliver happiness; it is not particularly good at solving endemic political problems.

The twentieth century has been a sobering reminder of democracy's limitations. The major democracies were often at war in a century marked by two world wars, the Korean War, the Vietnam War, all the little wars (many of which still rage), and above all, the long cold war. It has been a century dominated by gulags and killing fields, by death marches and final solutions, a century in which we have created the means of self-extermination and invented totalitarianism as a political creed. It still seems as though half the human race is bent upon destroying the other half.

Democracy survived the twentieth century, as Arthur Schlesinger Jr. has put it, "by the skin of its teeth." The unprecedented onslaughts of totalitarianism and human perversity nearly wiped it out.

The experience of the twentieth century lends support to the historical arguments against democracy. The first was powerfully articulated by Plato. And here we confront a great irony. Not only did the Greeks invent the first democracy, but Plato was himself a close associate of such defenders of the new democracy as Protagoras and especially Socrates, who argued that we find our natural fulfillment as participating citizens in the polis, the basis of who we authentically are. The exercise of citizenship educates us in the ways of those practices and excellences that make us truly human.

Plato didn't agree. His brief against democracy was that people are not equal, and even if they were equal they could not agree on a common course of civic action. It is fanciful, he said, to think that people really know what they want, that they can make rational judgments about justice, virtue and such matters, that they know what happiness is, or even that they really care much about politics. Politics is boring for most people. In short, the principle of ordering one's life is not to be found within individuals. Their true identity derives from allegiance to a civic order which they themselves are incapable of creating. So Plato's strategy was to devise an order that would relieve people of the burden of constantly deciding about political questions and arguing about their interests.

Plato's argument has proven devilishly resistant over the centuries. It was taken for granted throughout the Middle Ages. At the dawn of modernity, Thomas Hobbes offered another version of it. Like Plato, and indeed all political thinkers, Hobbes began with an assessment of human nature. Politics always follows ethics. Again like Plato, he thought humans to be frail and paltry creatures, with only intermittent glimpses of the truth of things, driven by self-interest and destined for a life that is, as he famously said, "solitary, nasty, poor, brutish, and short." To the question, What sort of government will work for so benighted a species? Hobbes answered: a great and fearsome sovereign, a great Leviathan, to impose laws and restraints. The weaker human nature, the stronger must be the political authority to threaten punishment and exact obedience.

This argument has been reprised in different forms in the twentieth century —by totalitarians of all stripes, by social engineers, by technophiles. All agree that democracy is unrealistic; it is based upon principles that are contrary both to human nature and to the nature of politics; it requires intellectual and moral capacities that the average citizen simply does not have. Early in the century sociologist Harry Elmer Barnes called for an intellectual aristocracy to control society. And Walter Lippmann said the citizen "lives in a world which he cannot see, does not understand, and is unable to direct." Citizens, he wrote in *Public Opinion*, are like a theatergoer who arrives in the middle of the third act and leaves before the last curtain. They have neither the capacity nor, for the most part, the desire to participate responsibly in public affairs.

Plato's argument was theoretical in nature, based on certain ideas about human nature and the political order. Another historical argument deals more with the practical antinomies of democracy, perhaps not so much an argument against democracy per se as an analysis of the difficulty of making it work in practice. Alexis de Tocqueville is the *locus classicus* here. Tocqueville feared that the demands of liberty and equality, the community and the individual, virtue and self-interest could not be reconciled. He worried a lot about the tyranny of public opinion, the natural tendency of democracy toward conformity, and the absolute sovereignty of the majority. "Despotism," he wrote, "appears to me peculiarly to be dreaded in democratic ages." And toward the end of his *Democracy in America*, he speaks plaintively of a kind of oppression unlike anything "which ever before existed in the world." He foresees "an innumerable multitude of men all equal and alike, incessantly endeavoring to procure the petty and paltry pleasures with which they glut their lives. Each of them, living apart, is a stranger to the fate of all the rest. His children and his private friends constitute to him the whole of mankind; as for the rest of his fellow citizens, he is close to them, but he sees them not; he touches them, but he feels them not; he exists but in himself and for himself alone; and if his kindred still remain to him, he may be said at any rate to have lost his country."

One could scarcely imagine a bleaker civic vision. What was Tocqueville forecasting—twentieth-century totalitarianism? The welfare state? Expressive individualism? Consumer culture? Mass society? America as it appears under corporate capitalism? Perhaps all of the above. The immediate point is that his analysis bears on the contradictory character of democracy. Tocqueville was not ready to sacrifice either equality or liberty. But he was never at ease with their contradictory character.

The passage of time has done nothing to mitigate this harsh existential side of democracy. In our time Isaiah Berlin has provided rich commentary on Tocqueville's analysis. In a September 1998 article in the *New Yorker*, Berlin was quoted by his biographer, Michael Ignatieff, as saying: "If, as I believe, the ends of men are many, and not all of them are in principle compatible with each other, then the possibility of conflict—and of tragedy—can never be wholly eliminated from human life." Berlin's famous distinction between negative and positive freedom casts Tocqueville's dilemma in a modern frame. Individuals should be left alone to pursue their own conception of the good life, consistent with the laws and the freedom of others.

Berlin was less optimistic than Tocqueville about democracy's prospects. While falling short of calling it conceptually incoherent, he was firm in his belief that democracy in no way relieves us of the burden of moral choice. And many of the choices are incommensurate. No amount of government intervention can change this; the Tocquevillian resort to citizen agency cannot change it; neither can easy appeals to virtue. What holds society together is not any kind of political or moral consensus but rather an ability to understand social life from different perspectives. In a radically pluralistic society, empathy becomes the great civic virtue. Canada is a dramatic case study, included at the end of this volume, of the incommensurability Berlin speaks of.

These historical arguments are strong and cannot be ignored. They account for the fact that democracy has not in the past been the political norm but rather the always at-risk exception and remains even today weakened by recurring crises of legitimacy. Yet it goes on. The arguments against it have not prevailed. Each year Freedom House publishes pie charts showing the new countries that have entered the democratic camp, a practice somewhat reminiscent of coloring the map red in the days of the British Empire. All the red parts were ours. In the past twenty years some thirty new democratic countries have emerged, so many new "red" patches on the global map. Freedom House's most recent study reports that eighty-eight countries, or 46 percent of the world's total are now democratic, defined as "maintaining a high degree of political and economic freedom and respect for basic civil liberties." This is the highest total in the twenty-six years these surveys have been conducted. Another fifty-three countries are ranked as "partly free." Fifty nations are considered not free. In terms of population, some four billion people live in free or partly free countries against two billion who do not. Democracy is clearly in ascent around the globe. Francis Fukuyama went so far as to claim, with Hegel-like assurance, that history has come home to roost in the arms of liberal democracy. Granted that Fukuyama may exaggerate, and notwithstanding that many of the new democracies are fragile shoots, democracy remains the political regime of choice nearly everywhere in the world. This is a truly amazing turn of events.

So there is no denying democracy's vitality and staying power. What are the reasons for its appeal? What are the roots of its endurance? How strong are its prospects? To find answers to such questions I undertook the conversations recorded in this book. I wanted to find out what others thought, the better to clarify my own thinking. Learning is an essentially dialogic activity.

What have I learned from these conversations?

To begin with, I've learned that one source of democracy's strength is its embrace of the very ambiguity, contradiction, and conflict decried by its critics. Plato feared chaos; democracy has proved that it can tolerate a large measure of chaos. Tocqueville strove to iron out the tensions within democracy; democracy accepts those tensions. Berlin stresses the uncertainty of moral choice; democracy lives with that uncertainty. Unlike other political theories that would transform human nature to some ideal mold, democracy accepts a warts-and-all humanity. This pessimistic anthropology is one of democracy's great strengths. It accepts that self-interest and passion are the mainsprings of human action; that tragedy and failure go with the territory;

that the engine of history is the conflict of wills. The raw materials of humanity are not very promising, but democracy takes them for what they are and in this realism finds a source of creativity. Democracy, in short, reflects the bent lines of humanity better than other forms of government do.

These conversations also reveal an interesting interplay between theory and practice. A body of opinion has always existed that would separate the two. Someone like Michael Walzer, for example, thinks that philosophy and politics are two quite different realms of discourse: the former cannot illuminate the latter, and the latter cannot enrich the former. I am hearing more Socratic voices in this book, the Socrates of the early dialogues who held up philosophical dialogue as a model of how political life should function. The peculiar excellence he exhorted his fellow Athenians to strive for was the habit of reflection as the guide to right action. His dramatic claim that he was wise in the sense that he knew nothing has a political translation: because in a democracy there are no absolute truths, no final answers, democratic truth must be forged through deliberation, through people's ability to think and act together. Moreover, in a democracy thinking and doing occur simultaneously, the restless motion from thought to action and back again endlessly. The unexamined life is not a democratic life.

The appeal of democracy as an idea struck me with force in my conversations with those who lived behind the iron curtain. It was touching to hear Martin Matustik speak of reading Kierkegaard and the Czech philosopher Jan Patočka even as he was on the run from the Secret Police; how their philosophies inspired the Velvet Revolution; and how their existential message provides a critical perspective on all political theories. In those circumstances one literally drew one's daily breath from ideas.

Or consider Merab Mamardashvili, in the dark days of the Soviet oppression. He drew hope from Plato and Kant and even Marx. "It is a great irony," Mamardashvili told me, "that Marx, who was a true philosopher of the Enlightenment, should have become the patron saint of one of the darkest societies in human history." From these sources Mamardashvili built a conviction of the active power of intelligence to shape reality, to distinguish between illusion and reality and to carefully balance the ideal and real aspects of experience. Above all, he drew hope from these intellectual sources for a better day. He was among that small band of rebel spirits who keep their thinking alive even though practice was prohibited.

Democracy in those dark times was a powerfully imaginative idea, a vision as it has always been, what Erazim Kohák calls an "audacious" vision. It is our task today, Kohák told me, "to rethink what democracy means, to rediscover all that was generous, all that was noble, all that was idealistic. Then democracy might have a future. Otherwise, I am not sure that it will and I am not sure that it should."

And, to be sure, the dialectic runs to the other way as well—from practice to theory. The practioners I interviewed for this book all acknowledge their debt to ideas. Thus Daniel Yankelovich working as a pollster has developed some sophisticated theories about public opinion, international relations, instrumental thinking, the role of elites in a democracy, even a definition of reality. When I queried him about his definition of reality, he answered by tracing the main outlines of philosophical thought in the twentieth century. No small problem with our democracy is that our dominant theories are at odds with our practice. Yankelovich is particularly indebted to thinkers like John Dewey, Hannah Arendt, and Max Weber. He was, for example, influenced by Weber's critique of instrumental rationality, the "master key" of modern societies.

So too, Dan Kemmis as a lawyer, mayor, and legislator keeps closely attuned to democracy's theoretical roots. Or Elmer Johnson, a citizen activist with long experience in the business community, who has been strongly influenced by such diverse works as Edmund Burke's *Reflections on the French Revolution* and John Rawls's *Theory of Justice*. From time to time he offers a rigorous course in ethics that covers all the major thinkers in that tradition. One of Johnson's central concerns is to develop a fiduciary ethic which stresses justice and the ideal of a common good as a counter to the excesses of capitalism.

The moral of the story here is that citizens in a democracy have to think about what they are doing, about the ideas that frame their practices. Above all, they must have such ideas. Otherwise, they will remain dependent on those who do. Our world is filled with a knowledge class whose expertise does not relate well to the experiences of ordinary citizens. This is a problem in democracy that can be solved, as many of my interlocutors have shown, only by establishing a more workable relationship between theory and practice.

A third reason for democracy's appeal is the by now indissoluble bond with the market economy. It may be too much to claim that the role of democracy is to make the world safe for capitalism or that economic freedoms are the basis of political freedoms. But earlier theorists such as Adam Smith and David Hume did say something quite close to that. For them the market determined natural liberties. And today it is axiomatic for Americans to think, in the words of George Will, that "as America becomes rich it also becomes freer and more egalitarian." This is not just a conservative opinion. It is mainstream thinking. College freshmen hold it as an article of faith.

So the claim that economics precedes politics, that economic freedoms bring political freedoms, has strong historical credentials. Democracy seems fated to swim like a companion fish by the side of capitalism. After all, the origins of democracy in Greece were rooted in economic reforms. And it is sobering to recall that two of the world's greatest democracies were based on a slave economy. What made democracy viable as it emerged at the dawn of the modern age was not so much the idea of democracy, which after all had been around for a long time, as the new economic and social factors that made it workable. Thinkers began to see that the market could deliver on what democracy only promised. It afforded opportunities for choice, conditions of equality and empowerment, greater well being, and so forth, that democracy as an idea could not. For good empirical reasons, the market economy came to be thought of as the practice of which democracy was the theory.

This point was dramatically brought home by a story a Hungarian friend told me in 1990. It is the story of the Gorenje freezer, and it goes like this. Before the 1950s people cooled their food with huge blocks of ice that were sold from horse drawn carts. The first refrigerators were made in the Soviet Union and appeared on the Hungarian market in the early 1960s. One effect of this new technology was to liberate women for jobs outside the home. At the time Hungary had the largest female work force outside Finland, and this in turn explained the expanding economy. In those years, Hungary enjoyed the beginning of what we remember as Goulash Communism. In the 1980s a new challenge arose in the form of the Gorenje freezer which was manufactured in Yugoslavia. Whereas the icebox limited meal planning to hours and the refrigerator to days, the freezer (which came equipped with a microwave oven) made kitchen planning possible for months in advance.

Hungarians were not slow to see the possibilities. Over the long holiday weekend commemorating the seventy-first anniversary of the Great Socialist October Revolution, more than 100,000 Hungarians went on a shopping spree to Vienna. My friend spent part of that weekend at the Austrian-Hungarian border observing a line of cars ten miles long winding slowly through the checkpoint. Every third or fourth car had a Gorenje freezer in it.

This freezer enthusiasm signaled important changes in how Hungarians regarded Communist Party power, the quality of life, and issues of legitimacy and citizenship. The freezer packed with frozen pork became a metaphor for a better way of life and a new relationship between the state and the people. What did the new way of life symbolized by the freezer have to do with semi-totalitarian taboos and an increasingly irrelevant paternalism? Why couldn't people make their own choices? "People wanted to know," my friend told me, "why they had to go to Vienna for those damn freezers."

Was the fall of communism due primarily to the appeal of democracy or the lure of the market economy? Clearly both. In what admixture? It is impossible to say. The alliance between democracy and the market economy is strong. But it is also highly problematic. The market may turn out to be democracy's nemesis.

I hear in the conversations in this book two further arguments for democracy, both of which go well beyond economic parameters. One might be called the ecological argument, although none of my interlocutors used precisely that terminology. Theories of democracy as they developed in the Enlightenment period were heavily influenced by modern science. As such they tended to be somewhat abstract, mechanistic and procedural—what came to be known as the liberal model of democracy. The body politic was conflated with the study of nature. It was assumed that human behavior could be understood like any other body in motion. Arthur Lovejoy has called this the method of counterpoise by which desired results are achieved in the political order by balancing forces and interests against one another.

This method was based on the science of celestial mechanics according to which the planets were held in their orbits by a balance of centripetal and centrifugal forces, either of which operating independently would cause the planets to disintegrate. Political theorists adopted a similar model and sought to accomplish social goals by artfully balancing competing egoisms. The two premises underlying the political method of counterpoise, Lovejoy states, are that "men never act from disinterest and rational motives, but that it is possible, nonetheless, to fashion a good whole, a happy and harmonious state, by skillfully mixing and counterbalancing these refractory and separately antagonistic parts." Modern science favored a mechanistic view of nature, put together like a clock. Political theory in its image viewed society in similar terms. Thus we came to use language like the machinery of government, political machines, a machine that would run by itself, the balance of powers, the competition for votes, power politics, and the like. As one commentator put it: "The framers of the Constitution were great clock makers in the science of statecraft, and they did, with admirable ingenuity, put together an intricate machine, which promised to run indefinitely, and tell the time of the centuries."

The ecological model of politics is quite different, a more holistic model which shifts the emphasis from mechanism to organism. It owes a lot to the evolutionary perspective introduced by Darwin and reflected in contemporary science's new self-understanding. It owes something to our renewed interest in ecological studies as well as what philosophers call the *Lebenswelt*, the life world of our lived experience. Experience is the key, what John Dewey called the "intercourse of a living being with its physical and social environment."

Two basic features of the ecological model are a fundamental connaturality between the human and natural and, second, a sense of nature as a self-governing community of diversity, conflict and harmony. We can think of the biosphere itself as a kind of democracy which teaches us important lessons about unity in diversity, harmony out of conflict, creativity, even about the democratic virtues of participation and deliberation. Above all, it teaches the lesson of connectedness, that democracy like nature has a metabolic mode of existence, engaged in a continuous exchange with all of its parts.

Dan Kemmis's bioregionalism is one example of the ecological perspective brought to bear on our thinking about democracy. He defines bioregionalism as "the philosophy of organic relationships" and speaks of agriculture as a metaphor "for nurturing and caring, for gathering disparate parts together into functional wholes." People and their physical spaces cannot be separated; a sense of place is essential to social health. Political thinking must take into account the ways we can appropriately inhabit our environment.

Another example of how the ecological model is influencing our thinking about democracy can be found in our renewed interest in civil society, social capital, civil investing, the public sphere, community, citizen empowerment, public forums, deliberative democracy, multiculturalism, and like topics which are much talked about in this book. On the surface this may look like politics as usual, different interest groups jockeying for their piece of the pie. But something deeper is going on. The language of participation is symbolic of multiple efforts in modern democracies to counter atomic individualism, narrow self-interest, and citizen passivity, values that predominate in the mechanistic model, with a more inclusive and interactive politics. It expands our vision of democratic possibilities and increases our capacity to build a public world. These ideas come together in the civil renewal movement which is the (largely untold) political success story of our time.

A final argument for democracy I hear in these pages is what might be called the ethical model. From an empirical point of view, democracy is always troubling, always falling away from its own ideals. But we would err to focus too narrowly on the empirical side of democracy. It has other meanings and there are other ways of thinking about it. We might reflect, for example, on how it functions powerfully as a template of our narrative selves. Democracy is the story that we find most satisfying to tell ourselves because it gives a certain coherence to our social experience and because it articulates certain hopes we have for the future.

When we move behind democracy as an empirical reality to discover how it works as what some thinkers call a "signifying practice" or a "performative ideal" then we rise to a new plateau of understanding. We think then of democracy as a vision, an ideal, a transcendent goal that can motivate mighty deeds. Democracy is not a pre-given but constantly evolves out of the ground of its past and against the horizon of its possibilities. Viewed thus, democracy is the only thing we have that resembles a meta-narrative, an ideal that conceptualizes the aspirations of large numbers of people. As such democracy is akin to a belief system and shares this with religion: both require a deep level of commitment, both introduce a dimension of transcendence into our thinking that carries us beyond the confines of the given.

Alexis de Tocqueville famously said that democracy "cannot be maintained without certain conditions of intelligence, of private morality, and of religious belief." It is unlikely that we will be able to regenerate our political experience without reference to the ethico-religious ideas of evil, hope, and love. William Connolly is one who blends such ideas into his thinking about democracy. Thus he can speak of religion as "a sense of reverence and gratitude for the essential ambiguity of things and the abundance of life over the different kinds of identity we construct out of it." He can appropriate Augustine to talk of difference and otherness, of belief and suffering, of hope and contingency. His is a very modern voice richly infused with voices from the past.

And hear Jean Bethke Elshtain on the close relationship between democracy and its ethico-religious roots. She tells us: "As an empirical matter democracy arose out of the matrix of Judeo-Christian morality. Ideas of equality, freedom, rights, the dignity of the human person, and covenanted relationships that issue into membership spring rather directly from that tradition. Democracy cannot be sustained without institutions of moral formation of which religions are preeminent." These institutions are our principal ballast against the winds of materialism that are blowing strongly through our culture, a hope against what Elshtain calls "econometrics and the marketization of identity, the fragmentation of personality into ever finer slivers of identity."

One of democracy's purposes is to clear spaces in which the spirit may flourish.

Delaware, Ohio
January 2000

PART ONE

The Anatomy of Civil Society

Headnotes

Benjamin Barber holds an academic chair at Rutgers University but he is also a public intellectual and activist. His leading premise is that democracy is an artifact, a human creation. The question then becomes: What must we do to make a viable and beautiful creation? To be sure, none of the interlocutors in Part I are strangers to ideas. They all advocate a theoretical sophistication. For example, Barber invites us to consider carefully the philosophical underpinnings of democracy in liberalism, in history, in modern thought. But for him the final emphasis falls on the pragmatic possibilities of democracy: on the values of participation, building community, the potential of technology to promote democracy, education, equality and justice, and increasingly on the nature of civil society.

In his own words: "Democracy is not a cognitive system concerned with what we know and how we know it but rather a system of conduct concerned with what we will do together and how we agree on what we will do. Democracy is practical not speculative; it is about action not truth. If we had certain knowledge about the ideal forms of human association, we wouldn't need democracy. Democracy begins where certainty ends. The political question is always: What do we do when we don't know what to do?"

Daniel Yankelovich in one sense steals the march on other voices in this collection: He has a proven formula for making democracy work better. As an expert in public opinion formation, he came early to see that unless opinion matures into judgment, the public will remain mired in confusion, wishful thinking, and error. So the question for him became: By what means does the public come to mature judgments about public issues? The answer to this question, he thinks, is vital to the functioning of a modern democracy.

Yankelovich's well-known formula comprises three stages. In the first, the public becomes aware of the problem through various techniques of consciousness raising; the second is the phase of working through, facing the hard choices and costs inevitable in reaching sound policy; and the third stage is resolution and political compromise. Yankelovich illustrates the deliberative process with the health care issue. Americans, he says, are aware of all kinds of problems in the health care system. They have many opinions and can be expected to emote quite eloquently on talk shows and in focus groups. But they have not yet begun to face realistically the hard choices that need to be made to change policy. They are far from having worked through the issue. This is the hard part, Yankelovich says. "It requires getting in touch with one's deepest values and coming to the realization that our conflicts are at bottom conflicts of value. And people naturally resist having to compromise or abandon cherished values." As a consequence, no facet of the health care issue has reached the stage of resolution.

The same is true of a goodly number of other public issues. Yankelovich sees a large work of education ahead of us—in the universities, in the media, in government. In short, we must rethink our public philosophy.

Daniel Kemmis is a political practitioner par excellence. As a lawyer, legislator, and mayor, he has followed the call of Jefferson for a nation of citizens deeply involved in public life. He believes that politics "is a transforming work. Only through the medium of politics can our highest potential as human beings be reflected." For Kemmis politics takes place at two levels: that of the individual committed to a vital sense of citizenship and at the level of the body politic with a renewed understanding of the polis. People and place are the two constituent parts of what it means to be a working democracy, people and place brought together in an organic relationship which he calls bioregionalism.

Kemmis has a lot to say about how our cities can be made better "units of inhabitation"; about developing public spaces ("politics is about space as much as people," he says); about corrosive individualism and an intrusive regulatory bureaucracy as enemies of democracy; about empowering citizens. And he establishes a novel relationship between politics and spirituality. "If we are serious about reclaiming politics," he says, "we must give up the bankrupt delusion that a humanly engaging politics can be created where wholeness, presence, or grace are strangers."

Making Democracy Strong

Benjamin Barber is something of a rarity on the American scene: a liberally educated academic. He is professor of political philosophy at Rutgers University where he also directs the Walt Whitman Center for the Culture and Politics of Democracy. He is the author of a number of scholarly books (including the much-discussed *Strong Democracy*), a published novelist, an accomplished musician, a director of off-Broadway plays, a world traveler, a wine connoisseur, and a popular lecturer. Not since Marshall McLuhan has an academic had a foot so firmly planted in the public world. I have for the past dozen years or so been carrying on a dialogue with Barber about the nature of democracy. We first met on a sunny autumn day in Minnesota where we were both attending a conference. I was working on a book commemorating the bicentennial of the Constitution at the time and began the conversation by asking Barber how he would diagnose the problem in American society at that juncture of our history. He said he thought of our democracy as a long distance runner with a heart condition.

"On the outside we are running stronger than ever and faster than ever," he went on to explain. "But on the inside we are wearing down and becoming much more vulnerable. We need attention. I sometimes think of our democracy as a baby. Not so much that it is young, but in the sense that it can take more of a beating than you think it can. Babies look frail, but they are tough little critters. American democracy, from that point of view, is wonderfully resilient. Think of all that we have been through in our history. So we are strong. But like a baby we are vulnerable. I would be a lot happier if the American people were more aware of the vulnerability and the fragility of their democracy."

This assessment indicated to me that Barber didn't think democracy was an inevitable development in history.

"Oh no," he said. "Quite the contrary. The inevitability of tyranny is more likely the case. Democracy is such a fragile and rare form of human organization. If we look at history, or at the world today, we see that there has never been much democracy anywhere. It is not a natural state."

"Is it worth all the trouble?" I asked.

"I have always believed that the best things about human life are artificial, in the sense that we create them. Democracy is not natural; it is an artifact. Like works of art, it is created. Despite the long tradition of naturalism and romanticism, the best things are not natural but man-made. So we must think of the state as a work of art. Liberty is a work of art. We are not free by nature. Natural things have their own rhythms; they live and die according to their own laws. Artificial things have to be tended."

"So you wouldn't agree with Rousseau, who said we are born free and enchained by society?"

"No. It's the other way around. We are born in chains and whatever freedom we are able to achieve is the result of the society we build."

"What prescription do you offer for attending to our democracy?"

"The only thing to do is make an ailing democracy healthier, a weak democracy stronger. The thrust of my writings, and especially in *Strong Democracy*, is to suggest to the American public that our democracy is a thin and frail shadow of what it might be. I want to say that some of the responsibility for that thinness lies in the philosophy that underlies our American system."

"What is that philosophy?"

"It is the philosophy of liberalism."

"How are you understanding that word?"

"Good question—because liberalism can mean many things, and there is much confusion about it today. We tend to think of a liberal as someone to the left on the political spectrum. I mean liberalism in its classic sense as a philosophy that puts the individual first—conceives of government as an instrument to serve these ends. The English philosopher John Locke was a major proponent of the philosophy, and it had an enormous influence on the founders of our country."

"It sounds like a good philosophy to me," I said.

"It is a good philosophy. But it is a limited philosophy. I contend that it seriously constricts the possibilities of democracy. Please understand that I am not attacking liberalism per se, nor denying its many virtues. What I am saying is that it is an inadequate basis for a strong democracy."

"How would the fuller democracy you urge differ from our current democracy?" I asked.

"It would rely much more heavily on citizen participation. A fuller democracy does not mean participation of all the citizens all the time in all forms of public life. But it has to mean government by all of the people some of the time, in at least some public matters, for it really to count. From this perspective, voting, which we take to be the chief symbol and often the last action of democracy, is actually in many ways the least important of our public activities. Most people seem to think democracy means voting, free elections, and the like, but that is only the starting point, not the terminal point."

"Are you trying to promote a lost democracy, or are you promoting an ideal you think hasn't yet existed?"

"That's a difficult question. Historians are always reminding me that the democracy I appeal to has never had a firm existence in the American tradition. I respond by saying that tradition is not one thing. It is rich and complex. There is a Madisonian tradition with a certain distrust of the public and Jeffersonian tradition which trusts and encourages the public to engage in civic action. I readily admit that the Founders were highly suspicious of democracy and built in all kinds of hedges. On the other hand, they believed deeply in the democratic principle, in the sovereignty of the people. I put it this way: although Jeffersonian democracy may not have the best historical credentials, it nonetheless is rooted in a powerful political rhetoric that has a historical base in Andrew Jackson, populism, and the progressive movement. That suggests to me it does have a real life in the American polity which can be called upon. So I don't see myself as simply inventing a utopian dream or trying to import from classical Greece or Rousseau or whomsoever a model of democracy that would be foreign to our experience."

"Speaking of Rousseau," I said, "he argued that democracies could only be small. The Founders, on the other hand, were trying to devise a democracy for a large, pluralistic, and commercial republic. It still seems a reasonable position to say that the kind of democracy you advocate has never had national prominence or real institutional footing in this country, even though it often does exist at the microlevel, in those many little republics and voluntary associations that Alexis de Tocqueville waxed eloquent about."

"You raise two questions: the historical question and the possibility question. Historically, you are largely right. It is easier to identify strong democracy at the local level. Tocqueville said the spirit of liberty in America was at the local level. The representative system was meant to rescue democracy from oblivion at the national level by permitting some form of democratic capability and also protecting us from the abuses of majoritarian tyranny. So I agree that strong democracy was most conspicuous at the local level and was weaker at the national level. One of the problems I am dealing with is whether or not modern technology and modern institutions might not facilitate a stronger democracy at the national level than was possible in a earlier age. One of the points Rousseau made was that constitutions have to be appropriate to the age. Our times have changed. Technology crosses time and space and makes possible national forums of participation. Traditionally we have looked upon politics as a spectator sport. Now the interactive possibilities of technology are considerable."

I then raised a question about the earlier distinction between the Madisonian and the Jeffersonian: "It is, after all, a distinction within a common frame of values. Both men bought into the philosophy of liberalism. So the distinction between Madison and Jefferson can't be a distinction between liberalism and democracy."

"Fair enough. Nor is that a distinction I want to invent. I don't want to argue that the strengthening of democracy requires the destruction of liberalism."

"That isn't clear from what you have been saying," I noted. "Nor is it always clear in your writings."

"I know. There is some rhetorical significance to that. Mark Twain once said that the best way to get attention is to start a fight. It's sometimes useful to overstate a case. But it isn't rhetorical. Despite the fact that I cherish the values that are associated with our liberal tradition, I am aware that there are real tensions between liberal values and democratic values. In fact they often conflict. To resolve those contradictions doesn't mean we have to destroy one side or the other. We may not have to live with the contradictions. But we do have to be aware that liberal values pushed to their extremes have a tendency to undermine public and democratic values."

"Because liberalism as you define it stresses individualism?"

"Yes. Privacy rights and property rights, which are classical liberal values, when pushed hard come up square against the democratic values of equality, participation, and community. I don't think these are contradictions that can be wished away or deviated from with ameliorative strategies. I want to look at these contradictions as part of the reality of America."

"Suppose you had a choice: liberal values or democratic values—take your pick," I proposed.

"The choice is not realistic, since in America we have always had both. I suppose that if the Bill of Rights were threatened, or if we lived in a society where privacy had disappeared and individuals were defined exclusively in terms of the communities to which they belonged, I might join the American Civil Liberties Union and say that we had better make the Bill of Rights our chief fight. In that narrow context I would have to choose liberal values because they are the basis of democratic values. But my sense is that, historically and politically, it is not rights and liberty and individualism that are seriously at risk—although they are always at risk to some extent; what now are at risk are the values of social justice, equality, participation, and community. Those are the values that need shoring up. That doesn't mean so much sacrificing liberal values as working out some compromises."

"Why do you think we as a nation resist these democratic values?"

"Because an active communitarianism does encroach upon our privacy, upon our right to do as we choose; it makes demands that in a wholly privatized society don't get made on us."

"One suspects that there is also a fear that too much emphasis on community and equality can lead to an oppressive socialism or, in the worst of cases, totalitarianism. After all, totalitarian states emphasize the same democratic values you do," I observed.

"There is a danger. But given our long liberal tradition I should think America is the least likely place for that to happen. On the contrary, we can afford a great deal more community and democracy than we have."

"I think you have agreed that liberalism is the condition of democracy?"

"Yes, if you agree in turn that democracy is the condition of liberalism. I would want to say that the values of liberalism were originally the product of a democratic civic culture. They don't have an independent prior existence."

"The received wisdom is that historically the liberal tradition preceded democracy," I said.

"That isn't true. Historically, monarchy preceded both of them. It was the democratization of monarchical regimes with the emergence of parliaments (think of the Magna Carta) that generated liberal values. Historically monarchies, dictatorships, and tyrannies come first, democratization comes second, and liberalism comes third, but then serves as a basis for further democratization."

"That's a clear way of putting it," I said. "So you would say that for someone like John Locke in the seventeenth century, liberalism was possible only because there was a prior sentiment of democracy for him to build on."

"Exactly. Locke can be seen as a democratic radical. I don't think Locke could have developed his liberalism had he not been deeply imbued with democratic values. That is another way of making my point that democratic values legitimize liberal values. It's easy to see that liberal values have no sanctity in a tyranny or a monarchy. The only states that have been able to sustain liberal values are democratic states. That is no accident."

"Then why didn't John Locke talk like Benjamin Barber?" I asked.

"Because Locke was up against a monarchical regime, and what had to be emphasized were liberation values. I work against a liberal tradition and want to emphasize democratic values. The historical circumstances in Locke's time demanded the logic and rhetoric of liberty. Our need today is not for emancipation so much as for forms of participatory communities that give liberty some substance and overcome the pathologies of alienation and individualism to which the value of liberty, pushed far enough, can lead—and indeed does lead—in twentieth-century America."

I asked Barber how he would define democracy. He cautioned me that we ought not be too theoretical when we talk about democracy.

"To be sure, we have to have some knowledge of concepts like power, rights, and justice. But democracy is not a cognitive system concerned with what we know and how we know it but rather a system of conduct concerned with what we will do together and how we agree on what we will do. Democracy is practical not speculative; it is about action not truth. If we had certain knowledge about the ideal forms of human association we wouldn't need democracy. Democracy begins where certainty ends. The political question is always: What do we do when we don't know what to do? It is the tyranny of an excessively theoretical approach to transform a discussion of politics into a discussion of knowledge."

I accepted Barber's caveat but still pressed for a definition of democracy.

"I can give you a political definition but not a philosophical one."

"That will do."

"Politically we may define democracy as a regime / culture / form of social or civil association where we make decisions, choose common conduct, and create or express common values in the practical domain of our lives in an ever-changing context of conflict of interests and competition for power—a setting, moreover, where there is no agreement on prior goods or certain knowledge about justice or right and where we must proceed on the premise of the basic equality both of interests and of the interested."

Because of his radically pragmatic concept of democracy, much of Barber's recent work has been an attempt to revitalize the notion of civil society as the taproot of civic life. "Americans are caught in a squeeze today," he explains, "big government on the one hand and big business on the other. Although it is ultimately accountable to the American people, the government is seen as an almost foreign body: a threatening sphere of quasi-professional politicians and bureaucratic managers who have lost much of their authority as authentic voices for the public they supposedly represent. On the other hand, the private sector, representing the market, and constituted by private individuals and corporations, speaks for the public only inasmuch as it aggregates the voices of individuals and companies—private prejudices and special interests given a 'public' status they do nothing to earn. Not only is the public left voiceless and homeless, but those in government who still try in good faith to receive counsel from the now phantom public don't really know where to turn since so-called public opinion polls canvass private prejudice while special interests represent themselves and only themselves. Politicians turn into 'professionals' out of touch with their constituencies, while citizens are reduced to whining antagonists of the men and women they elect to office or clients of government services they readily consume without being willing to pay for it."

Barber refers to this as a two-celled model of government. What he proposes is a three-celled model with civil society the middle term between the two monopolies of state and corporation.

"Civil society, or civic space, occupies the middle ground between government and the private sector. It shares with government a sense of publicity and a regard for the general good and the commonweal; but unlike government it makes no claims to exercising a monopoly on legitimate coercion. Rather, it is a voluntary and in this sense private realm devoted to public goods. It shares with the private sector the gift of liberty, it is voluntary and is constituted by freely associated individuals and groups; but unlike the private sector, it aims at common ground and consensual (that is, integrative and collaborative) modes of action. Civil society is thus public without being coercive, voluntary without being privatized. It is in this domain that such traditional civic institutions as foundations, schools, churches, public interest, and other voluntary civic associations properly belong. The media too, where they take their public responsibilities seriously, are part of civil society.

"Democracy is precisely that form of government in which not politicians and bureaucrats but an empowered people use legitimate force to put flesh on the bones of their liberties; and in which liberty carries with it the obligations of social responsibility and citizenship as well as the rights of legal persons. It is that form of government in which rights and responsibilities are two sides of a single civic identity that belongs neither to state bureaucrats nor private consumers but to citizens alone. Civil society is the domain of citizens: a mediating domain between private markets and big government. Interposed between the state and the market it can contain an obtrusive government without ceding public goods to the private sphere, while at the same time it can dissipate the atmospherics of solitariness and greed that surround markets without suffocating in an energetic big government's exhaust fumes. Both government and the private sector can be humbled a little by a growing civil society that absorbs some of the public aspirations of government, without casting off its liberal character as a non-coercive association of equals."

I said that by this criterion we seem to have a pretty vibrant civic life. Foundations, churches, public interest groups, schools, and other civic and voluntary associations abound in the land.

When I put the question to him Barber answered with a story: "Awhile back I gave a lecture on citizenship and civil society. Afterwards a lady raised her hand and said: 'You shame me sir! You are so right. Being a citizen in civil society is vitally important. But I have to tell you, what with my chairing the church bazaar committee, my service at the hospital, my assignment on PTA, and now I've been elected head of my block association, I just don't have time to be a citizen.'"

I thought the story reflected the ambiguity and confusion people feel about their civic identity.

"Precisely," Barber said. "People occupy civic space all the time. But they don't know it. They think they are acting privately when in fact they are acting publicly. So language is important. What we call things counts. Part of our task is a reconceptualizing and a repositioning of activities and institutions already in place. We need to understand our civic engagements not as private activities, but as nongovernmental public activities, and we need to call the spaces we share for purposes other than shopping or voting *civil society.* When the free space that is civil society goes unrecognized, we begin to treat the activity that takes place within it as private activity that is on a moral par with the most selfish forms of commerce. This is how associations concerned about the good of all people—for example, labor unions and environmental organizations—lost their identity as public interest groups and reemerged as special interests whose aims are indistinguishable from those of the for-profit corporations with which they compete."

When we understand this, Barber believes, civil society will create a genuine public force. "With the notion of civil society as a mediating space between government and private sectors theoretically reestablished, we can raise in a concrete fashion the practical question of how to secure a genuinely public voice in American political debate. For, quite simply, the public voice is nothing other than the voice of civil society."

I asked Barber how we could recognize a genuine public voice. He noted the following characteristics: commonality, deliberation, inclusiveness, listening, lateral communication, imagination, empowerment, and provisionality.

"Does any one of these have priority?"

Barber said if he had to choose one it would probably be deliberation. That is so important to the democratic process.

"The public voice is deliberative, which means it is critically reflective as well as self-reflective; it must be able to withstand reiteration, critical cross-examination, and the test of time—which guarantees a certain distance and dispassion. Like all deliberative voices, the public voice is dialectical: it transcends contraries without surrendering their distinctiveness (just as a good marriage between strong individual partners makes them one without losing their two-ness)."

"Let's go back to the Constitution. Is it a liberal document or a democratic document?" I asked.

"It is mostly a liberal document which makes a fuller democracy possible."

"What do you think the principal shortcoming of the Constitution is?" I asked.

"It engenders by its very nature a sense of public purposelessness. As a document of compromise it was intended to do that as a way of circumventing any particular purpose. I think of America as a Noah's ark in which everything comes in twos—a two-house Congress, a two-seat-per-state Senate, a two-sided trial system, a two-party system, et cetera. That of course was intentional and for good reasons. But it doesn't favor the values of a strong democracy. And however well it might have worked historically, we have to seriously reexamine our constitutional system today. What was a source of strength in the beginning has in many ways become a cause of faction and weakness in today's circumstances—many of which were not and could not have been anticipated by the Framers. Three examples illustrate my point. At its founding America faced a future of bounty and seemingly infinite resources; it no longer does. It was an insular nation that had little truck with foreign nations; it no longer is. It was largely non-urban and that, of course, is no longer the case. Scarcity of resources, globalism, and urbanization, to take only these three examples, have drastically altered the nature of our problems and, more importantly, the nature of any solution to them."

"Are you calling for changes in the Constitution?"

"Less constitutional changes than institutional changes. And these suppose more a change in our attitudes than a change in the Constitution itself. The original Constitution was a compromised response to conditions that existed then. Today we must compromise the compromises and find a way to adapt the republic to new conditions of finitude, boundaries, and interdependence."

"What would you say is the Constitution's principal strength?"

"One of the great things about the Constitution is that it not only strikes a balance, but it leaves a great deal of room for moving the balance around. It never gets too specific. If you look at, say, the Weimar Constitution written after World War I, it specifies everything right down to traffic laws. You know that will break. The American Constitution is in the best tradition of *res publica* or a *politeia,* which is the Greek word for a constitution: it offers a set of fundamental principles which guide public life, but it doesn't give much detail. It leaves a lot of the responsibility for carrying it out to us. That means that we can lose our democracy. But it also means that we can make democracy a lot stronger within the framework of the Constitution. It's an extraordinarily flexible document which depends heavily on the civic virtue of the people. To make the Constitution work requires a people with civic virtue. But that concept doesn't have much resonance with the American public today. Part of revitalizing democracy means rehabilitating that term, reintroducing the vocabulary of civic virtue. Citizens in this perspective become something more than bearers of private interest."

I was curious about the role of education in building a strong civic society.

"I think we have missed the boat on education. To educate for civic virtue in any vital sense would require a revamping of the whole system," Barber said.

"Let's imagine you had a charter to revamp our system. How would you proceed?"

"That's a dream."

"Dream on."

"Well, let's start with where we are. There are two models of the university being purveyed today to address the current crisis in education. Mirror images of each other, one calls for a refurbished ivory tower, while the other calls for an uncritical servitude to the larger society's aims and purposes (read whims and fashions). Neither is satisfactory. We may call the first the purist model and the second the vocational model. The first is favored by academic purists and antiquarian humanists and is an embellishment on the ancient Lyceum or the medieval university. In the name of the abstract pursuit of speculative knowledge, it calls for insulating the university from the wider society: Learning for learning's own sake—not for life, not for democracy, not for money; for neither power nor happiness; neither career nor quality of life; but for its own pure sake alone. To the purist, knowledge is radically divorced from time and culture, from power and interest; above all it eschews utility.

"The vocational model abjures tradition no less decisively than the purist model abjures relevance. Indeed, it is wildly alive to the demands of the larger society it believes education must serve. Where the purist rejects even the victories of modernity (equality, social justice, universal education) as so many diseases, the advocate of education as vocational training accepts even the ravages of modernity as so many virtues—or at least as the necessary price of progress. The vocationalist wishes to see the university go prone before modernity's new gods. Service to the market, training for its professions, research in the name of its products are the hallmarks of the new full-service university, which wants nothing so much as to be counted as a peer among the nation's great corporations that serve prosperity and material happiness."

"Are you saying that neither model serves a civic purpose?"

"Exactly."

"What model would you propose?"

"What I wish to urge is a far more dialectical model of education: one that refuses to prostrate itself, its back to the future, before the ancient gods of the canon, but is equally reluctant to throw itself uncritically, its back to the past, into the future as envisioned by the new gods of the marketplace. This argument suggests not that the university has a civic mission, but that the university *is* a civic mission, is civility itself, defined as the rules and conventions that permit a community to facilitate conversation and the kinds of discourse upon which all knowledge depends. On this model, learning is a social activity that can take place only within a discursive community bringing together reflection and experience. On this model, education is everywhere and always an ineluctably communal enterprise."

"The university is a civic mission. Help me think through that claim."

"I mean to suggest much more than that democracy and education are parallel activities; or that civic training and the cultivation of knowledge and judgment possess a parallel structure. I am arguing that they are the same thing: that what distinguishes truth, inasmuch as we can have it at all, from untruth is not conformity to society's historical traditions or the standards of independent reason or the dictates of some learned canon, but conformity to communicative processes that are genuinely democratic and that occur only in free communities. My argument here goes well beyond Jefferson's instrumental formula making education the guarantor of liberty. It suggests that liberty is the guarantor of education; that we not only have to educate all persons to make them free, but we have to free all persons to make them educable. Educated women and men make good citizens of free communities; but without a free learning community you cannot educate."

"Your thinking seems quite clearly to bear the influence of John Dewey."

"Yes, Dewey, but also of Walt Whitman who even more than Dewey refused to wall off democracy from life, or life from poetry, or poetry from democracy. The center at Rutgers is named after Whitman—it is also the name of my university chair—because I saw in him a philosopher of democracy resisting the ethos of a gilded age. This was also a way of making it clear that my chair and my center were concerned with the broader issues of civic culture and arts and humanities and not just with political science, narrowly speaking. I regard *Democratic Vistas*, Whitman's essay on the problem of American democracy, as one of the great contributions to American democratic literature. In this sense, it's not just Whitman's instincts and his poetry but his actual writing on democracy that I am honoring."

"Are you a communitarian?"

"To the extent that learning entails communication. Communication is a function of community. The equation is simple enough: no community, no communication; no communication, no learning; no learning, no education; no education, no citizens, no freedom; no freedom—then no culture, no democracy, no schools, no civilization. Cultures rooted in freedom do not come in fragments and pieces: you get it all, or you get nothing."

"In a word, education is a function of community, or as Dewey put it, 'the school must itself be a community life.'"

"Right. But let's be mindful of how traditional Dewey's position is. Dewey's conception of education is often deemed progressive, yet in fact it harks back to classical and neoclassical models of *paideia* and *Bildung*. *Paideia* was the term the Greeks used to encapsulate the norms and values of public life around which citizenship and learning were organized. To be an educated Athenian was to be a free and participating citizen. These were not two distinctive roles, two parallel forms of training; they were a single identity revolving around common norms each individual made his own. Imagine Socrates recommending a canon to his pupils, or telling an Athenian youth that what he learned in the Lyceum was not meant to apply to life beyond the bleached stones where the two of them sat in the sun conversing. The German Enlightenment term *Bildung* possessed the same unifying cultural thrust; it brought together under the rubric of life, learning, and self-reflective experience the same ideals of the fully developed citizen of a civil cosmopolis. The education of Emile (Rousseau) or the education of the young Werther (Goethe) was a lifetime task of which schooling represented only a phase. Emile did not imagine his pupil could separate the cultivation of his civility from the reading of books; Goethe never conceived that Werther could or should wall off his life from his learning."

"Do you think Dewey might have approved some kind of canon?"

"The trouble with the purist's canon is that it renders knowledge a product stripped of the process by which it is endowed with its quickening vitality and its moral legitimacy. The canon does not produce the cultural education the Germans called *Bildung; Bildung* produces the canon, which consequently needs to be no less flexible and mutable than the life processes that make it. The trouble with the vocationalist's servitude to society is that it fails to distinguish society or society's fixed conventions from the free society and the unique educational prerequisite that condition freedom. A free society does not produce *Bildung,* which is always critical of it; *Bildung* produces a free society, keeping it from ossifying and perishing—helping it to overcome its most difficult contradiction: the institutionalization and petrification of the spirit of freedom that animates it."

"So what does the future hold?" I asked, putting the conversation on a different tack.

"Ask me a harder question."

"Let me put it this way: how sanguine are you about the prospects for strong democracy?"

"I am a pessimist of the intellect but an optimist of the will."

"What does that mean?"

"As a citizen and a human being who wishes a better world, I am an optimist. Hope springs eternal. If people in Buchenwald could dream of a better day, then I can live in difficult times in America and dream of a richer democracy. It could happen; it is possible if only we work hard enough. But as a social scientist, as a historian, as a cold-blooded observer looking at the trends and tendencies of our times and projecting them into the future, I have to say it is going to be a rough haul. Democracy has never been more than a hope against hope. Liberty is always at risk and never guaranteed. When did democracy ever have a good day? Maybe today is its best day. Even so, our chances are less than 50 percent."

"The prospect seems to make you very sad," I said.

"My sadness comes from the fact that the best qualities of America come out in the private realm but they ought to shine in the public arena. I would transpose the virtues of the little republics to the national government, which is another way of saying that I want to import more of the values of classical republicanism. We have inverted the classical relation of public to private, which gives our society an eerily schizophrenic character. At the private level lots of good things happen: people are creative, energetic, idealistic, religious, charitable to the needy, and all that. But something very peculiar happens when we move over to the political domain. Then people shed their creativity and ideals and vision and become distrustful and cynical. We don't trust politicians much, and we don't trust government much. We think of it narrowly as a means of arbitrating interests that can't be squared in the private realm, so it is a necessary evil. We tend to think the purpose of government is to clear the way for the pursuit of our private interests. What strong democracy is all about is restoring to the political sector some of the energy and luster that we find in the private."

"Strong democracy seems to mean strong government for you," I noted.

"No. It means a strong citizenry, strong participation, strong civic community, strong identity of Americans with their neighborhoods. What I want to do is bring government out of the cold, not by making everything government, but by making it part of a larger public-political space in which we carry out those 'we' activities that define us as citizens—citizens of both our neighborhoods and the national community. To make government a mere appendage to all that is good and valuable in our democracy has very antidemocratic implications. To put all the goodies in voluntary associations, as some conservative writers tend to do, is to insulate government and nudge it in the direction of fascism. Let's think of the private, the public, and the governmental as all part of the larger political order in a sense that they are all parts of the *polis*. I am not really very interested in government as such. But I am interested in the political and the public."

"Hasn't it been one of the better instincts of Americans to reduce the role of government?" I asked.

"No. That attitude actually aggrandizes the role of government. It leads to bloated bureaucracies and isolates government from public control. That is very bad. If Americans had anything near the respect for government that they have for their voluntary associations, and invested proportionate energy into it, then we would have a much healthier democracy."

"Don't we do that?"

"I don't think so. I don't know anyone who refers to their church as 'them' or 'they.' They say 'we.' But the government is always 'them.'"

"Apparently you can't subscribe to the thesis that democracy takes place in the little republics?" I suggested.

"I can't leave it there. Democracy better also take place in the big republic or we are going to lose the little republics. Let me give you a nice illustration. We know Alexis de Tocqueville for his famous book on democracy in America. But he wrote another book on the *ancien régime* in France in which he showed how the French villages and municipalities had been from medieval times governed in a relatively autonomous and relatively democratic fashion. Townships had considerable self-determination, and their meetings involved the local aristocracy, the merchants, and the peasants. They were not unlike the New England town meetings. At the same time there was on top of this a growing bureaucratic, oligarchic, court-oriented monarchy that eventually smothered the life out of the local democracies. Tocqueville saw that as inevitable and, of course, it led to the French Revolution, which was an attempt to sweep away the whole system and start over again with a new national democracy. We know that experiment failed, but Tocqueville's point is that the autocratic government of the old regime ultimately sat on and squeezed the breath and life out of the little republics. I can see that happening in America. Yes, we have lots of good manifestations of public life. But if you have sitting on top of that a gigantic federal bureaucracy—the Pentagon, the IRS, the FBI, and other mammoth institutions—they will ultimately squash the local communities which are by and large vital and which we rightly cherish. We can't settle for a vital public life at the one level and a numbing bureaucracy at another level. In the long run the two cannot coexist. What we have to do is bring together the two levels in a stronger democracy; we have to breathe some of the fresh air of local energies into the national government."

One of Barber's recent books is *Jihad vs. McWorld: How the Planet Is Both Falling Apart and Coming Together and What This Means for Democracy*. Here he considers the possibilities of democracy in a global setting. He anchors his analysis on a metaphor from W. B. Yeats, who said that we are caught today between the "two eternities of race and soul, a backward look to tribal loyalties and a forward look to a cosmopolitan future."

"The first scenario," Barber says, "rooted in race holds out the grim prospect of a retribalization of large swaths of humankind by war and bloodshed: a threatened balkanization of nation-states in which culture is pitted against culture, people against people, tribe against tribe, a Jihad in the name of a hundred narrowly conceived faiths against every kind of interdependence, every kind of artificial social cooperation and mutuality: against technology, against pop culture, and against integrated markets; against modernity itself as well as the future in which modernity issues. The second scenario paints that future in shimmering pastels, a busy portrait of onrushing economic, technological, and ecological forces that demand integration and uniformity and that mesmerize peoples everywhere with fast music, fast computers, and fast food—MTV, Macintosh, and McDonald's—pressing nations into one homogenous global theme park, one McWorld tied together by communications, information, entertainment, and commerce. Caught between Babel and Disneyland, the planet is falling precipitously apart and coming reluctantly together at the very same moment."

Might it not be, Barber wonders, that Jihad and McWorld have a common denominator of anarchy, the lack of a common will, an enmity toward democracy?

"After all," he says, "Jihad and McWorld operate with equal strength in opposite directions, the one driven by parochial hatreds, the other by universalizing markets, the one recreating ancient subnational and ethnic borders from within, the other making national borders porous from without. Yet Jihad and McWorld have this in common: they both make war on the sovereign nation-state and thus undermine the nation-state's democratic institutions. Each eschews civil society and belittles democratic citizenship; neither seeks alternative democratic institutions. Their common thread is indifference to civil liberty. Jihad forges communities of blood rooted in exclusion and hatred, communities that slight democracy in favor of tyrannical paternalism or consensual tribalism. McWorld forges global markets rooted in consumption and profit, leaving to an untrustworthy, if not altogether fictitious, invisible hand issues of public interest and common good that once might have been nurtured by democratic citizenries and their watch-dog governments."

What is lost in the global battle between Jihad and McWorld, according to Barber, are the virtues of democracy and the ancient practices of citizenship.

He is particularly critical of the economic motif that now governs world affairs, and is especially critical of the claim that democracy and markets are the twin forces in the creation of a better world. That market freedoms nourish democracy is an argument that has been made since the time of Adam Smith and David Hume. Barber doesn't buy it. He says: "Capitalism needs consumers susceptible to the shaping of their needs and the manipulation of their wants while democracy needs citizens autonomous in their thoughts and independent in their deliberative judgment. Capitalists may be democrats but capitalism does not need or entail democracy. And capitalism certainly does not need the nation-state that has been democracy's most promising host."

What Barber fears most is the "soft" tyranny built into the homogenization of culture on a global scale, what he calls "the malling of the planet," including cyberspace. He doesn't mince words on this point.

"The great myth of capitalism," Barber contends, "has been the idea that all markets do is license and legitimize choice. Markets empower people to choose, to vote with their dollars, D-marks or yen. This myth blurs two crucial issues: the character of choice and the supposed autonomy of wants. Certainly, markets open up brand name choice. But, at the same time, they close down broader choices. The old example still stands: In many American cities you can choose from twenty-five models of automobiles, but you can't choose public transportation. You can choose a Big Mac or a Whopper on the run between errands from work, but you can't choose to sit down for a three-hour meal with the family. You'd be fired."

Barber's critique is far from self-evident and he has been accused of being biased against the deeper social and even spiritual aspects of capitalism. For example, Fareed Zakaria, managing editor of *Foreign Affairs*, reviewed the book in *The New Republic* and made the point that while capitalism surely does have its tawdry aspects, it has qualitatively improved the lives of many people who otherwise would be condemned to the short and brutish life of Hobbes's jungle. Zakaria puts it this way: "Conspicuously absent from his account of civil society are private firms. In fact, he sees corporations as actively hostile to civil society. . . . Barber must know that the concept of civil society emerged in Europe in the 18th century in part to describe private business activity. . . . How can one speak about organizations that provide individuals with personal autonomy and personal dignity, and shield them from the whims of the state, without mentioning private enterprise?"

That is a telling criticism. I asked Barber how he would answer it. He told me: "I know there is a school of thought that sees the market as part of civil society, but this two-celled liberal public / private model is one that my entire life's work has been devoted to challenging."

Thus are we brought to the heart of one of the major debates of our times: the role of a market economy in promoting democracy. At this point in history we are far from a satisfactory answer to that question.

How the Public Learns the Public's Business

Daniel Yankelovich is one of the keenest social observers in America today. As the founder and long-time president of the polling firm Yankelovich, Skelley, and White, and cofounder with Cyrus Vance of Public Agenda, he has had an unusual perspective on the changing mores of the country and the mysterious ways in which ideas inform social policy. He has, over the years, developed a compelling theory about public learning, about how ideas work in a democratic society.

In a long conversation in his New York apartment we discussed his views. "As an undergraduate," he began, "I was a philosophy major and got interested in certain schools of thought which deal with what we know and how we know it. It was all a lot of fun and had a somewhat abstract character then. But when I got into the real world the abstract terms of epistemology like *knowledge, opinion,* and *judgment* became more concrete for me. I realized one day, for example, that we had no way of distinguishing between the two concepts of public opinion and public judgment. I saw that the lack of such a distinction was causing a lot of mischief."

"What kind of mischief?" I asked.

Yankelovich gave this example: "We know other governments are very interested in American foreign affairs, particularly as to how this might affect their own policies. But public opinion polls can mislead them. For example, when polls ask, 'Would you come to the aid of Europe if it were invaded?' and the majority of Americans answer, 'No way,' this is terribly misleading and fateful to positions allied governments might take.

"To think that what the public thinks is what is measured by the polls is totally superficial and misleading. Public opinion plays a role in America that other countries don't understand. And I don't think our own public policy elite understands it. For most of them, the American public is another country. In fact, they might know other countries better than they do their own! I really entered the problem of public learning through a growing concern about the misjudgments that foreign leaders and our own foreign policy thinkers were constantly making by misreading public opinion polls, by interpreting them too literally. I remember one day saying to myself, in a grumbling way, that somebody should work on this problem. Then it occurred to me that I was the logical person to do it."

The formation of public opinion, Yankelovich points out, is "more like a biological process than a physical one. It evolves, goes through stages, matures gradually. We have to know the stage of development on any given issue, or the polls will mislead us. For example, 7 percent of Americans support national health insurance. But what does that mean? Does it mean people feel strongly about the issues or that they have settled views? Do they have opinions or have they reached a judgment? There is a big difference.

"In the early stages opinions are unstable," Yankelovich says, "They flip-flop at the slightest provocation. People have not thought through the consequences of their views. Today, for example, most of the public remains mired in wishful thinking on protectionism and health care, resisting any attempt to confront with realistic information the costs and trade-offs each entails. Political candidates who act on the results of opinion polls on these issues will soon feel the ground give way under their feet. On the other hand, there are issues on which public opinion has matured. People's views are solid and stable, not mushy."

I asked for an example of a non-mushy opinion.

"I want to cite one that may seem surprising," Yankelovich answered. "Many policymakers fear that the American public is reverting to a pre–World War II form of isolationism. But the American people have actually thought through the isolationism vs. internationalism issue. They agree with those who urge that with the end of the cold war we should give greater priority to our domestic concerns without, however, abdicating our responsibility as leader of the free world."

I asked Yankelovich to explain more fully the distinction between public opinion and public judgment.

"There are several distinctions to be made." he answered. "Public judgment contrasts with public opinion in several important respects. Public opinion has come to mean what public opinion polls measure: the vagaries of the public viewpoint at a moment in time, however vague, confused, ill-informed, and clouded with emotion it may be. Public judgment, on the other hand, represents the public's viewpoint after all elements of mere opinion have been distilled from it. Public judgment reflects the public's viewpoint once people have had an opportunity to confront an issue seriously and over an extended period of time. For public judgment, as distinct from public or mass opinion, to prevail, it is necessary that an issue catch people's attention, that they be exposed to the arguments for and against various positions, and that they think deeply enough about the issue to accept the consequences of their own beliefs.

"Typically, this process of converting mass opinion into public judgment takes months, if not years, and often involves strenuous debate and perhaps several distinct changes in outlook. It is curious that we do not have adequate semantics to describe this distinction, which is so vital to the functioning of a modern democracy.

"In the public policy tracking I have done over several decades, issues of public importance always seem to go through three phases. The first is when the public becomes aware of a problem, the phase of consciousness-raising, if you will. The second is the time of 'working through.' And the third is that of political compromise, when some resolution is hammered out. American culture is terrific at consciousness-raising. If anything, we overdo it. The media is good at beating the drums and getting everybody excited. Then they go on to the next issue as though that were the end of the job, leaving everybody in a state of high anxiety and unenlightenment. In a democracy, that is a disaster; it maximizes public awareness and public ignorance at the same time. To be excited about an issue but fail to think it through makes for the worst kind of citizens. A state of moral frenzy is not public judgment."

It struck me that the "working through" phase was the most difficult step in the process of reaching public judgment. Yankelovich agreed. I asked for an example.

He obliged with the following: "One of my favorite examples is when increasingly in the 1970s women said to their husbands: 'I think I'll go out and get a job, dear, which means you are going to have to do more work around the house.' It takes fifteen seconds to impart that information. It may take months to work it through. The classic example is 'working through' death. The information content is quickly imparted: a loved one is going to die. But it may take years to 'work through' the cycles of grief, anger, depression, and lack of realism before we can put our lives back together.

"The reason I like the grief reaction example is because it makes clear that there are distinct steps in the process of coming to terms with an issue. A couple of years ago I was at a conference in Sweden on the future of the welfare state. It was a particularly grim affair. At one point I turned to a friend and said: 'I don't understand what is going on here. Why are these people so gloomy?' He told me they were in a state of mourning. These were people who had spent their lives fighting for public housing, health care, and the like, and they were now facing the reality that they might have been on the wrong course. Before they could begin to face alternatives, they had to go through this period of grief reaction.

"I am always startled after all these years to realize that the concepts of public judgment and 'working through,' organized around choices and alternatives, are so unfamiliar and new to so many people. You would think them self-evident in a democracy, that someone who called attention to them would be accused of having a grip on the obvious, of platitudinous thinking. The fact that they are not platitudes tells us something about the state of our major institutions, about the media, about the universities, and about our political process. This is a failure of understanding—an intellectual failure. It is part and parcel of the positivism and parochialism of our institutions that they fail to understand the most elementary and fundamental aspects of our democratic society. We are trying to cope with great social complexities in too narrow a framework of thinking, with a philosophy born of another era and in circumstances that no longer apply."

I was curious about Yankelovich's use of the word *philosophy* in this context. He explained that he didn't so much mean formal systems or philosophical schools as they are taught in the universities. He had in mind something like what the Germans call a *Weltanschauung*—philosophy in the sense of a world view, a general conception we have of reality.

Our prevailing philosophy, he emphasized, is inadequate for the problems we face. "The dominant philosophy held by the experts on whom we most depend—economists, defense analysts, bankers, industrialists, journalists, government officials—can best be described as a 'missiles-and-money' sense of reality or what I often refer to as our culture of technical control. This philosophy assumes that what really counts in this world are military power and economic realities, and all the rest is sentimental stuff. It has overly constricted the domain of what is real and transformed the large political and moral dilemmas of our time into narrow technical questions that fit the experts' own specialized expertise. This process of technicalizing political issues renders them inaccessible to public understanding and judgment because the public exists in the very domain of reality that is excluded. To narrow issues artificially is to exclude the bulk of the citizenry from the policy-shaping process. Sad to say, our most prestigious institutions of higher education that train our elites impart to them a distrust of the general public—the masses, the *petite bourgeoisie*, the faceless electorate, and so forth. Or, if not an active distrust, at least an astonishing remoteness—as if the well-educated experts were a class apart, sharing a rarified culture and a pool of knowledge the uninitiated could not possibly hope to comprehend. This mentality is so much a part of our contemporary zeitgeist that it is difficult for us to realize how very arbitrary and one-sided it is."

We discussed health care as an example of an issue that has been manipulated by technical elites but has not matured in the public's mind. People are well aware of it. A majority know that costs are going through the ceiling, that many have no insurance. They are at the ready with charges of greed, waste, and corruption. But they are weak on specifics, often unaware of the true costs of health care or the consequences of different proposals. We hear, for example, vague references to European plans or the Canadian system. But how many know what the Canadian system is? Or what it costs? Or what it delivers? Or how viable it is? As a matter of fact the Canadian system is arguably a very bad one and in any event one in much trouble.

Says Yankelovich: "Health care is a particularly vivid example of the disorderly manner in which the public comes to focus on choices. Among leaders and experts hardly a day passes without a new idea for coping with the crisis. But the public remains oblivious to most choices."

They are aware of a range of choices but are a long way from actually making them. People have opinions on malpractice suits; there has been a good deal of consciousness-raising on healthy life styles, not smoking and the like; people know about HMOs; and so forth. But between the awareness and any effective public policy a degree of unreality exists, a resistance to choice work, what Yankelovich calls a "barricade of wishful thinking."

So the situation looks much like this, he concludes: "People feel a sense of urgency about changing the health care system but haven't even begun to confront realistically the hard choices that need to be made. Unfortunately, policymakers are largely unaware of the depth and intensity of the public's resistance. Policymakers know that Americans are deeply concerned about the adequacy, safety, and affordability of health care coverage. But they incorrectly infer that this means voters are ready to accept the consequences, including the costs, of changing the existing system. The public is in the throes of working through the issue and it is, let me stress, hard work because wrestling with any complex issue—be it abortion, the death penalty, or whatever—requires getting in touch with one's deepest values and coming to the realization that our values often conflict. And people naturally resist having to compromise or abandon cherished values. So no facet of the health care issue has arrived at the stage of resolution."

"Will it?"

"It will if the national debate is productive."

"Is it productive?"

"Over time it may be. But the odds are that many years and many crises will have to pass before the American public fully accepts the need to ration, regulate, reform and even revolutionize health care so that it preserves some semblance of a right rather than a consumer good, without bankrupting the nation. What we basically have to do is alter our definition of reality."

The phrase "our definition of reality" caught my attention.

"What is the American definition of reality?" I asked.

"Well, that's a philosophical question," Yankelovich said, "so I'll give you a philosophical answer." Again, he paused, a bit longer this time, before proceeding. "The whole Anglo-American tradition of philosophy is off in a special corner. I spent most of my academic years in that corner. When I studied philosophy at Harvard, the department was dominated by people with a very strong logical orientation. This is sometimes called positivism and it influences every profession and misleads every profession. And it is still the dominant philosophy, which surprises me for it is so arid and sterile a line of inquiry that I would have thought it would have petered out long ago. Anyway, I decided it was a dead end for me. Don't get me wrong. I am not knocking philosophy. In fact, if I were prescribing the ideal curriculum, I would have a good chunk of philosophy in there, but in a larger context with other modes of thought and with less emphasis on the endless knitting and weaving of arguments and counterarguments and some generous place for modes of thought that accommodate judgment, wisdom, and wit."

I thought it was highly ironical, to say the least, that in this most democratic of societies our major institutions are distorted by intellectual methodologies and attitudes whose consequences lead in antidemocratic directions.

Yankelovich explained this dilemma as a conflict between the aims of subcultures and the ethical pull of the larger society. The larger society tends in a democratic direction whereas the subcultures tend to be privatistic and elitist. "Americans have an enormous amount of respect and deference for elites," he said. "Some Americans who think of themselves as elites are as remote from the concerns of the average person as any French aristocrat was before the Revolution. The academic profession is organized in an elitist fashion. So is business. We have many baronies within our democracy. Many of them are as autocratic as any medieval barony. The legal profession is perfectly comfortable with the adversarial method, even though there is widespread opinion that it favors the perpetrators of crime rather than the victims. The relationship between a subculture and the mainstream is complex, and the ways they mutually nourish and sustain one another far from clear. But this is what gives America its dynamism and creativity. And ours is a very dynamic and creative society."

"But is it cohesive?" I asked. It seemed to me the presence of many subcultures without a restraining public ethic would tend to tear the fabric of society apart.

"Oh yes, I think it is cohesive. Very cohesive in fact. Precisely because of its great ethnic and geographic diversity, American society has overemphasized its coherence around a handful of social values which have extraordinary power and breadth. Take one of the central ones—the notion of equal opportunity. Everyone has a chance, but not everyone will succeed. Those who succeed are not necessarily those who are richer or smarter. We do not have a meritocracy in that sense. The myth is that of effort. In making this effort you can fail or succeed because there is a large measure of luck involved. There are social critics who want to reform society because luck plays such a large role in it. I think that is a profound misreading of the American value system. Americans cherish the system precisely because there is so much luck in it. You never know. That is why people don't want punitive income taxes for the rich. You never know. Someday you might be rich. This runs very deep in the ethos. So I think the basic social and political values of American society have an inner coherence, even though we don't all think the same way. The coherence comes not from everyone thinking the same way but from diverse thinking being organized around a handful of core values."

Yankelovich cited the example of bilingual education. "This touches a very sensitive cord because it runs against the central ethic of the melting pot and the idea of one language. Acquiring that language is part of the effort we have to make to become an American. An issue like this introduces incoherence far more than does prayer in the schools, abortion, or affirmative action. These issues are very much around the core of our basic values like equal opportunity. We expect affirmative action issues and we expect them to be divisive. But we are geared to deal with them. We instinctively recognize that bilingual education poses the threat of incoherence."

The example made the point that we have to step out of our subcultures in order to deal with issues of public import. But it still left open the question of how we do this. We all belong to and have allegiances to various subcultures which we can assume, in important respects, to run against the public interest. It would seem to indicate the need for large-scale reform in our major institutions.

"That is my concern," Yankelovich said. "The question is: How can we create institutions that will permit us to do a better job of working through issues? The teaching institutions would be one candidate for doing this. But they don't. They lecture. They impart information."

"Could they do it?"

"Sure they could. But they would have to be different. They would have to see their role differently and organize themselves differently. They would have to develop a different mind-set. If you talk to a professor about public education, he either turns his nose up, or if he engages in it at all he lectures his audience with the intention of raising their level of information a little closer to his own. That is not 'working through.'"

"Are you saying that educational institutions have a responsibility to get major social issues on the public agenda and help the public think through them?" I asked.

"I am saying something more specific. I am saying even more narrowly that academic disciplines like the social sciences have an intellectual obligation to understand their subject matter, which is the structure of society, and to impart that information to their students. But they have failed to do this. It isn't a failure of intelligence per se, but due rather to the values of the subculture—in this instance, the subculture to which the professoriat belongs. The values of the subculture have been a seduction. The aping of scientific concepts, epistemologies, and language has led disciplines like sociology and political science down the garden path for years. The notion that an academic discipline is responsible only to its peers has been a seduction. The great practical success of the physical sciences has been the ruination of the social sciences. I meet young faculty members in sociology departments who almost weep in frustration because if they do interesting and important work it will count against them for tenure. They have to play a game. I think that is a scandal. And we are not even asking the universities to do something outside their own mandate. Oddly enough, while there has been plenty of criticism of the press, the medical profession, and secondary schools, the universities have gotten off lightly."

"They were criticized in the sixties," I noted.

"But when the dust settled it was business as usual. The point I am stressing is the obligation of those in positions of power to balance the requirements of their particular subculture with the requirements of the larger culture. That balance has been badly skewed for a variety of reasons—ideology, self-congratulation, isolation, etc."

"What about the media?"

"It's exactly the same situation with the media. They are involved in entertainment and in news. Public education is neither. The essence of news is not to repeat yourselves—almost by definition. In the news business, you don't harp away at the same thing because then it is no longer news. The very virtues of news coverage work against public education. The media have a fetish for information, a 'these-poor-saps-don't-even-know-where-Nicaragua-is' mentality. When I do surveys and report them to journalists, it's laughable. You'd be amused if you sat in an audience with journalists. I can give a presentation that brings wonderful data and insights to bear on a given subject, and they couldn't care less."

"There are some very perceptive and analytic journalists on the scene. Don't the best of them meet your criteria?" I asked.

"Even when they are giving more than information, they still think they are giving only information. Even the most gifted journalists are perceived as just being smart. They have a lot of information and are, in addition, smart. They are not perceived as doing something different."

"Don't they help shape public judgment?"

"They are giving points of view, and that is the first step. But in order to develop judgment the points of view must generate real dialogue. Collective judgment comes from dialogue. I see that happening now in a very interesting way. There is a debate going on among leaders about industrial policy. It's a real debate because there are a number of points of view. You have conservatives who don't like the idea and think that market forces can do whatever needs to be done. You have liberals who want to use the resources of government to help support certain industries in a selective way. You have economists who believe that the traditional economic theories of fiscal and monetary policy are all that is required. So we have a three-way debate in which each participant accuses the others of gross naïveté. Conservatives accuse liberals of trying to pick winners and losers and plan the economy— and so on, back and forth. In the give-and-take, each side is refining its point of view. The debate goes on at two levels. In the written statements of the protagonists there is a sharp, vitriolic tone. The layman wonders how they can ever get together, or how a layman can possibly understand such complicated issues. But just below that level one can detect a core of agreement emerging because the different parties are influencing one another. Now the interesting question is: How do you take that debate, which is very important to the general public, and move it onto the public's agenda?

"This debate suggests that we are doing a pretty good job at reaching some agreement among elites. There is in the United States an invisible university. It is enormous. The faculty of that invisible university consists of consultants, institutes of various sorts, and foundations. They hold innumerable meetings, and discussion is going on all the time. I probably speak at one such meeting a week. Part of what is missing in all of our institutions is that we don't have a good mechanism for translating what goes on in the invisible university for the general public. What I try to emphasize is that in the 'working through' process we need choices. Alternatives have to be spelled out."

"We've talked a lot about the failure of institutions," I said. "What must they do then? Or perhaps we need new institutions to do the job?"

"It is sobering to think that there is no institution in America whose imperative is to engage in this 'working through' process. The political system is the closest. But it is too gross and more concerned with interests. Maybe one reason the presidency is so powerful is because it is the only institution that is concerned with the common interest. It accomplishes the 'working through' process in a quite significant way. A 'bully pulpit' is one way to lead people through. It took a Richard Nixon to change our ways of thinking about Communist China. Even so, when it comes to serious issues that concern the public as a whole, we don't have any institution whose specific mandate enables it to mobilize its energies to focus on those problems."

"Can the invisible university serve this function?"

"The invisible university is an informal way of doing that job for elites, but not for the general public. Let me give you a striking example of where the process breaks down. The invisible university has been at work on the budget deficit. There have been innumerable meetings and discussions, and it gets into some pretty arcane economics. The relation between the Third World debt, international exchange rates, and variable-rate mortgages is not the most self-evident thing in the world. So the invisible university has brought the elites of both liberal and conservative persuasions to agree that something ought to be done about the deficit. But they haven't gotten the point across to the general public."

"Do you have a solution?"

"We have got to re-think our public philosophy."

"Where do we start?"

"Well, we are up against a mystery here. We have to begin by unraveling it. I mentioned earlier that I have for years been bewildered about why these ideas I am talking about are not part of our core vocabulary of democracy along with freedom of opportunity, due process, equality before the law, and so forth. These concepts are not particularly subtle or elusive. Indeed, they are as plain as the need for giving greater attention to protecting the environment or taking better care of our nation's children. Why are we so reluctant to embrace ideas that protect and strengthen our democracy? Why they are neglected and ignored poses for me a genuine mystery."

In his *Coming to Public Judgment: Making Democracy Work in a Complex World,* Yankelovich identifies the source of this resistance in something he calls "epistemological anxiety." The idea here is that when dominant status systems and modes of knowing are threatened, we humans, as though by instinct, resist whatever it is that is threatening them. For a long time now, our culture has favored an instrumental mode of rationality that privileges expert knowledge and the status that derives from it. We imbibe these patterns from early childhood on. They are embedded in our language and in our social practices. They constitute a powerful weltanschauung, the very breeding ground of our Culture of Technical Control.

"People are subject to epistemological anxiety," Yankelovich explains, "when the styles of knowing that have become second nature to them are questioned. Our cognitive styles and modes of knowing are part of our basic equipment for coping with the world and controlling the environment. Anything that threatens loss of control creates anxiety. I mean by epistemological anxiety the feeling that your special way of making sense of the world is being threatened. Inevitably, one's first impulse is to protect against such anxiety. If logical people are told that their logic is irrelevant in situations where logic has always worked for them before, they will understandably resist, unless they are given powerful reasons for thinking otherwise. And these powerful reasons would probably have to be couched in logical terms to be persuasive to them. If factually minded people are told that the facts do not count—once again in situations where the facts have always counted, they will naturally resist. If such people encounter situations where logic or factuality does not seem to work, it is hardly surprising that anxiety is aroused.

"The instrumental rationality associated with the Culture of Technical Control—logical, factual, analytic, focusing on how and why things work, time and space bound, valuing clarity and order and narrative—generates a set of matching values. I remember my surprise, as a philosophy major in college, to learn how influential the value of certainty was in the history of philosophy. So many of the questions we studied as students revolved around the question, 'How can you be *sure* you know x, y, or z?' More than three hundred years of modern European and American philosophy exhibit a clear preference for knowledge that is certain (even if trivial) over knowledge that is less certain, even if important to living. Philosopher John Dewey wrote an influential book, *The Quest for Certainty*, explaining powerful trends in philosophy in terms of this quest. When immersed in this literature, I first became aware that lack of certainty causes many people to feel uncomfortable and anxious."

And he adds: "The key to the mystery of why there is so much resistance to the concept of public judgment lies, I believe, in its tendency to create epistemological anxiety. It suggests that the dominant modes of knowing associated with the Culture of Technical Control may not be as powerful or inclusive as its devotees have believed, and that for some important purposes, other modes of knowing, including public judgment, may be superior."

One source that has been particularly helpful in unraveling the mystery of epistemological anxiety is contemporary German thought.

"Like many Americans trained in social science and philosophy, I have been deeply affected by German social thought. My interest in German philosophy did not end with my formal education. Quite the contrary; I have found myself reading more German thinkers in recent years than I did in college and graduate school. Three strands of German thought have particularly influenced me: that of Martin Heidegger and his student, Hannah Arendt, who emigrated to America in 1941 but who continued to think, and to write, in German; the contributions of Max Weber, to whom all students of social thought are indebted; and the work of the so-called Frankfurt School founded by Max Horkheimer, Theodor Adorno, and others, culminating in the contemporary work of Jürgen Habermas. These three tributaries, flowing into one, reflect an outpouring of insight that no student of society can ignore—

especially in the United States where these seminal thinkers deserve to be better known than they are."

"What have you learned from the Germans?" I asked.

"The important lesson derives from the long history of the German critique of instrumental rationality. From this critique we can gain a better understanding than we now have of where this form of thought fits within the larger scheme of human modes of comprehension. If one principal defect of instrumental rationality is its excessive narrowness of outlook, its tendency to mistake a part for the whole, then we need a sophisticated critique of its strengths and limitations to know how to compensate for its shortcomings."

Yankelovich finds Max Weber particularly important. "The social thinker who has looked into this distorting tendency of modernism with the greatest prescience is German social scientist and philosopher Max Weber who did his great work in the early part of this century. For Weber the most destructive element in modernism is not its economic power relationships but its tendency to give instrumental rationality precedence over all other forms of thinking, feeling, and valuing.

"He describes instrumental rationality as the systematizing, objectifying, and technicalizing mentality that dominates industrial culture. Weber saw the growth of instrumental rationality as the master key to modern history, and he did not like it. His fear was that the dynamism of this world view would ultimately destroy the quality of life in Western civilization. At one point in his writings he describes this effect as 'an icy-cold, polar night.' He predicted that it would shape the social character of humanity so adversely that the typical individual would become a 'heartless expert, a spineless pleasure seeker.'

"In his most familiar metaphor, Weber describes the effects of instrumental rationality as an 'iron cage' that imprisons the human spirit and cuts us off from the deepest sources of our being. Through the unfolding of instrumental rationality, Weber discerns an ultimate despair as it stripped life of mystery and charm, destroying what the English philosopher Edmund Burke had called 'the inns and resting places of the human spirit.' Weber says, 'With the progress of science and technology, reality has become dreary, flat, and utilitarian, leaving a great void in the souls of men which they seek to fill by curious activity and through various devices and substitutes.'"

"How important is Habermas?" I asked.

"Not only has Habermas carried the critique of instrumental rationality further than his predecessors, more importantly he has systematized a theory of knowledge that, without rejecting money-and-missile realism, highlights other, more relevant modes of comprehension."

"What is his message?"

"The gist of what Habermas is saying, as I understand him, is that instrumental rationality developed its great influence in relationship to the physical sciences. When it is haphazardly applied to political life, it distorts all that it touches. This factor of distortion derives not only from a crucial difference in subject matter but also from a difference in purpose. Historically, the objective of natural science and of instrumental rationality was to dominate nature. But the objective of political life is not, or should not be, to dominate anything. Political life concerns the conduct of human affairs and interactions among people. When we confront the issues of humans living together we encounter questions such as: How can we keep from dominating and destroying each other? How can we reinforce the human bonds that hold society together? Clearly these judgments are not properly arrived at through techniques designed for domination and control. Such judgments should represent the results of what Habermas calls 'communicative action.' Communicative action takes place in a setting of public discussion that leads to constructive and healthy forms of public action."

"What about Hannah Arendt?"

"She took us back to Kant and Aristotle to remind us of a long tradition of political philosophy, a tradition in which the practical, political abilities of the citizenry are required for self-governance. These are abilities that were once better recognized in Western thought than they are today. They have been lost under the domination of instrumental rationality and its money-and-missile offspring."

"How can we import the best of German thought into an American context?" I asked.

"One thing we could do is develop institutions devoted to promoting the formation of public judgment. In the United States, there are now several such institutions devoted to this objective. One is the Aspen Institute, a second is the Kettering Foundation, and third is the Public Agenda Foundation. In its programs of 'thought-leading-to-action,' the Aspen Institute concerns itself with leadership publics. In its seminars it seeks to meet the conditions I have described above under the heading of forming public judgment, though it describes its processes in other language. The Public Agenda, often in concert with Kettering, focuses more sharply on the general public. Its purpose is to prepare issues and to conduct communication campaigns in which the conditions for public judgment are met. The Aspen Institute has been doing its work for many years on an international scale. The Public Agenda is a newcomer, and confined to the United States. Let me attempt a one-sentence summary. If, thanks to German thought, the culture of technical control that now dominates our thinking can be seen in proper perspective, reduced in importance, and partially replaced by processes designed to arrive at public judgment, then the future of democracy will be well served and we owe a debt of gratitude to the outstanding German thinkers I have mentioned."

"How do we sum up Daniel Yankelovich's thinking?" I asked.

"My abiding assumption is that there can be no effective public policy without an effective citizen role in shaping it. Policies cannot succeed without the acceptance, cooperation, and understanding of citizens. Virtually every important domestic change in the United States has been bottom-up. It has come from the public, not the leadership. From civil rights to the women's movement to tax revolt, this has been the case. To an astonishing degree, the public has been the leader, and the leadership has been the follower."

"Is that the story of America?"

"To an astonishing degree," Yankelovich said as we concluded the conversation.

Politics in a Different Key

As we walked along the embankment of the Clark Fork River in Missoula, Montana, Mayor Daniel Kemmis said to me: "We are going to have to start doing politics differently or we will self-destruct."

Kemmis rose to national attention for doing politics in a different way, and his 1990 book *Community and the Politics of Place* was well received. I had come to Missoula in the month of May to follow him around for a few days and have some conversation as his busy schedule permitted.

"For one thing," Kemmis said as we continued our walk along the river, now rushing with spring force out of Hellgate Canyon, "we have to do a better job with our public spaces. Politics is about space as much as people. The two are inseparable. Ever since I became mayor, I have worked hard to create a park system on both sides of the river. Right now we are bogged down in a controversy over a footbridge that is a key part of the plan. One alternative would be to have the bridge footed on one of the small islands in the middle of the river, and some environmental groups think that would disturb the wildlife. On the other hand, the bridge is essential to the plan both practically and aesthetically. The debate goes on, but we are making progress." He pointed to an abandoned mill. "The city has acquired that parcel of land," he said. "The mill will be torn down, and the property will become part of the redeveloped river front."

We spent a long afternoon of my first day in Missoula on the riverbank. It didn't take me long to grasp that the Clark Fork River and the extended park along its banks was a metaphor for Kemmis's philosophy of politics. I asked him to elaborate on his philosophy.

"I follow Jefferson who called for a nation of citizens deeply involved in public life. If I were to put a name on my philosophy, I would call it bioregionalism, which brings people and place together in an organic relationship.

One comes to this philosophy more or less naturally out here. I was born on a farm on the high plains of Eastern Montana, and except for eight years in the East where I did my undergraduate work and studied law at Harvard University, I have spent my whole life here first in law practice, then as a member of the Montana legislature, and for the past four years as mayor of Missoula. There is a strong sense of place here. In our local mythology, Montana is referred to as 'the last best place.' I moved back to Montana in 1972 just as the state's constitution was being revised. The new preamble reads very much like the U.S. Constitution. It opens with 'We the people . . .' and so forth. But there is one phrase that is different and stands out: 'We the people of Montana, grateful to God for the quiet beauty of our state, the grandeur of its mountains, the vastness of its rolling plains. . . .' I think with those words the authors struck an indissoluble bond between the people ('we the people') and the place itself. People and place are the two constituent parts of what it means to be a public, a republic, a *res publica*. People define themselves in relationship to one another through the medium of a place, a region, a territory. The people of Montana so defined themselves, as the words of the preamble make clear."

Kemmis draws an image from Hannah Arendt to clarify his point. "What politics has lost," Arendt says, "is the power to gather people together, to relate them and separate them in due proportion." In *The Human Condition* she wrote, "The weirdness of this situation resembles a spiritualistic seance where a number of people gathered around a table might suddenly, as through some magic trick, see the table vanish from their midst, so that two persons sitting opposite each other were no longer separated but also would be entirely unrelated to each other by anything tangible."

What is missing, says Kemmis, is the table around which we can gather for deliberation and interactive conversation with different others. What is missing is a practice of politics that reaches deep into the subsoil of our lives together, a politics that can recoup a vital sense of citizen agency and reconstitute the public sphere. We are fast losing this sense of the public in this country.

Kemmis traces our dilemma to the founding period, to the debate between the Federalists and the Republicans. "At the Constitutional Convention the delegates wrestled with the question of whether citizens themselves could work out solutions to such problems as those posed by Shay's Rebellion or whether government was the only agency that could do so. Should the burden of solving public problems be the responsibility of citizens or government? In a letter to Madison, Jefferson, who was at the time ambassador to France, made his position clear. 'In the final analysis,' Jefferson said, 'peace is best preserved by giving information to people rather than by giving energy to the government.' Such information he called the most legitimate engine of government. Jefferson was, to be sure, advocating public education in the strongest sense of the word, education that would enable people to understand and enact the common good. Jefferson's version of republicanism advocated a face-to-face, hands-on approach to problem solving.

"The Federalists, on the other hand, advocated what can only be termed a politics of disengagement. They wanted to separate citizens rather than bring them together, relying on the machinery of government, 'a machine that would run by itself.' Thus at the very beginning of our nation two quite distinct points of view were etched into our national consciousness: Jefferson advocated public education and civic virtue as the foundation of government; Madison could not place such trust in human nature which by his estimate was too infected with self-interest to be a reliable basis of society and so opted instead for an elaborate system of checks and balances to take the place of what he called 'the defect of better motives.' This was the beginning of what Michael Sandel has called the procedural republic. In substituting self-interest for civic virtue, Madison reversed a cardinal tenet of the civic republican tradition. He also reversed the traditional belief that republics should be small in scope. On the contrary, the extensive territory of the frontier dovetailed neatly with Madison's theory of checks and balances, of one faction playing off against another, an excellent hedge against tyranny. More space would guarantee more factions and thus more checks and balances and thus would the fabric of society be tightly bound. Jefferson on the contrary saw those same spaces as a generator of civic virtue. The land, the sturdy yeoman, the virtuous citizen, was Jefferson's formula, and I share his sentiments."

At this point I raised some obvious objections. Isn't it far-fetched in this day and age when technology runs rampant and less than 3 percent of Americans are farmers, to tie civic virtue to agriculture and the sturdy yeoman? That leaves most of us out of the picture and paints our common civic project into a corner of futility. What relevance does Jefferson's pastoral model have in the kind of society we live in today? Wasn't Jefferson laying it on a bit thick when he wrote to John Jay that "the cultivators of the earth are the most valuable citizens. They are the most vigorous, the most independent, the most virtuous." And wasn't Jefferson's anti-business attitude offensive, especially when we recall that commerce and civic republicanism historically were closely allied and developed side by side? Not that I am unsympathetic to the Jeffersonian outlook. I have my little shelf of Thoreau, Wendell Berry, and Gary Snyder. I teach about environmental ethics. And I have my summer hideaway, in a beautiful valley, where I go to get in touch with cosmic rhythms. But nothing draws yawns from students more surely or glazes over their eyes with the clear evidence of boredom than even the slightest reference to Jefferson's bucolic ideal. I wondered how Kemmis would answer these objections. His answer surprised me.

"Of course we can't all be farmers," he said. "One can read Jefferson as a starry-eyed romantic, but I read him differently. I read him as making a point about public philosophy, particularly about public space. Indeed, I would argue that we have to read cities back into Jefferson's philosophy in a constructive way."

That struck me as a paradox. Kemmis explained his position this way:

"No, Jefferson's point is not far-fetched. Not at all. I am willing to wager that we won't begin to solve our runaway social problems until we buy back into Jefferson. What he was talking about was the problem of alienation, disconnectedness, and anonymity which he tied to commerce. His analysis has turned out to be largely correct. We have indeed created a society that undermines civic virtue and morals as Jefferson predicted it would. Jefferson was appalled by the thought of large numbers of people making their living by depending solely upon the choices of other people with whom they had no social or moral ties of any kind. And so should we."

I asked how Kemmis proposed interpreting Jefferson as including cities in his praise of agriculture.

"This brings me back to my philosophy of bioregionalism," he answered, "the philosophy of organic relationships. One way to read Jefferson's praise of agriculture is to think of agriculture as a metaphor for nurturing and caring, for gathering disparate parts together into functional wholes. One could use architectural imagery to make the same point, or medical imagery, as I sometimes do. But I am quite comfortable with Jefferson's metaphor."

I was reminded of some similar remarks on culture by Hannah Arendt that Kemmis might have called up to support his position. In her brilliant essay "The Crisis of Culture: Its Social and Its Political Significance," Arendt notes that culture derives from the Latin word *colere*—to cultivate, to dwell, to take care, to tend and preserve. Its primary reference was to nature and the human effort to make nature a fit and fitting place for human habitation. But it soon came to take on larger meanings. It came, for example, to refer to the "cult" of the gods; religion too is a kind of tending and caring. By Cicero's time the word culture came to embrace the works of intellect as in "a cultured mind" or even "the culture of politics." And as such it is the perfect image for public life, for citizens are engaged in a labor analogous to that of the farmer: they make things grow, they solve problems, they harmonize discordant parts. Viewed in this perspective, agriculture has less to do with the distinction between the rural and the urban than with the *res* that unites the two. We are not talking about country versus city but about real politics which resides in that unique blending of city and country which constitutes the polis. "This," says Kemmis, "is fundamental to any healthy conception of politics."

His interpretation of Jefferson was now beginning to sound less paradoxical. "Bioregionalism," Kemmis went on, "is closely related to the concept of inhabitation. To inhabit a place is to dwell there in a cultured way, which is to say with the habits and practices peculiarly appropriate to that place. Cities are places; they must be inhabited in just such a practiced way; they call forth appropriate habits of practice."

Kemmis draws some points about cities from Jane Jacobs's *Cities and the Wealth of Nations*. If we think of cities as "natural units of inhabitation" then we must think of them as organic wholes, as ecosystems. It is no accident that the root of the word for economics and ecology is the same—*oikos*, a home, a neighborhood, a *res publica*, a common world. In this perspective cities include the surrounding countryside and vice versa. The republican idea of a city-state is apropos here. If we think of cities as the primary economic and political entities, "units of inhabitation," then we will not be so enamored of the artificial boundaries we draw between cities and countryside. "City limits" is a pejorative, exclusionary term because it implies that at some point the city ends and something else, some other economic and political unit begins—the township, the county, the country. "This is very devastating thinking," says Kemmis. "But it is mainstream political theory. We have come to treat cities as purely derivative, the neglected stepchildren of state and nation. Politically we have no experience whatever of 'city-regions' or 'city-states.' Yet from its very inception, politics has been rooted precisely where Jacobs argues that economics is rooted: in the city-region, the city-state, the *polis*. This is the root of all politics. Cities are the natural units of habitation, the original *demes*, not the nation-state, not the globe, and they need more political power." Kemmis wrote a book on this subject, *The Good City and the Good Life*, published by Houghton Mifflin in 1995.

It is a subject worthy of attention. Americans have never been able to develop an adequate urban theory and in practice often have made an uninhabitable mess of their cities. We can think of Rome, Florence, or Paris as great cities. But we don't think that way about American cities. We think of the urban landscape as blighted; we regard the city with fear and suspicion, the seat of all sin and corruption. But we are not totally comfortable with pastoral imagery either. We seek a middle ground by cordoning off vast tracts of suburbs, a habitation somewhere between the city and the country, but not being either it demeans both.

"Our impoverished thinking is reflected in the reduced power of local governments to determine their own policies and shape their own future," Kemmis observes. And he adds: "This is especially true in the West, which has odd implications for a region which was the last of America's old frontier. If bioregionalism means anything then it makes sense to begin with the place where we live, to understand what it means and then try to construct a way of being public that would fit that place."

It occurred to me in passing that we Americans frequently deplore the loss of a historical sense, a time sense, but less frequently do we acknowledge a loss of space sense. We can be alienated in both senses. I asked Kemmis if he would go so far as to equate our loss of a public sense with the loss of a frontier in American life.

"Yes," he answered. "While the frontier was open, Jefferson's vision was a live option."

"When did the frontier close?"

Kemmis said there were various accounts. Perhaps the best known is that of Frederick Jackson Turner, who in 1893 delivered a paper to the American Historical Association in which he said, in a much quoted opinion: "Up to and including 1880 the country had a frontier of settlement, but at present the unsettled area has been so broken into by isolated bodies of settlement that it can hardly be said to be a frontier line." Turner, like Jefferson, recognized that the frontier was an essential ingredient in the development of the American character, and that without it the American psyche registered profound seismic disturbances.

Kemmis cites two symbolic indicators of the end of the frontier. One was the 1896 election campaign between William Jennings Bryan and William McKinley. Here in quite stark contrast were pitted against one another the values of the agrarian populist movement (Bryan) and well-financed commercial interests (McKinley). The McKinley campaign spent unprecedented amounts of money, and henceforward Madison Avenue was to be a permanent feature of American politics. A further wedge was driven between the governing and the governed classes. The other story concerned Teddy Roosevelt. In 1886 he left his ranch in Dakota Territory, and by 1898 he was leading the charge up San Juan Hill. From republic to empire in little more than ten years.

"For me," Kemmis said, "the real closing of the frontier was in 1887 when Congress passed the Interstate Commerce Act which launched the age of regulatory bureaucracy. In my mind it marked a significant departure from civic virtue and republican self-government, a major step in keeping citizens apart, shielding them from the necessity of direct, face-to-face problem solving."

Kemmis tells this story to illustrate the point he was making. "The citizens of Bitterroot Valley wanted to sell themselves stock in order to raise money for investment in local businesses. They had done so many years earlier and had managed to make some good investments and add jobs to the local economy. But when they decided to issue new stock, they found that the securities regulations were almost insurmountable. Not only did they have to meet the requirements of federal and state securities laws, but they also faced the obstacles of the Investment Company Act of 1940. These were neighbors trying to raise money from within the community to help the economy and therefore to help themselves. What they were finding, to their great frustration, was that they were not going to be allowed to treat each other like neighbors. They were going to have to act as if they were strangers to one another."

There was a tinge of sadness in Kemmis's voice as he spoke. I asked him if he was pessimistic about our civic capacities. He said that experience left him convinced "that our way of being public is a deepening failure." That is not an unfamiliar complaint in social analysis. I wondered if Kemmis thought the cause of this problem might be bureaucracy.

"It's Arendt's point about the missing middle. Much of our political life in this century had been a battle between individualism and regulatory bureaucracy. What is largely ignored is cooperation as the middle way. As individuals we privatize values; as clients of the bureaucratic state we are conformists; and the middle ground is polarization not cooperation." Kemmis quoted William Janklow, a former governor of South Dakota, who said in America today anybody can block anything. He cites an arm's-length list of first-hand experiences he has had that prove the governor's point. One especially caught my attention.

The town of Alberton in western Montana wanted to have a trace race to attract some tourists to the community. Kemmis explained that a trace race is a relay race with the first leg in kayaks through the rapids of a mountain gorge, the second on mountain bikes over rough trails to the top of the mountain, and the third down the mountain on hang gliders. Dangerous to be sure, but not out of character for the adventuresome inhabitants of that place. Eventually the plan was shelved because of the possibility of a lawsuit if someone were injured. "We are protected against ourselves whether we want to be or not," Kemmis commented. "We cannot any longer take responsibility for our actions, directly and face to face. And because we cannot take responsibility for our actions, our range of activity is narrowed. What we can accomplish together is limited in ways that frustrate us deeply. Thus it is, as Alasdair MacIntyre has said, that the politics of modern societies oscillate between a freedom which is nothing but a lack of regulation of individual behavior and forms of collectivist control designed only to limit the anarchy of self-interest."

Again, the missing middle.

On my first Monday night in Missoula I attended a city council meeting. City council meetings might be described as the engine rooms of democracy. Here we descend from the lofty theory of the bridge and the expansive vistas from the deck to the dimly lit, sweaty, nitty-gritty of political action where vital initiatives are taken, where compromises are hammered out, where the infrastructure of our civic lives is nourished and attended to. After all, in modern societies there would not be much democracy if the water lines aren't working properly or the power goes out. Democracy at this level is, as it was on this particular Monday night, about where to put a traffic light, how many feet to widen a street, how to control growth along the Rattlesnake Creek and about budgets, endlessly about budgets. From its inception democracy has been intimately bound up with commerce, and that remains true today. At this particular meeting Kemmis had presented his budget for the coming year to council. It was a bulky volume about the size of the New York phone directory and must, I thought, have drawn the mayor deep into the intricacies of regulatory bureaucracies. On this night in Missoula as in thousands of similar meetings across America, the business of democracy went on, conducted by the citizens themselves, bearing the full burden of their humanity.

Later, I asked Kemmis what was most satisfying about his job as mayor.

"Presiding over city council meetings," he smiled. In a more serious vein he began to talk about Missoula Vision 2020, a long-range planning document developed under the mayor's initiative.

"It is a good example," Kemmis said, "of a community facing its problems and articulating its ideals. People of all sectors of the community participated in one way or another in producing the report. This is a political initiative as promising as we could humanly hope for."

At this point Kemmis did not seem so pessimistic about our civic capacities. I told him that.

"I have always believed that politics is a transforming work," he said. "Through politics we are brought from a state of savagery to a state of civilization, and only through the medium of politics can our highest potential as human beings be reflected. There are two levels upon which this transforming work must occur. On the individual level, it requires a revitalized sense of what might be meant by citizenship. On the level of the body politic, it implies a renewed understanding of the polis."

I asked how he would evaluate the two levels.

"We begin with the recognition that the meaning of citizenship is profoundly corrupted. People who customarily refer to themselves as taxpayers are not even remotely related to democratic citizens. Taxpayers bear a dual relationship to government, neither half of which has anything at all to do with democracy. They pay tribute to the government, and they receive services from it. So does every subject of a totalitarian regime. Then there is the idea of a concerned citizen as if citizenship were essentially a form of grievance. Or the hopelessly confused phrase 'private citizen,' which is the civic equivalent of dry water. Standing by itself, which it rarely does, the word 'citizen' evokes all the weariness and unhappiness we associate with public life, so that most of us would not readily, let alone enthusiastically, call ourselves 'citizens.' So we have to face these corruptions and reclaim the rich political meaning of citizenship from the rubble of a political culture inhabited largely by sullen taxpayers."

"Are we doing that?"

"I see evidence that there is emerging a greater sense of citizenship in which adversaries learn to solve problems through face-to-face collaboration. This sense of citizenship is based on a renewed understanding of what it means to be a neighbor. In Old English a neighbor was a 'near dweller.' Neighbors are people who find themselves living in adjoining places and this in turn implies relationships of interdependence and collaboration. A neighbor is someone we live with. We may not like that neighbor or that place; we may well wish we were elsewhere with more agreeable neighbors. But realistically the practice of being neighbors draws together the concepts of place, of inhabitation, and of the kinds of practices from which civic virtues evolve. I detect a renewed sense of place in America and therefore a revival of citizenship."

"And is that place the city in the sense you described it earlier?" I asked.

"It is," he answered. "That is the *res publica,* the common thing we will together."

This brought us to the second level of the transforming work of politics: a renewed understanding of the polis.

"I've already talked at some length about my ideas on this," he said.

"Do you have anything to add?"

"Let me recall here a striking image I have borrowed from Kurt Schmoke, the former mayor of Baltimore. Schmoke has spoken of his vision of Baltimore becoming a 'city in grace' which seems to me rich in political resonance. The idea of a city in grace is appealing for two seemingly unrelated reasons. First, it answers to a deep longing for a spiritual dimension in public life. In our prevailing political culture, this longing produces one of two results. The first is alienation from public life because it does not fulfill this spiritual need. People do not like politics, or public life in general, because it does not engage their highest or deepest instincts. So they either abandon citizenship altogether, or they import into politics a narrow, essentially mean-spirited religiosity which in fact only worsens the prevailing gracelessness of public life, thus driving new multitudes into alienation. This has been all too much the legacy of the New Right, just as alienation from an inhumanly secularized public life has been the legacy of liberalism. Against this background, Mayor Schmoke's explicit commitment to nurturing some form of grace in public life comes as a rare flash of both spiritual and political wisdom.

"But Mayor Schmoke's vision is appealing for a second, equally compelling reason. Put simply, his dream seems to be (if only barely) within human reach. In its concreteness lies its hope. That concreteness is intimately connected to the nature of the political entity of which he speaks. A city in grace, while barely imaginable, could actually occur on the face of the earth because a city is a real, living organism, and therefore capable of something we might call grace. We can imagine governors or presidents borrowing Mayor Schmoke's rhetoric and speaking in similar terms of the political entities they govern. But states and nation-states are abstractions to which we cannot easily apply any of the key concepts discussed here: not wholeness, not presence, not grace, and therefore, not, I will argue, civilization or citizenship. If we are serious about reclaiming politics, we must give up the bankrupt delusion that a humanly engaging politics can be created where wholeness, presence or grace are strangers. If the idea of a 'city in grace' is to be more than a ringing sound bite, then we have to give full weight to both of its nouns. We need to ask what a city might have to do with grace. Grace is such a prolific concept that no one understanding can exhaust its meaning. But surely some part of grace has to do with a way of acting in the world which is strikingly appropriate to the time and place."

The idea was new to me. I told Kemmis I would need some time to absorb it. "So will I," he said.

I had one final question for him: "Is Montana still the last best place?"

He took a while to answer. "It could be," he said finally. "It could be."

He thought about my question a little longer, then went on: "I think it was John Maynard Keynes who said that the political problem is to combine economic efficiency, social justice, and individual liberty. Those are the goals we have essentially laid out in our Visions Report, but no one would expect them to be realized in anything but an imperfect manner. I think with our resources here, our traditions, and latent political will, we have as good a shot at it as anybody. An enduring sense of possibility seems to dwell in this place."

On my last afternoon in Missoula, I drove the few miles to Bonner where the Blackfoot River meets the Clark Fork. The Blackfoot was elevated to mythic status in Norman Maclean's *A River Runs Through It* which I had recently read—a haunting tale about beauty and death in the land of the Big Sky, about helping and about those for whom there is no help, about the difficulty of friendship and the river of good and evil that runs through the human heart.

It was a fitting place to reflect on the image of the city Kemmis adopted from Mayor Schmoke. This quote from the novel seemed the appropriate one: "All good things . . . come by grace and grace comes by art and it does not come easy."

Democracy is such a good thing. It too comes by grace and art. And it does not come easy. In Montana or anywhere else.

PART TWO

Technology and Capitalism

Headnotes

We often talk about democracy in a vacuum, as though it existed more or less independently of other social forces. Matters become murkier when we realize that democracy is inextricably interwoven with institutions that may or may not favor democracy. In fact, one of the paradoxes of democratic society is that most of the institutions in that society are not in and of themselves very democratic. The military is certainly not. Religious, legal, and educational institutions don't tend to be. And so forth. In Part II we discuss the market economy and technology, two powerful shapers of modern society which stand in a highly ambiguous relationship to democracy.

Consider the wondrous market. Some think it the very foundation of democracy; some think it is the enemy of democracy; and many seem to conflate the two. The end-of-history school of thought sees in the triumph of the market economy the triumph of democracy itself; economic freedom is one with political freedom; democracy and capitalism have become virtually interchangeable terms.

Elmer Johnson has long wrestled with the relationship between democracy and capitalism. From one perspective, capitalism has been a great success. Adam Smith would marvel at the economic miracle we have wrought. On the other hand, capitalism must take much of the blame for our most egregious social pathologies: it encourages a predatory ethic and adversarial excesses that are deplorable; it unleashes a rampant commercialism that is ultimately self-destructive; and its attack upon traditional values is vicious.

Johnson advocates a restoration of the fiduciary ethic that made capitalism possible in the first place, the use of the law to promote responsible corporate governance, and a return to the nonmarket sources of moral behavior. Johnson says: "While there are many reasons favoring a market order over alternative forms of economic organization, the ultimate justification of a market order is that it provides a necessary condition to the full possibilities for lives of moral worth."

Consider now technology. Again we are plunged deep into the dark country of ambiguity. In ancient Rome the temple of Janus faced east and west to symbolize the hope of dawn and the day's ending at sunset. In his two faces were inscribed the mysteries of time itself: youth and age, life and death, permanence and chance. In twentieth century society technology plays a Janus-like role as the focus of our highest hopes and our worst fears.

Many technophiles speak confidently of electronic republics, the empowerment of people through the Internet, and a more democratic diffusion of knowledge. Michael Kinsley, who works for Microsoft and edits the on-line magazine *Slate*, stated their case well. In one breath he notes that technology has made many of the software programmers where he works rich while still young *and* the widely shared belief, indeed passionately held belief, that today's technology revolution is also "a revolutionary advance for human liberty." His logic is tight, and typical of technophiles: technology makes people rich, being rich constitutes an advance in human freedom.

Well, maybe. But those who do not share this optimism have good arguments on their side too. A great many of our anxieties and frustrations do stem from the technologies we have created. Freedom can be threatened as well as enhanced by technology, and in an increasingly panoptic society the threat seems often greater than the enhancement. Minimally, our technological creations are difficult to control, and in the worst case scenario they have the power to destroy life itself.

Arthur Kroker shows us the somber side of technology. He invites us to think hard about whether it is or is not on the side of democracy. "We are the first citizens of a society that has been eaten by technology," Kroker claims. "We are a culture that has actually vanished into the dark vortex of the electronic frontier. Now everyone comes under the spell of digital reality." Everywhere we look today there is unabashed adulation of the technological juggernaut as a new form of salvation. But what we don't attend enough to is the authoritarianism implicit in technological advances. This is where the political question arises: If we lose a critical perspective on technology then is politics nothing more than a naked instrument of the will to power, of absolute control? Kroker sees a lot of fascism associated with technology.

What is the bottom line? According to Kroker, "Democracy in the sense of consensus formation through debate, discussion, public deliberation, and participation is long dead. With the advent of electronic technology, voters have become mere servomechanisms to a process of virtuality that in effect guarantees their disappearance in the political process. Democracy lives now as an image effect of an earlier time." And this: "Our political predicament is how to be simultaneously a new race of techno-mutants in the name of an expanding freedom. All the usual approaches to ethics and politics have been canceled out."

Does Kroker overstate his case? He might. But it is one we would do well to ponder.

Mark Kingwell works in the existential shadowland where capitalism and technology impinge on our understanding of happiness. Popular culture beams a single message: Be happy. We have shelves of self-help books, drugs, and a mighty advertising industry that "represent the kind of technological, shortcut thinking that makes happiness hollow and cynical in our culture." What can be done about this? Kingwell argues that we must break loose from the philosophy of thin utilitarianism that is at the basis of our therapeutic culture and its market-based idea of happiness. He turns our attention to a "more robust theory of happiness, a more expansive vocabulary of happiness, and healthier practices of happiness" that can be found in Stoicism and ancient Greek thought with their emphasis on character and virtue. Kingwell writes: "The only possible way the notion of happiness can be reclaimed from the machinery of manipulation and self-indulgence is to recast it as the possession of a virtuous character and the performance of virtuous action."

Finally, Kingwell marks a connection between our weak notions of happiness and our legitimation concerns about democracy. He draws on Aristotle's theory of virtue and Habermas's notion of dialogic partipation to reinvigorate our thinking about justice (the biggest political problem of our time, according to Kingwell) and citizenship. We need the stronger remedies of such thinking to get beyond the shallow utilitarianism that holds us in its grip.

Is Democracy Compatible with Capitalism?

Elmer W. Johnson is a partner in the Chicago law firm of Kirkland & Ellis. He joined the firm in 1956 and has been a partner since 1962. He served as a member of the firm's managing committee from 1971 to 1993. Mr. Johnson also served as general counsel for International Harvester Company during its reorganization from 1981 to 1982. From 1982 to 1983, he served as special counsel to the chairman of Ameritech Corporation in connection with the break-up of AT&T. From May 1, 1983, to June 30, 1988, he held various offices at General Motors Corporation with responsibility during all or most of that period for the legal, operating and public affairs staffs. In May 1987, he was elected executive vice president and a director of the company and served as a member of the Executive and Finance Committees of the board. On July 1, 1988, he retired from General Motors and returned to the private practice of law at Kirkland & Ellis.

Johnson has published widely on ethical and social issues, and in the early 1990s he directed an interdisciplinary study project on public policy and the future of urban transportation. When I interviewed him, his report, entitled *Avoiding the Collision of Cities and Cars: Urban Transportation for the Twenty-First Century,* had just been published. We began with some talk about that report. It is pretty grim reading and documents in great detail what many already sense: to wit, we are overly dependent on the automobile at a cost we can ill afford. The report calls for "habit changing strategies and a new transportation ethic for the twenty-first century." The conversation soon enough turned to the larger ethical and social issues that define the actions of America's corporations about which Mr. Johnson offers many insights.

A particularly thorny issue is the relationship between the corporation and democracy. We recalled that Alfred P. Sloan, the legendary president of General Motors, wrote a good book on his experiences called *My Years with General Motors*. I asked Johnson if he might write a similar book.

"Sloan did write a good book," Johnson said. "I recommend it to anyone studying business. But I don't have any plans to write such a book."

Johnson offered this brief history of his years in Detroit: "I went to General Motors in 1983. Little did I know it would be a decade of great change and upheaval. We would have to go back to the '20s to find anything comparable. One of the first things I did was seek out a senior executive to get briefed on the industry. We had lunch in one of the company's well-appointed dining rooms. I felt very much the novice, so I asked: 'What is the most important thing going on in the industry now?' The older executive said to me: 'By the 1990s there will be only six automobile companies in the world. Only the largest will survive. Only they have the resources and organizational ability to exploit a global economy.' I believed him. After all, the first 200 years of the Industrial Revolution marked a steady evolution toward the large corporation with an ever greater division of labor and hierarchical complexity. It seemed logical that this evolution should continue. But the 1990s have come and gone and that executive could not have been more wrong. Today we have not six automobile companies but 160. So I came to the sober conclusion that the evolution of the large corporation had ended. In fact it had ended over ten years before I came to GM. I soon realized that I was caught up in a changing global environment. One of history's most remarkable organizational achievements—the large public corporation, governed by an independent board of directors—has served society for most of this century as an unrivaled creator of wealth and employment.

"If Adam Smith had risen from the grave and paid us a visit in the late 1950s, he would have marveled at the economic miracle we had wrought and at the tolerable working order of the fiduciary ethic that made it possible. We can attribute the success of managerial capitalism partly to the evolution of laws governing managers, responsibilities toward investors, partly to business schools for professionalizing management, and partly to the introduction of compensation and incentive arrangements that work to align the corporate interest and the manager's self-interest. But by the 1960s cracks had begun to appear, and now the symptoms of decay have grown serious. Now the corporation is an endangered species, and we must take strong measures if we are to preserve and renew it."

"What are some of the symptoms of decay?"

"There are two kinds: generic and specific. Among the generic causes I would cite bureaucratic rigidity. Because they were so successful, corporations became smug and inattentive; top management became more remote from operations, and boards grew more passive. They trained few middle managers to exercise the kind of peripheral vision and integrative judgment required for bottom-line accountability in operating units, and management responsibility became fragmented and diffuse. Younger executives did not make, and were not expected to make, difficult trade-offs involving market, technology, and costs. These cultures also discouraged frank, open debate among executives about the problems they faced. There was a clear perception among the rank and file that top management did not receive bad news well. But a basic law of nature made itself manifest. Human beings and organizations are apt to grow fat, dumb, and comfortable in the absence of external shocks to the system."

"And those shocks came?"

"Yes, a number of specific ones. One of them was the explosion of information technology which gives small companies equal access to information and reduces transaction costs so greatly that large, hierarchical organizations no longer enjoy their former advantage. As a result, many big corporations are considering divestment of assets or decentralization of operations that can be carried out less expensively and more flexibly by autonomous suppliers.

"A second force is the advent of flexible manufacturing, which allows companies to make highly differentiated products on a single assembly line. For example, if auto assembly operations are most efficient at 200,000 cars a year, modern technology permits a manufacturer with only one plant to turn out, say, five distinct models of 40,000 cars each and compete effectively with a manufacturer with five plants, each of which produces 200,000 cars of only one model.

"Third, the emergence of worldwide markets enables formerly small, high-cost manufacturers like BMW to achieve optimum levels of production efficiency by catering to a global market niche.

"Fourth, we have witnessed a moral revolution in the workplace. Traditionally, we assumed that manufacturing efficiency required absolute management control over the production process. Management did all the thinking and decision making; workers carried out orders. Over the last decade, however, we in the United States have begun to see that the advantage enjoyed by many of our global competitors lies not so much in their automation skills and efficiencies of scale as in all their thoughtfully designed efforts to em-power workers, give them a greater sense of job satisfaction, and elicit their enthusiastic commitment to quality and company.

"Finally, we have experienced a profound evolution in corporate capital-ism—the professionalization of the investment function and the emergence of the institutional investor. The growing importance of forced savings in the form of public and private pension funds has accelerated this development. Average savers no longer decide how to invest their savings in the stock market; they don't even decide how much to save. Companies, unions, gov-ernments, and educational institutions have pension plans that tell workers how much of their income will be saved and invested for the future. The plan's administrators then choose professional investors. Unfortunately, this system shows numerous symptoms of ill health."

"Was all of this apparent to you when you went to General Motors in 1983?"

"Not really. When I joined General Motors I thought of it as a career. I didn't think I would ever return to my law firm. In the beginning I was so busy that I didn't really see the whole picture. I had responsibility for several staffs and worked long days. It was a stunning education. So intense. So new. I was on the fast track, and after two years Roger Smith, then CEO of General Motors, called me in and said he wanted me to take over Canada. I asked why. So I could get my operational stripes. And Canada was the easiest place to earn them. 'It's hard to fall on your face in Canada,' Smith told me. 'But,' I protested, 'I don't want a job where I can't fall on my face.' I knew I was a can-didate for the chairpersonship, but after about four years I was convinced that Roger Smith's strategies were failing and I thought I knew why, or at least some of the reasons. In April of 1987 I expressed to him some of my doubts. He countered by making me executive vice president and putting me on the board. I said to myself, well, maybe this way I will have a chance to do some-thing. In due course I presented a white paper which contained my diagnosis of what was wrong with GM and what I thought it would take to fix it."

"What did you recommend?"

"My prescription included new blood in the top 500 (I thought about 100 of them should leave); decentralization and revamping the committee system which ate up incredible amounts of time. It is ridiculous to try to manage a half million people—beyond human scale. It kills hope and results in dead people coming to work each day. I had concluded that GM's problems were not the result of just ten years of bad luck, but of thirty years of bad corporate culture in which the middle and upper management had become so self-assured, so insular, so complacent, so arrogant that they thought they were beyond the reach of the competition and even the external environment. There were only two ways I saw to break this logjam at the top. The leveraged buyout was the principal mechanism of the '80s. But I zeroed in on the board of directors. Where are they? What are they doing? Why aren't they bringing a fresh perspective to bear on corporate culture? It is their duty to monitor top management and step in where necessary. Yet they just sat there feeding at the same trough."

"Which the corporate culture encouraged?"

"Yes, the club mentality prevailed. Management has so many ways of neutering the board, first of all by picking the members. It's a mutual admiration society. A good old boys club."

"How did boards get that way?"

"As the control mentality grew, CEOs selected and groomed their directors with great care, and often, by increasing the number of directors, they decreased their individual influence. Significant stock ownership was not required for board membership, and those who questioned the CEO's judgment or policies were often excluded from the inner sanctum—the nominating and compensation committees. As boards of directors grew larger, meetings tended to become mere formalities, often degenerating into slide shows or theatricals carefully scripted by the chairperson. There was little or no time for give and take on the issues. The chief executive often became the sole mediator between the board and management.

"Other factors worked against board effectiveness as well. Most boards developed close social ties that tended to restrain their monitoring function. The outgoing chief executive often continued to serve on the board after retirement. Outside directors seldom met alone to discuss management issues, and when they did, the retired chief executives membership on key committees inhibited free and open discussion. After all, the old chief executive often picked the new, and the two usually stayed in close communication. Given the way boards operated, even a CEO who understood the need for radical reform was up against almost insuperable odds, especially if he was a career insider. How could he suddenly change colors and repudiate his predecessor, the man who had given him his job? That predecessor still sat on the board, after all, and had selected many of the other members. Short of a clear crisis, it would be imprudent or futile to fight such odds.

"Perhaps my experience as a lawyer over the last twenty years has warped my view—lawyers don't spend a lot of time with companies where everything is going well. In all fairness, I should also point out that every board I've ever worked with had at least a few diligent, independent members who did their best to carry out their responsibilities. But the board culture generally prevented them from achieving a critical mass at the critical moment."

"How was your report received?"

"With stony silence."

"Did it damage your chances for the chairpersonship?"

"I suppose. About six months before I left I told Smith I didn't care about the CEO position. I wanted to be part of a great team. He told me I was still a leading contender for it. But he was telling four or five other people the same thing. I told him I thought this was very destructive. By January 1988 I had come to the end of my rope. I was exhausted trying to change the place. And I began to seriously wonder whether I was in the right place."

"Did you lack the requisite political skills?"

"As defined by the corporation, perhaps. The team was my focus, not personal preferment."

"But surely all corporate executives have to be team players?"

"That is true up to a point. Then what I call the giraffe principle of corporate leadership kicks in. The higher up the hierarchy you go the more your neck sticks out above the others. The process ends in acute CEO-itis."

"Was the experience disillusioning for you?"

"Yes, although it happened little by little."

"Could it be that you were somewhat naive?"

"Maybe in the sense that I was too much swayed by my experience in my law firm where we had a collegial governance system. But I was not naive in maintaining my ties to my law firm. This gave me a good deal of independence while at GM. And it gave me an out. I could always go back and, of course, did. In that sense I was not naive."

"Do you think you left GM a better place?"

"I did. I identified a lot of good people and put them in key positions. They will be influential for years to come and have already done a lot to cut down on the old tunnel vision and move the company into the twenty-first century. I think it will now be easier for GM to recruit talented young people. I also raised questions about how GM impinged directly on the public interest, particularly in the areas of safety, environmental impact, and energy use. I think some good will come of my efforts in that direction. I might have even done something for family values by making the company reexamine its policy of moving management every two years or so. Does this policy serve some overwhelming corporate purpose? I asked."

"Isn't it now clear that the market economy is still the best economy? Everyone everywhere is singing the praises of capitalism, especially since the collapse of communism."

"True. With the collapse of communism, capitalism's chief competitor seems to have disappeared. A little more than half a century ago, we were in the grip of a global depression, and the future of democratic capitalism hung in the balance. It appeared that socialism might well be the ultimate fate of the free world. At about that time, Friederich A. von Hayek, a forty-year-old Austrian economist who had distinguished himself in business cycle theory, did something almost impossible for an economist. He wrote a passionate book: a soul-stirring polemic called *The Road to Serfdom*. It was addressed to socialists of all parties, and its purpose was to force them to think through the dire consequences of their theories: how socialism would gradually paralyze the driving forces and smother the creative powers of a free civilization."

"What was the gist of Hayek's argument?"

"Hayek's thesis is that socialists have a fatally wrong conception of reality: namely, that a central authority can actually garner all the relevant knowledge necessary to inform individuals in what direction their multitudinous efforts must aim so as to maximize the total wealth of a society. History has amply demonstrated that only a spontaneous market order can perform this extraordinary feat. Hayek, indeed, has turned out to be a prophet in his own time. He is right to pay tribute to the marvelous coordinating function performed by market systems. He rightly excoriates the socialist planners for their fatal conceit: their absurd idea that a central authority has the knowledge to perform this function.

"Capitalism has raised the material well-being of the masses of citizens in the advanced societies of the world to levels that were never dreamed possible, and this despite the population growth of the last two hundred years. The deliverance of the masses of people in democratic capitalist societies from grinding poverty has been accomplished not by pursuing equality but by harnessing the energy of private self-interest. Capitalism also decentralizes power and responsibility. All utopian forms of economic organization, dedicated to achieving greater economic equality, require centralization of power. In the process, the managers of the centrally ordered economy tend to be corrupted by their power, and the system breaks down. Each day we hear fresh evidence of the depth and breadth of corruption in the bankrupt socialist economies of the former Soviet Union and Eastern Europe."

"This sounds like the market model is the one to which all nations should aspire."

"I'm afraid not. I've recounted the blessings of the market and the reasons for its success. But we periodically forget that the market ceases to be a blessing when it gets out of hand, as it has in our country over the last decade."

"What are some of the symptoms of this?"

"For one thing, we have been on a credit binge in both the public and private sectors. Our government went on a public spending spree in the 1980s and raised the level of the annual budget deficit from $28 billion in the late 1970s to the current level of about $300 billion per year. At the same time, these legislators substantially deregulated much of our private financial system. In the process, the titans of our banking industry developed an expansive new market share mentality that replaced good old-fashioned credit judgment. This enabled our entire populace to go on an unprecedented spending spree of their own. In the world of big business, we greatly extended the role of the market. We created something called the market for corporate control. The device for playing in this market was the junk-bond financed, bust-up takeover. It enabled a lot of investment bankers, lawyers, takeover artists, and managements to become multi-multi-millionaires overnight by churning wealth instead of creating it.

"This credit binge is now over, and we are in the first stages of a long hangover. We have yet to figure out the nature and extent of the mess. It will take years to sort out. Even if the market doesn't turn us all into predators, the commercialism of the last ten years has certainly turned many more of us into full-time consumers. The stores are always open. Everything is for sale, including human companionship and conversation. Today's marketers intrude into every nook and cranny of our lives to promote artificial and obsessional wants. They relentlessly drive home the message that joy lies in goods. Each year they spend $130 billion in advertising, all tax deductible. Given the intensity of our devotion to individual getting and spending, it is not surprising that the gulf between rich and poor—a gulf not inherent in capitalism, by the way—has widened very significantly over the last ten years. The connection between the privatism of the unbridled market and the loss of family and communal values shows up in increasing levels of child abuse, drug addiction and crime, and the deterioration of physical and social infrastructures, social pathologies we are all familiar with."

"This is the bad news."

"Which is further complicated by the emergence of a global market economy that seems destined to subject every country to its domain and discipline. It seems no longer possible for a society to maintain a distinct culture and traditional values. If this is true, we are in a terrible fix. It would mean that all participants in the global economy are in a race to the bottom: namely, that those governments requiring the least protection of environmental and worker interests will be most likely to attract capital investment; that as wealth and income are distributed on the bases of one's prowess in the competitive jungle and one's luck in the lotteries of family wealth and genetic endowment, the concentrations of wealth and poverty will become intolerable; and that the interest of future generations will inevitably be sacrificed to the buying power of the living."

"So the market is at best a mixed bag?"

"Very much so."

"How do you see the relationship between democracy and capitalism?"

"There is a real but somewhat complicated relationship. Market societies long predate such democratic arrangements as the widely extended rights to vote and hold office. The political preconditions of markets have much more to do with the rule of law, the sanctity of property rights, and the enforceability of promises. However, it is probably the case that democracies flourish only in those societies where the organization of economic life is left largely to privately owned (nongovernmental) enterprises operating under conditions of free competition for the consumer's dollar. Democratic life requires a certain level of stability, prosperity, and personal autonomy that the market makes possible."

We had here, I felt, reached ethical bedrock in our conversation. As a veteran professor of business ethics, I have long tried to impress upon my students the ancient wisdom that economics is a branch of moral philosophy. To try to make sense of capitalism (or any economic system) without situating it in an ethico-philosophical context is a futile endeavor. No economic order, and certainly not capitalism, free-floats in a value vacuum. Value neutrality does not here apply. Adam Smith had this in mind when he called the market model "the natural system of perfect liberty and justice."

Benjamin Rush called commerce an instrument of "humanizing mankind." Alexis de Tocqueville was of the opinion that commercial culture encourages us "to try to attain that form of greatness and happiness which is proper to ourselves." Charles Montesquieu thought commerce would "soften barbaric morals" and induce peace among nations. If nations engage in trade, the chances of war lessen. President Eisenhower echoed Montesquieu when he advocated trade with the Soviets as a means of containing their ambition for world domination. "Commerce," wrote Montesquieu in the *Spirit of the Laws*, "is a cure for the most destructive prejudices; for it is almost a general rule, that wherever there is commerce, there we meet with agreeable manners. . . . Peace is the natural effect of trade. Two nations who traffic with each other become reciprocally dependent; for if one has an interest in buying, the other has an interest in selling; and thus their union is founded on their mutual necessities." One of the best cases for the nexus between the market and morality was made by David Hume.

Hume's strongest argument rests on his analysis of commodities and the close connection he postulates between commerce and culture, art and civility. Commodities were not for Hume, as they were for Marx, a kind of fetishism; nor were they symptoms of a rank materialism, as they were for Matthew Arnold. Rather they were a high expression of human creativity directly related to our most civilized achievements. The argument, in simple form, is this: commerce produces commodities; commodities produce refinement; refinement produces virtue. "The ages of refinement," Hume said, "are both the happiest and most virtuous." Hume makes a brilliant connection between the mechanical and the liberal arts: "The same age which produces great philosophers and politicians, renowned generals and poets, usually abounds with skillful weavers and ship carpenters. We cannot reasonably expect that a piece of woollen cloth will be brought to perfection in a nation which is ignorant of astronomy, or where ethics are neglected." The spirit of excellence first aroused by commerce will carry over to art and science with the result that "profound ignorance is totally banished, and men enjoy the privilege of rational creatures, to think as well as act, to cultivate the pleasures of the mind as well as those of the body."

No one has made this particular argument as cogently as Hume. One finds elements of it in the Greeks, and the medievals were quite conscious of the connection between theoretical and practical activities. But after the Renaissance, this integral manner of construing values is largely lost, and never expressed as forcefully as in Hume. Industry and knowledge are "linked together by an indissoluble chain," he said, to increase and show faith in our humanity. These qualities, both reason and experience show, are found to be "peculiar luxurious ages." There is nothing foppish or effete in Hume's use of words like "refinement," "luxury," "pleasure." He associates them with commodities and associates commodities with high culture. Hume's human-ism is robust and unequivocal. Commerce and knowledge work in tandem "to increase our humanity"; they are the chief characteristics that distinguish a civilized age from times of barbarism and ignorance.

Hume emphasizes, as always, the advantages of commerce for the political order: "But industry, knowledge, and humanity are not advantageous in pri-vate life alone; they diffuse their beneficial influence on the public to render the government as great and flourishing as they make individuals happy and prosperous. The increase and consumption of all the commodities are advan-tages to society." The converse is also true, that "in a society where there is no demand for such superfluities, men sink into indolence, lose all enjoyment of life, and are useless to the public." Hume's argument now looks like this: progress in commerce leads to progress in the arts, which in turn "is favorable to freedom and has a natural tendency to preserve, if not produce, a free gov-ernment."

I got somewhat carried away with my digression on Hume. But I did not forget that I was having a conversation, not giving a lecture. I asked Johnson what he thought of Hume's analysis. He said that it was good provided that we bear in mind the limits and provisos that Adam Smith pointed out. I then asked Johnson if he thought the emerging nations could look to capitalism for a model.

"The new leaders of Poland, the Czech Republic, and Hungary, as well as those that are emerging in the republics of the former Soviet Union, have mixed emotions about our brand of capitalism. They are searching for ways to create market economies that avoid our consumption-goods hedonism and our extremes of wealth and poverty. Perhaps they've been re-reading Rousseau."

"Rousseau? What did he have to say?"

"Here is an interesting historical insight. Over 200 years ago, when Poland was undergoing one of its periodic political reformations, its leadership called on Rousseau for counsel. Not being the bashful type, he told them exactly what to do. Here is what he told them: 'In reforming your constitution, if your only wish is to become noisy, brilliant, and fearsome, and to influence the other peoples of Europe, their example lies before you; devote yourselves to following it. . . . Try to make money very necessary, in order to keep the people in a condition of great dependence; and with that end in view, encour-age material luxury, and the luxury of spirit which is inseparable from it. In this way you will create a scheming, ardent, avid, ambitious, servile and knavish people, like all the rest; one given to the two extremes of opulence and misery, of license and slavery with nothing in between. I know that men can only be made to act in terms of their own interests; but pecuniary interest is the worst, the best, and most corrupting of all, and even, as I confidently repeat and shall always maintain, the least and weakest in the eyes of those who really know the human heart. In all hearts there is naturally a reserve of grand passions; when greed for gold alone remains, it is because all the rest, which should have been stimulated and developed, have been enervated and stifled.'"

"An alarm already sounded by Plato."

"Plato talked about the division of labor and the natural harmony of the simple market economy in the *Republic*. The city of sows, as he pictured it, whose simple needs were harmoniously met through the exchange system just didn't work for long. The city of simple needs soon became the luxurious, feverish city of hedonistic consumption. The invisible hand of the market was inadequate to curb the acquisitiveness and concupiscence of the citizens. Thanks to Plato, Rousseau, and others, we have known for a very long time, but have forgotten, that market systems have serious weaknesses."

I said that we seem also to have forgotten Adam Smith's ideal of a commercial humanism. Or perhaps it was a false ideal to begin with. Smith thought that the market economy would promote civilized behavior and a range of respectable virtues.

"True, but we must remember that Smith also cautioned that the market system, even though it be the best available system, is fraught with serious weaknesses and must be restrained by a regulatory web that strengthens the fiduciary ethic within our intermediate institutions and protects important social interests. For the market to be a humanly workable system it must draw heavily on moral wellsprings that predate the market itself, on virtues of compassion, self-restraint and judgment that may indeed be supported or even strengthened by the market but for the flourishing of which the market is not sufficient."

"Say more about these intermediate institutions and the fiduciary ethic."

"As far as I am concerned, that is the heart of the matter. I began studying this problem many years ago. It soon became apparent to me that there is no such thing as a self-regulating economy. The market economy, like all economies, must be undergirded by the intermediate institutions (i.e., those between government and the individual, such as family, church, the corporation, and the media organizations) that give structure to our economic and social life and that flesh out the natural hierarchy of the social bond. This conception, with its emphasis on the fiduciary ethic that sustains these institutions, is logically a subsection of an overall theory of justice that comprehends an ideal of the common good. In this regard I have been strongly influenced by such diverse works as Edmund Burke's *Reflections on the French Revolution,* Emil Brunner's *Justice and the Social Order,* and John Rawls's *Theory of Justice,* as well as by Alan Gewirth's excellent essay, "Political Justice," in *Social Justice,* edited by R. B. Brandt. To state my case very briefly and much oversimplified: These thinkers take into account in their conceptions of a just society the twin principles of (a) the equal freedom of individuals for rational and moral development and (b) the common good of the organic community. They recognize the tensions between these two principles and the danger of swallowing up individuality in some large corporate whole. But they also recognize the fundamental compatibility of the two principles in that the development of the individual can only flourish in community. Some of these writers envision an ideal of hierarchic community, as do I, in which the diverse and complementary gifts and unequal capacities of individuals are made to work together for the common good. It is in this context that I submit my conception of a structured market order. The general idea is to organize our economic life in such a way as to combine the individualist and corporatist aspects of the common good."

"Are you talking now about what is referred to these days as business ethics?"

"In the deepest sense, yes."

"But the specter of Plato's city of sows beggars our best efforts to construct such an ethic."

"Yes. The predatory ethic prevails. As that great moralist James Earl Carter once put it: 'Life is unfair.' God endows relatively few, through no merit of their own, with the best of brains, good looks, family nurture, inherited wealth, energy, and the right breaks at the right times, while he endows the vast majority, through no fault of theirs, with a pittance of one or more of these component conditions of the good life. To make matters worse, the favored few tend to prey on the ignorance and bondage of the many.

"In *The Battle for Human Nature,* Barry Schwartz, a psychology professor at Swarthmore College, argues that the disciplines of economics, evolutionary biology, and behavioral theory have converged on a frightening conception of human beings as self-interested, rational, economic individuals living in a world of social Darwinism very much to their liking, a conception that has come to be so widely accepted that it threatens to undermine the traditional conception of humans as moral beings who are obligated to choose the right, regardless of self-interest. As the modern conception becomes ever more pervasive, Schwartz says, our social lives and democracy itself are tainted and transformed by the market mentality: everything becomes a commodity. Thus, a false conception of humans becomes a self-fulfilling prophecy. Yet the commercialization of noneconomic goods is ultimately self-destructive. Society cannot hold together, and even the market cannot exist, without conventions of social responsibility and mutual trust."

"And against this predatory ethic you posit a fiduciary ethic."

"Yes. My historical perspective indicates that what accounted for the success of the market system was the ability of corporate managers to act primarily not out of self-interest but as fiduciaries. I tend to see this matter from the angle of my own profession, the law. Consider the successive waves of social legislation that, by imposing fiduciary responsibilities on the corporation and its managements, have put a very different face on U.S. capitalism over the last sixty years, a much more human face: the legal reforms of the 1930s and '40s to protect investors, to institute a social security system and to bolster the power of unions; those of the 1960s and '70s to provide social safety nets in the areas of health care and retirement, to better ensure product safety and safety in the workplace, to create equality of employment opportunity and to protect the environment; and even that of the 1980s, to protect employees and communities in connection with plant closings. It turns out that a chief virtue of democratic capitalist societies is their ability, not shared by command-and-control societies, to adapt and evolve and become more just.

"This indicates that our particular brand of market order, in which the large corporation plays such a prominent role, presupposes a fiduciary ethic on the part of corporate managers; that the principal impetus for an elevated fiduciary ethic has come not from the operation of the market but from the efforts of reformers working cooperatively through the machinery of law and self-regulation; that this machinery has performed the schoolmaster function of educating business leaders (and I might add, lawyers and accountants as well) to their responsibilities as fiduciaries in society; and that this education has in turn improved the workings of our market order, so that the market does a much more effective job of taking into account, and in fact placing a premium upon, the ethical caliber of corporate managers than would otherwise have been the case. Without the widespread trust and confidence generated by this elevated fiduciary ethic, corporate managers would not have been able to mobilize the savings of investors, or bring about the complex scale of employee cooperation and hierarchy entailed by the large modern corporation, or account for the production of an ever-increasing share of total goods and services."

"You seem to be advocating a kind of legal paternalism."

"Of a special kind. As the constitutional scholar Walter Berns has said, the law can lend support to the moral dispositions of a people. It is not the whole answer but it is part of the answer. My profession has done a lot to keep the market in its proper place. The law is not just another business. It is a profession whose code of ethics holds out a higher end than the bottom line. As a result we are not simply hired guns that can use every trick and incivility in the books. We are also representatives of a judicial system whose ideals have to do with the approximation of a just society."

"How do you respond to members of your profession who don't think in such ideal terms? You surely cannot see great merit in our trigger-happy, litigious society."

"No. I deplore it. I deplore the excesses of an adversarial culture. Instead of using the law for the structuring of responsible corporate governance, we have created the total adversary society. The idea is that justice will be furthered by group conflict. These forms of paternalism, instead of calling forth elevated codes of fiduciary responsibility and evoking the best qualities of leadership, have produced an atmosphere of legal warfare, with the conflicting parties speaking only through lawyers. As a result, more and more people spend more and more time not in producing more wealth but in arguing over how to divide up a rather static level of wealth."

"How has this sad state of affairs come about?"

"The legal profession has been taken over by plaintiffs' lawyers who control state legislatures and make reform next to impossible. If we could place limits on punitive damages we would take a giant step toward a less harrowing society in which all of us at any given moment can literally lose our shirts. Our confused state points up the incoherence of contemporary jurisprudence, the lack of unifying first principles. In the economic arena we observe the trend toward a more paternalistically supported market order. In the sexual arena the trend has been away from paternalistic restraints toward ever more market freedom. I happen to believe that the first trend is the more healthy one. I assert that paternalism has unfairly been given a bad name. I realize that the very word stirs up unhappy memories of the prohibition era. Let me be clear that I am not about to propose the wholesale enactment of a broad variety of sumptuary legislation. I do contend, however, that we need to develop a jurisprudence of legitimate or justifiable paternalism if we are to stem the twin evils of our time: Leviathan government and rampant individualism."

"You make your case eloquently."

"But I don't want to overstate it. The time was when we looked to the law to provide structural, paternalistic support of such institutions as church and family on the theory that these institutions were necessary props to a high civilization. We long ago shed ourselves as a society of the authoritative influence of church. In recent decades we have questioned the legitimacy of marriage and family, and their future has been questioned. What I have been trying to suggest is that in our corporate-dominated market economy, and in the weakened state of other moral institutions, we must use the law in ways that promote responsible corporate governance, both in terms of the directors' fiduciary responsibilities to stockholders and investors and in terms of the corporations' fiduciary duties to the public in ways that resolve conflicts without resort to costly, inefficient litigation."

"Would you agree that we must go to deeper sources of morality than the law to solve our social problems?"

"Indeed. I believe a society is in a serious state of decadence when its members come to depend primarily on either the market or legal paternalism or any combination of the two for generating and sustaining an adequate ethic. As one who subscribes to the Judeo-Christian tradition, I believe in the primacy of the life of the spirit, in the incredible power of the God-inspired hero, whether the famous prophet or statesman or the little-known teacher or author, to arouse and transform the many from their ignorance and apathy and self-indulgence so that they are enabled to lead lives of freedom and dignity and moral worth. Next to this source of moral power, paternalism and the market are not even poor seconds. While there are many powerful reasons favoring a market order over alternative forms of economic organization, the ultimate justification of a market order is not that it generates or sustains an ethic, but rather that it provides a necessary condition to the full possibilities for lives of moral worth, namely the freedom to choose."

"Thus the spirit of Adam Smith lives on in Elmer Johnson."

"I am an admirer of Adam Smith. He was a great moral educator. Let me offer one of my favorite quotes from *A Theory of Moral Sentiments*. Smith wrote there: 'How selfish soever man may be supposed, there are evidently some principles in his nature, which interest him in the fortune of others, and render their happiness necessary to him, though he derives nothing from it.

The greatest ruffian, the most hardened violator of the laws of society, is not altogether without it.'"

"Some final questions now about the role of education. Is law a good preparation for the business world?"

"Not particularly. Certainly not trial lawyers. I was a business lawyer, which helped somewhat."

"Is business school a good preparation for business?"

"Business schools have been very influential. But in major universities they are reconsidering their role. I suspect the MBA syndrome has had its day. The business major will survive but I would hope in the context of a more liberal education. When I taught a course on business ethics at Colorado College in 1979, over 25 percent of the students were majoring in business. How sad, I thought, to be squandering the best opportunity they will ever have for an education in depth and breadth."

Once again, Johnson touched a nerve. In courses on business ethics, my pitch on the relationship between business and liberal education runs along these lines: Liberal learning and the business world have never been on very cordial terms in America. They wave at one another from opposite sides of a deep abyss and occasionally reach across for a ceremonial handshake. But the distrust abides. The professorate has traditionally adopted a posture of disdain for commerce. Businessmen tend to regard academics as woolly and quite unsuited to the demands of the "real" world.

One consequence of this standoff is that our educational efforts have long been impaled on the horns of an ugly dualism. On the one hand, there is a rankly instrumental view of education according to which its chief purpose is to train the young for the marketplace. On the other hand, the proponents of the liberal arts define education more purely as knowledge for knowledge's sake, as the study of those subjects of intrinsic interest, as mental discipline, or whatever. However liberal education is defined, it is pretty well hived off from practical consequences. The common understanding of liberal learning as conceptual formation lives on amid the many recent attempts to restore the shattered unity of knowledge. It is a view reflected in the rhetoric of countless college catalogs.

Something about this notion of liberal education is deadly. It is narrow, reductionist, and arrogant; it omits large elements of experience from consideration; it ignores the emotions and other noncognitive processes of the mind; it ignores the body, action, and play, and virtually the whole realm of practical knowledge. It is in fact a very illiberal view of the liberal arts. And when liberal education itself becomes illiberal then other segments of experience want for a liberating perspective, for a reasoned place in the spectrum of human values. Dialogue between our different cultural institutions then breaks down, and we take up arms against foes who are largely imaginary.

The time could not be more opportune for a rapprochement. One might envisage a kind of cross-pollination in which the weaknesses of the one might be healed by the strengths of the other. Generous infusions of philosophy, theology, history, and other liberal subjects could help corporate leaders develop a more adequate basis for what they are doing.

Business is more than just business. Money is more than just money. Somewhat analogous to medieval grace, wealth is a metaphor of vitality that directs human energies toward transcendent ends. It must be socially scripted for common purposes. Business has moral, spiritual, and aesthetic aspects as well as purely economic ones. But those in business don't often understand these larger dimensions of what they do.

It is self-evident that corporations command immense power in our society. Our best hope for a better future rests with them. They clearly command the economic and technological resources. It is now necessary that they develop greater intellectual resources—a more liberal understanding of their role in shaping values and forming the public interest. Corporations are now engaged in the war of ideas as much as anyone else. Their effectiveness depends on how well they grasp and relate to broad culture and intellectual trends.

Of course, any rapprochement must be a two-way street. Educators will have to rethink their relationship to society in general and to the business world in particular. They will have to enter into closer dialogue with themselves and with corporate leaders. Above all, liberal educators must reexamine their own product: the kind of student they are sending forth into the world. It may be true, as it is often charged, that college graduates are on a whole a rather feckless lot who are immature and poorly prepared to take up creative roles in the business world. Academics might well heed the advice of French philosopher Henri Bergson. He was once asked to address a congress of teachers. Ill at the time, he sent a one-line message: "Educate your students so they can think as men of action and act as men of thought."

There is no clear-cut distinction between liberal and career education. Truly liberal education is all of a piece, moving in constant and often indistinguishable flow between its theoretical and practical poles. As George Santayana put it, "Everything ideal has a material base and everything material has an ideal fulfillment." There is no longer any convincing way of drawing sharp distinctions between education as an intellectual exercise, as moral formation, as professional training.

Johnson agreed with all that.

"Do you see similar self-questioning going on in law schools?"

"Not as much. We are not likely to see major reforms there. The law is too complex. We are always adding new fields."

"What is the best undergraduate preparation for law?"

"Poetry."

I drew a breath of surprise.

"I cite my own experience here. As a high school student my strengths were in math and the sciences. When I applied for a scholarship to Yale I was told I was too weak in the humanities. In my last year of high school I was tutored intensively in English literature. Not only did this qualify me for the scholarship but it became my major field of study. And, of course, most of the great English literature is poetry."

"Why is this such a good preparation for law?"

"Because lawyers deal with the written word. We need to write well and think clearly. Read well. Analyze well. When I write something I go through three basic stages. I get it out of my head on paper any old which way. I then begin to sort it out and organize it logically. Then comes the final rewrite for condensation, sparkle, style, brevity. When I consider how I work, I realize this is exactly what I did as an English literature major."

"One might argue other disciplines can teach that."

"I agree. I was a history minor. And, as I have indicated, studied a lot of ethics and social philosophy. But, and this is a big difference, it is the primary purpose of literature to teach us about language. No other discipline has that as its primary purpose."

Good news for English departments I thought, as I saw Elmer Johnson to his plane.

The Fate of Democracy in an Electronic Age

On the cover of Arthur Kroker's *The Postmodern Scene: Excremental Culture and Hyper-Aesthetics* (written with David Cook) is a replication of Eric Fischl's painting *The Old Man's Boat and the Old Man's Dog*. It depicts an open boat on a rising sea with five nude bodies in various poses of sexual attraction and revulsion. They appear to have experimented with all the known forms of indulgence and reaped the bitter fruits of unhappiness. Entering the painting from the right foreground is a Dalmatian dog with one paw lifted and its mouth open in an expression of agonized baying.

There is an air of decadence and impending doom about the painting. It conveys a strong flavor of exhaustion, dead power, and ambiguous sexual energies, with undertones of panic and despair. The painting fascinated me as a key to Kroker's books, many of which I have been reading in the recent past. In addition to *The Postmodern Scene*, he has written or coauthored *Spasm: Virtual Reality, Android Music and Electric Flesh; Data Trash: The Theory of the Virtual Class;* and *The Possessed Individual: Technology and the New French Theory.* These and other of his works are somewhat offbeat and unorthodox in style but rich in analysis of the postmodern self and the direction of technology in the late twentieth century.

Cogitating Canadians, sitting on the northern rim of the American empire, have made something of a specialty of probing the role technology plays in society. Marshall McLuhan comes first to mind. McLuhan's studies on the media and technology began to appear at mid-century, and for three decades he lobbed explosive bolts of insight into our self image as a technological society. His *Understanding Media*, first published in 1964, remains a classic in the field. Some view Kroker as the firstborn of McLuhan's vast progeny.

On a rain-swept fall day I flew to Montreal for a conversation with Kroker at Concordia University where he teaches political philosophy. I began with some questions about the Fischl painting. "It expresses the pestilential spirit of late twentieth-century society," Kroker said. By pestilence he means a tortured state of mind that is equally divided between entropy and hyperactivity, ecstasy and dread, piety and cynicism, primitivism and hyper-imaging. "We are a culture of excess," Kroker explained, "and at the same time a culture that is rapidly running down. The decade that stretches before us is like a shimmering uncertainty field in quantum physics: its politics intensely violent, yet strangely tranquil; its culture conspiracy-driven, yet perfectly transparent; its media seductive, yet always nauseous; its population oscillating between utter fascination and deep boredom; its overall mood retro-fascist, yet smarmingly sentimental."

Kroker often uses modern paintings to illustrate technological themes. For example, he uses Giorgio de Chirico's *Landscape Painter* to show how our society has metamorphosized into a "geometry of signs"; Mark Gertler's *Merry Go Round* to convey the strange mix of automation and hysteria in postmodern politics; Max Ernst's *Robing of the Bride* to underscore the price we pay for bonding our experience to the rhythms of technology; and René Magritte's *False Mirror* to emphasize "the nuclear structure of our experience" and "the algorithmic logic set in motion by the computer."

"We are the first citizens of a society that has been eaten by technology," says Kroker. "We are a culture that has actually vanished into the dark vortex of the electronic frontier. Now everyone comes under the mythological spell of digital reality."

In this perspective, we are well beyond the traditional and benign view of technology as the sum of those tools we humans use to advance our ends and interests; well beyond the more recent view that technology is a kind of epistemology which creates unique forms of perception and ways of knowing; beyond even the notion of technology as virtual reality if taken in the mere sense of a substitute reality.

"Sure, technology is that," Kroker agreed. "We can put on head sets and data suits and in various ways wire ourselves into technological reality. We can get into the virtual experience of the expanding universe of digital reality with its spiraling arms, teleonomic logic, infinitely curving space, warp jumps, and multiple time zones. But that isn't the whole story. If we are to understand electronic technology profoundly, we must see it as a life-form."

This is the real meaning of virtual reality. Kroker elaborates: "Technology comes alive, actually acquires organicity. In the course of evolution we had first the animal species, then the human species, and now the technology species that speaks not the language of the social but the language of bio-technology—a species that has its own vocabulary (operant code cloning, sequencing and transcription, recombination); its own aesthetic (virtual reality); blood (electricity); logic (combinatorial); evolutionary principle (chaos theory); diseases (worms and viruses); medical therapeutics (computer vaccines and disinfectants); and cellular membranes (electronic networks)."

Kroker comes on strong. One suspects at first that he is speaking metaphorically, drawing sweeping analogies between biological life and technology. But he is not speaking metaphorically.

"What is unique about our turn-of-the-century experience," Kroker insists, "is that we are witnessing the emergence of technology as a living species existence. The fusion of technology and biology has given rise to living androids, a momentous evolutionary rupture in which technology substitutes its own genetic logic for the heretofore ascendant generic history of the human species. We are the first citizens of the culture of biotechnology. Our genes have escaped their long evolutionary imprisonment in the body and have inscribed themselves in the labyrinthine electronic highways of our recombinant culture."

This language wasn't connecting readily to any of the categories available in my mental files. Like someone waiting for a traffic light to change, I expected that soon Kroker might say something that would let me proceed along more familiar conceptual avenues. I asked him if he could do some translating for me, make matters a little clearer. He showed me the preface to his book *Data Trash* (written with Michael Weinstein). That didn't help at all. At this point Kroker suggested lunch. When we were settled comfortably in one of the little bistros for which downtown Montreal is renowned, I turned the conversation to what I had come primarily to discuss, to wit, the impact of the new technology on democracy.

Kroker's analysis of this question runs on several threads. One thing we notice about society today, he said, is a strident technophilia and a concomitant rise of what he calls "cyber authoritarianism." Everywhere we look is unabashed adulation of technology, an almost hysterical and utterly uncritical infatuation with new and emergent technologies as a form of salvation. It's hard to find anyone these days, especially in the mass media, who takes a critical stance toward our most powerful technologies. Who opposes the automobile or jet airplane? Look how assiduously we cultivate the technology of money and behold how computer technology has invaded the command centers of our culture with scarcely a dissenting voice. We are as lemmings to the sea.

"So," said Kroker, "the first thing we must note is the shutting down, the silencing of all perspectives critical of technotopia. Everyone believes as an article of faith that technology brings progress, greater freedom, better democracy, and so forth."

That's because, and here he paraphrased McLuhan, technology requires utter human docility and acquiescence as benefits an organism that wears its brains outside its hide and its nerves outside its skin. Think of the computer, Kroker said, and what it does to memory.

"The computer has no memory if by memory we mean the presence of political judgment and aesthetic reflection. Perfectly recalling everything in the cold language of data, it is incapable of mediating politics and history. Computer memory is always cynical, always about the actual disappearance of embodied memory and the vanishing of aesthetic judgment."

Kroker thinks this all adds up to a "radically diminished vision of human experience, a disintegrated conception of human good." This is where the political questions arise. If we have no critical perspective on the ethics of technology, when technology slips away into virtuality, then we begin to see some rather frightening political implications. The question we have to grapple with here is this: What does it mean when human experience is made virtual without a sustaining ethical vision or a viable political program? However we answer the question we must begin with the premise that technology has created a new political order.

I wanted to know more about the authoritarian mind that Kroker associates with technology. Lunch was now over, and as we made our way back to his office, Kroker explained it this way: "What we observe," he said, "is the development of a techno-fascism that equates freedom (and other traditional humanistic values) with technology. The deep belief here is that technology increases the possibilities of freedom. This soon escalates to a form of fetishism that we observe from MIT to Silicon Valley. It has a deep deterministic strand: technology is not only good, it is inevitable. This produces a new class structure—what I call the virtual class of elites. They have everything to gain by a technologically mediated society. The logos of leading corporations are: adapt to cyberspace or you're toast; get on the information highway or you will be flattened. Belief in technology is not itself in question."

Then there is what might be termed liberal fascism. Kroker follows Michel Foucault here and calls attention to the varied and subtle ways in which power conspires to discipline members of society—and holds us in unsuspecting bondage. Foucault speaks of the carceral society, and Kroker of the bunker state, to convey the ways in which we are constantly being controlled: tax systems, austerity programs, unemployment and inflation, welfare programs (one of the best control measures yet devised), electronic monitoring, propaganda, and so forth. "The dominant mood of liberal fascism," Kroker says, "is cynical piety—the attitude that what we are doing to you may hurt but it is good for you."

Liberal fascism is at root antidemocratic because when combined with techno-fascism it reduces the language of democracy to the language of technology—an infinite circle of polls, focus groups, advertising, sound bites, simulacra, image creation, and political posturing. French philosopher Jean Baudrillard says that all politics now function in the language of simulation. "The political class has virtually no specificity," says Baudrillard. "Its element is no longer that of decision and action, but that of the video game. The essential is no longer to represent, but to circulate. Politicians try desperately to do this. Their interaction more and more assumes the form of special effects, of mood and performance. Even their ideology does not appeal to our profound convictions. It either circulates among us or it fails to circulate."

"At the level of structural logic," Kroker sums up, "a fundamental ungrounding, a deconstruction of democratic categories has taken place. And at the level of practice, the virtual class has pitted the powerful machinery of the surveillance society against all those not benefiting from the intensive knowledge industries. What this means is that the virtual class imposes a structural logic that is in principle antidemocratic and in practice basically fascistic."

Then, finally, there is the phenomenon of retro-fascism of the kind that wasn't supposed to happen again. But, says Kroker, it has "returned with a vengeance fueled by the dual forces of primitivism and hyper-technology. It emerges whenever there is economic depression, widespread social discontent combined with some form of national humiliation." He cites as manifestations of retro-fascism the rise of Ross Perot in American politics, Berlusconi in Italy, the Reform Party in Canada, the Bosnian Serbs, the former Soviet Republics, and the religious right.

Neo-fascists are driven by ideology, the will to purity, a strong punitive instinct and an ability to play to resentments and fears. A secret longing for the death camps lies not far beneath the surface. "Neofascists," says Kroker, "see enemies everywhere and favor direct action over discussion and negotiation. They fill the political vacuum by trumpeting strong leadership, coercive discipline and unrealistic images of a golden past. But it is an adventure in self-annihilation and it spells the end of democracy for sure."

I wondered if Kroker saw a bright side to the technology he had so far described in chillingly macabre terms. "Are there any liberating aspects of technology?" I asked.

"There are some, but they are limited," he answered. "I think electronic publishing would be an example. This represents a grass-roots effort to make possible international dialogue at a high critical level. The notion of virtual communities has some merit, the ability to transcend ourselves. Such developments are at least interesting. There are many creative interventions in the media scape. In Amsterdam, for example, hackers organized a digital city. They created the city of Amsterdam in virtual language with fifty or sixty thousand people discussing what the shape of that city should be. Also, European artists are quite advanced in thinking about the possibilities of the electronic body. I know about a project in Cologne on virtual feeling. It is an attempt to create an electronic body, and to create a common sensorial framework in which such bodies can actually feel one another. *Tele-existence* has been coined to describe this. The general idea is to transplant images of your body around the world and download them. In Paris I went into a darkened room with a futon in the middle and on it the living image of a person. You could get on the bed and lie together with that person in an embrace of virtual sexuality. We have here a real fusion of human flesh and electronic flesh. Not just an imaging system. A real body emerges. Virtual sexuality is a reality."

I asked Kroker what he thought about the possibilities of electronic democracy. "This is more dubious," he said. "This tends to be pseudodemocracy. It is firmly under the control of politics as usual with built-in suppression circuits and choices that are predetermined to filter out undesirable perspective. It's like Clinton at an Ohio town meeting saying, 'I feel your pain.' Such posturing is media politics at its worst. The message is one with the dominant ethos: Adapt to technology or you're toast."

"But at least you are allowing for some emancipatory possibilities," I said at the risk of repeating myself. "You would allow for a minimal technological humanism."

"It is possible that humans can be honored partners in the process of technological liberation," he admitted. "But I think it is more likely that humans will be reduced to servomechanisms with their flesh and minds fed into the harvesting machines of gigantic image combines. Human flesh is being harvested today on a large scale. Democracy in the old-fashioned sense of face-to-face consensus formation through debate, discussion, public deliberation, and participation is long dead. With the advent of electronic technology voters have become mere servomechanisms to a process of virtuality that in effect guarantees their disappearance as players in the political process. Democracy lives now as an image effect of an earlier time."

I asked for an example of image harvesting machines, and Kroker gave several: "Shopping malls, TV talk shows, computer consoles, rock videos: all quick-time processing machines for harvesting the body of its organic juices, and draining bone and tissue into an indefinite spiral of telemetry. [It's] no longer a consumer model of economy, but an exterminatory one working in the language of harvesting not information but the large-scale archiving of body parts, dreams, and projects; and certainly not communication but a violent strategy of dissuasion for disappearing communication into serial data flows."

I said it all sounded quite weird.

"Not at all," Kroker answered. "It is the most common way in which we live. We are busily computing the whole human experience into gigantic databases, archiving it as informational content then resequencing, recombining, and resegueing these databases to create new mutant forms of human experience and indeed a new form of human history itself. We are becoming quite adept at reconfiguring databases into recombinant futures. Most advertising is based on the idea of a recombinant culture. It is not about buying products but about feeding us into the lip of the electronic net."

"Did Marshall McLuhan foresee all of this?"

"McLuhan was very prophetic," Kroker said. "He understood a processed world and media logic. But the downside of McLuhan was that he was an apologist for the virtual class. McLuhan after all was a Renaissance scholar and steeped in scholastic philosophy, so he was a technological humanist despite himself even though he was much disturbed by the whole specter of technology. His controlling metaphor is from Poe's story, *A Descent into the Maelstrom*. The effects of technology are comparable to the descent into the maelstrom: they make us somewhat delirious, induce a sense of helplessness but paradoxically sharpen our intellectual curiosity and resources."

In Poe's story, an old sailor recounts to some companions how he had been at one time caught in a fierce storm off the coast of Norway. The storm created a giant whirlpool that began to pull him under. After initial panic, Poe's sailor takes up a philosophical attitude toward his predicament. He becomes reflective, indeed calculating about the storm around him, the dangers and risks it creates but as well the hope it offers. He observed, for example, that large bodies were sucked into the vortex more quickly than small ones, that spherical bodies sank sooner than others, and that cylindrical bodies stood the best chance of survival. The sailor therefore lashed himself to a water cask and threw himself into the raging sea. And so he was saved. In McLuhan's analogy, technology had plunged us into the vortex, but we can think in the eye of the storm. We can study its slope and strength, its force and direction to determine the conditions of our survival. Thought becomes a kind of lifeline.

McLuhan's analogy carried for me a moderately uplifting humanistic message. I asked Kroker if he felt he were in a maelstrom.

"Definitely," he said.

"Are you trying to create lifelines?"

"No," he said. "I don't believe we need lifelines to get us out of technology. We need to get deeper into technology to understand it better."

"But if you eschew humanism," I protested, "then you have to be some kind of technological determinist. That's the only alternative I see."

"I don't eschew humanism," Kroker responded. "I am saying that our traditional understanding of humanism is insufficient. We might call it a weak-humanism."

"What kind of humanist are you?"

"I would call myself a hyper-humanist."

"Meaning . . . ?"

"That we have to push the premises of classical humanism beyond their limits to effectively bring modern technology under ethical judgement."

"Is this strategy working?"

"We don't know how things are going to turn out," he answered. "Where I am now is that the ideology unloosed by technology is an ideology of facilitation. It says to us: These image harvesting machines provide many freedoms such as improved interactivity, new knowledge, greater communication, more possibilities for self-development And indeed more democracy. I see such promises as sucker bait, a seduction strategy. In fact when the human species feeds itself into virtuality, then what comes out is the grim, hard-nosed politics of consolidation. We see it now in the Internet. That's exactly what is happening. People are now calling for the privatization of the Internet. It has to be commercialized as quickly as possible. Government has to get out. The time for dreamers and utopians is over. Forget the soft talk about the relationship between technology and democracy. Now is the time to consummate the marriage between technology and pan capitalism. That's the political bottom line."

The thought occurred to me that in the evolutionary scheme of things we might be preparing ourselves for a more immaterial mode of existence, perhaps elsewhere in space, perhaps cloning ourselves for extraterrestrial existence. That could be the point of the strong idealistic strand in Western humanism from Plato to Teilhard de Chardin who postulated a noosphere as the term of our evolution. Kroker thought there might be something to that.

"We have in effect already cloned ourselves," he said. "It is now possible to implant micro-computers directly into the body. This to me is the story at the end of the twentieth century: we have developed a technology that has species existence with its own autonomous logic, power of self-replication and purposes. This has been our historical fate. Bear in mind that the question of technology is coeval with the identity of Western culture itself. Technology and logos were fused from the beginning. Technology was our way of being in the world."

I told Kroker that his analysis must make him very nervous.

"Nervous and also very angry. But I am not a determinist. Let's say I am a resister. My political strategy is that we first have to know the ground politics occurs on. I try to understand the deep idiomatic language of technology, to get deeper into the vortex, so to speak. Canadian philosopher George Grant said the limits of technology are ultimately the catastrophes contained within it. I call attention to the catastrophes. I am a practitioner of crash aesthetics."

Anticipating my next question, he explained crash aesthetics as a method of understanding technology by becoming it, getting the epistemological jump on it so to speak, thereby exposing the contradictions in the virtual class and the catastrophic possibilities of technology itself.

"This is our political predicament as I see it," Kroker went on, "to be simultaneously a new race of techno-mutants in the name of an expanding freedom. All the usual approaches to ethics and politics have been canceled out, so now we are forced to travel in hyper-reality at crash speeds without the guidance of traditional ethical guidelines. So we are in new territory, forced to develop a politics of impossibility that would simultaneously insinuate itself within the command logic of virtual reality while dislodging itself from the hegemony of that reality. So it's a politics that operates under a double sign of appropriation and resistance, immersion and displacement, speed and memory. Crash aesthetics is about the recuperation of the body, morally rearmed, technologically fit for riding the envelope of high tech."

"Isn't this a dangerous gamble?" I asked.

"It probably is," he allowed "but it is the only way that I can see to negotiate any ethical strategies within technology that might have some chance of success."

I asked Kroker if he saw his writing as a form of resistance.

"Yes," he answered, "but because technology is so pervasive, I find myself forced to write in a hyper-deconstructive mode. The questions I ask are: How can technology be brought to the bar of experience? What is the quality of the human condition? What mode of subjectivity makes it possible for people to sustain themselves in the absence of the great unifying principles of existence? Amnesia is our condition today. We are agents of forgetfulness and have become incapable of questioning the horizon before which we are enucleated. We live in a world overshadowed by the signs of inertness and melancholy, of anxiety and vacancy. What we have to do, in short, is rescue experience from its imprisonment by technology."

I asked if activism had a place in Kroker's scheme of resistance. He said that he thought activism was one of the strategies that opened up possibilities for political democracy. "I was living in the States in the '60s," he said, "and was active against the Vietnam War and in the McCarthy campaign. I was in Indianapolis when Martin Luther King was shot and in Los Angeles when Bobby Kennedy was shot, and it struck me from that point on that American democracy was doomed, that liberal democracy had embarked on a catastrophic phase. I left the States shortly after that."

"Is living in Canada better?"

"It's different and it is different in interesting ways."

"What are some of the ways?"

"We don't live in a superpower. We have the luxury of living in a shadow culture. We have a bilingual country, a parliamentary political tradition, less violence, better social benefits, vast spaces. But I think the main difference is that we don't feel the oppressive weight of technology so keenly. The United States is the technological society par excellence, the world's first digital culture. But of course we feel it keenly enough. Don't get me wrong."

"Would you say Canada is a freer country?"

"I think so. At least to the extent as I just mentioned that it is a less technological society. After all, Canada is based on two refusals of modern culture:

the Tory refusal of the American Revolution and the Quebec refusal of cultural homogeneity."

"So what can we look forward to?"

"The choice at century's end is between liberal fascism and retro-fascism. Two different sign systems are now in place. It will be interesting to see which system stabilizes."

"But it's a Hobson's choice, isn't it?"

"Basically."

"What about the humanistic and democratic possibilities you hold out?"

"That's for the long run."

There didn't seem to be any place I could take the conversation now. Darkness had fallen and it was still raining. I said goodbye to Kroker and went out into the wet city to catch a cab back to the airport. As I flew home, the image of Poe's sailor kept turning in my mind. Cruising at 35,000 feet gives one a good perspective on the technological maelstrom.

Happiness and the Pursuit of Democracy

Happiness exists, Camus wrote, so why refuse it?

Why indeed.

Happiness has clearly been one of the centerpieces of our philosophical and religious traditions. Everyone agrees on its importance. We all seek it. But we don't all find it. Could it be that we do not know exactly what we are looking for? On a question so large, definition takes on great importance.

Mark Kingwell, a young philosopher at the University of Toronto, discovered this when, in the course of a lecture on utilitarianism and happiness, a member of the audience interrupted him. "But sir," she asked, "how do you define happiness?" Kingwell, like any well-turned-out Ph.D., could think of a number of definitions, and he rattled off a few of them in response to the question. But in retrospect he realized that they weren't good answers—too semantic, too glib, too beside the point really of the widespread preoccupation with happiness in our culture.

He decided the subject was worthy of further investigation and in due course published a complex, somewhat uneven but very fine book entitled *Better Living: In Pursuit of Happiness from Plato to Prozac* (forthcoming in an American edition entitled *In Pursuit of Happiness*). "The happiness question," Kingwell writes, "is a good one, indeed a very good one. It is both answerable and important, and not just for instrumental reasons either. We can speak meaningfully about happiness, and we can do so with intelligence and with reasonable prospect of results."

Kingwell begins his study not on the high ground of philosophy as one might expect but in the rag and bone shop of popular culture. Too many of the ladders to the high ground, to push Yeats's metaphor, have collapsed under the weight of abstraction and intellectual senility. Moreover as a political philosopher, he considers popular culture part of his turf and writes widely about it. He says in his defense: "One cannot shirk the terrible duty of philosophy: to descend into the messy streets of what we sometimes call, misleadingly, 'the real world.' It is there and only there, that the genuine battles over identity, happiness, and the good life can be fought and, possibly, won."

So Kingwell pans through the hard scrabble of popular music, advertising, pop psychology, self-help books (with titles like *Become Happy in Eight Minutes*), movies, TV shows, shopping malls, novels, magazines, college textbooks, the World Wide Web, perfume bottles, and even the drug culture. They all beam a single message: Be happy. Kingwell went so far as to enroll for a one-week course at a happy farm called the Option Institute. Located in the Berkshires, and one of several personal development centers around the country, it is run by one Barry Kaufman (known as Bears) and his wife Samahria Lyte. The Institute actually promised to make its clients happy for a fee of $1,275. Kingwell was curious about how that could be done. How does one learn to be happy? He records his experiences of that week as straightforwardly as the material permits, but absurdity and irony infect the script from the start (when he is told by an aide that "this is a terrific opportunity to pursue growth in a supportive atmosphere") and remains to the end when Kingwell leaves the Institute to drive back to the airport in his rented Sentra, overcome with a vague nausea induced by the self-exposure, narcissism, and psuedo-democracy, the "manufactured emotion and enforced intimacy" that dominated his week at the Institute. The problem with places like the Option Institute, Kingwell concluded, is that they represent "the kind of technological, shortcut thinking that makes happiness hollow in our culture, the same cynical hard sell masked as benevolent healing that spills off the shelves of the self-help section."

How, he wonders, have we come to this pass? How did we arrive at a place where we think we can distill happiness into bottles, form it into little pills, and sell it? We founder about seeking answers in a sea of symbols and signs, of simulacra and semiotics; in global economies and information systems; in technological wizardry, the antics of postmodernism, and the pyrotechnics of cyberspace. And it is a wearying business. Kingwell rightly asks: Where did we go wrong?

One false step was taken, he thinks, when at the dawn of the modern age, the idea of happiness came to be understood in rank physicalist terms and human beings viewed as mere pleasure-pain machines. Thomas Hobbes sets the pace here. Hobbes was born in 1588 as the Spanish Armada was approaching English shores. So frighted by the prospect was his mother that the young Thomas was born two months prematurely, on Good Friday morning, April 5. Hobbes later recalled: "Unbeknownst to my mother she gave birth to twins: to myself and to fear, which has been my constant companion throughout my life."

Fear was the passion that drove him as he believed it drove all humans in a ceaseless and futile pursuit of peace and happiness. Hobbes experienced the Age of Anxiety long before the era was so-named. Hobbes was well connected in the scientific circles of his day. He was particularly taken with Galileo's idea that science was the study of bodies in motion, and he extended this insight to his analysis of society and human nature. We humans are also bodies in motion, governed by one inexorable law: appetite or the desire to increase pleasure and aversion or the fear of pain. We are condemned to the slippery slope of always seeking to satisfy our desires, what Hobbes calls "a perpetual and restless desire of power after power."

Thus are we trapped in the circle of anxiety. Why do we act this way? Because we are weak, unruly, and contradictory. But Hobbes's pessimistic anthropology soon runs up against a painful paradox: the more we strive to satisfy our desires the more we fail because desires by definition multiply faster than our capacity to satisfy them; the more power we create for ourselves the more fear and envy we inspire in others who in turn threaten us, thus creating more fear and anxiety. And so on without end.

Hobbes is famous for his psychological hedonism, as his view of happiness has come to be called. And he is important because his philosophy flowed rather directly into the broad stream of utilitarianism, unquestionably the most influential ethical theory of modern times, and thence in a direct step to our therapeutic culture and its market-based idea of happiness. Hobbes's pleasure-pain principle was, after all, an earlier formulation of the greatest happiness principle. For utilitarians the raison d'être of government, law, and morality is to provide the greatest happiness for the greatest number.

This was the view behind Jefferson's argument that the only aim of government "is to secure the greatest degree of happiness possible to the general mass of those associated under it." And John Adams's similar claim that "the form of government which communicates ease, comfort, security, or, in one word, happiness, to the greatest number of persons, and in the greatest degree, is the best."

Kingwell identifies a number of flaws in utilitarianism. To begin with, it furnishes the philosophical foundation for "the attempt to create a kind of earthly paradise of rationalized pleasure, social coordination, and algorithmic governance: a utopia of collective, complete and constant happiness as vivid and enticing in prospect as any vision of heaven." But immediately we come up against the Hobbesian paradox. Such a view of happiness cannot be sustained. What we see clearly in our consumer, fun-seeking culture is that the happiness principle leads to large scale unhappiness. We are, Kingwell writes, "a culture suffering from a bipolar disorder, with manic and depressive episodes following each other by hysterical turns, binging and purging, sometimes existing in close proximity and annexing cultural forces in what looks like an attempt to destroy the opposite. Pleasure and its denial are, for us, locked in a Manichaean battle." Kingwell calls this "the pathologizing of happiness," the cynical manipulation of artificially created desires in the name of psychological health.

Another problem with the greatest happiness principle is its inability to bring the individual and the community into a satisfying relationship. If individuals are reductively defined as pleasure-seeking atoms, then what sense can we make of civic society, participatory democracy, or responsible citizenship? If individualism always trumps community and individual identities are effectively shaped by the ideological imperatives of a consumer culture, the consequences would seem, on the face of it, devastating for a democratic polity.

It is clear to Kingwell that we need a more robust theory of happiness, a more expansive vocabulary of happiness, and healthier practices of happiness. At this point he turns to the Stoics, to such texts as *The Consolation of Philosophy* by Boethius and Epictetus's *Enchiridion*. This is a smart move for a couple of reasons. Not only have the Stoics been much neglected by modern thinkers, they also constitute our strongest reservoir of moral thinking, the principal fount of the great tradition of cosmic humanism. The Stoics turned to nature for stable moral guidance rather than to traditional religions or to society or even to philosophy. "Live according to nature" was their rallying cry. "Always think of nature," wrote Marcus Aurelius, "as one living organism with a single substance and a single soul." We are all part of the teeming energy that constitutes the divinity of the universe, a subtle harmony of rationality, law, eros, and soul-stuff.

Stoicism is blessedly free of the notion of the self as a pursuer of interests. It doesn't get bogged down in a maze of preferences or the squirrel cage of ceaseless desire satisfaction. Most of our desires are wayward and ought to be curbed rather than yielded to. Stoicism's great ethical principle is, as

Epictetus articulated it, the principle of control. "There are things which are within our power," he said, "and there are things which are beyond our power." The trick is to distinguish between the two, control what is in our power, and be indifferent to what is not in our power. Note how very different this principle is from that of Hobbes, and how it points to a very different moral universe. We move from a hedonistic to a eudaemonistic concept of ethics. Stoicism emphasizes character and such virtues as strength of will, detachment, discipline, simplicity, intelligence, authenticity, civic commitment and self-sufficiency. We come in Stoicism to the notion of happiness as virtue.

I must say in this context that Kingwell is somewhat dismissive of Thoreau. *Walden*, he says, rings "false"; it is a new form of "soulful, poetic elitism"; it is "somewhat indulgent." This is not right. Much better, I think, to place Thoreau in the Stoic tradition, and see him as perhaps the most Stoic of modern writers whose voice grows stronger by the minute. Thoreau's message is that the natural world is our home, the place we indwell and must tend with care. Thoreau undertook a great experiment in self-discovery and local politics. He created a meaningful world by closely observing nature, by participating in nature, and by describing nature in richly textured and analogical language. It was an experiment in appropriation, in what Kierkegaard called taking authorship of one's life.

Kingwell seems too inclined to see Thoreau as a romantic visionary, indulging in a pastoral fantasy or, even worse, an oddball, a kind of nineteenth century hippie rejecting society. But that is to get Thoreau wrong. He was, I would argue, a radical empiricist before William. James made that expression popular, a good materialist of the Stoic kind. Thoreau wasn't arguing that everyone should go to the woods; he wasn't trying to impose artificially a pastoral ideal on an industrial society. I read Thoreau to be making the same point the Stoics made, which is to say: nature is the ground of our deepest meanings. He was elaborating a philosophy of organic relationships.

Be that as it may, Stoicism puts before us the clear, hard-edged questions concerning the quality of life, the good life, the life that is worth living. "Why do you mortals seek happiness outside yourselves when it lies within you?" asks Epictetus. It is the right question. Thus Kingwell is led back to the Greeks where these questions received their first (and some would say best) answers. He at this point lays his philosophical cards on the table. "The only possible way the notion of happiness can be reclaimed from the machinery of manipulation and self-indulgence is to recast it as the possession of a virtuous character and the performance of virtuous action." So there you have it, a version of virtue ethics first articulated by Aristotle. This is the idea that morality is not so much to perform certain actions according to certain principles as to possess a certain character. This moral syllogism now obtains: since the happy life is the good life and the good life is a virtuous life, the happy life is therefore a virtuous life. "Happiness is an activity of the soul expressing complete virtue," as Aristotle somewhat archly put it. What he had in mind was happiness as the development of a set of excellences appropriate to our nature.

The going gets a little heavy here. But Kingwell enlivens his analysis throughout with a number of existential flourishes. He tells us what he likes to eat and drink. He worries about his love life. He pens some hilarious send-ups of academic life, particularly that modern form of the Spanish Inquisition known as the job search. And, of course, the many illustrations he draws from popular culture help the reader along to the finish line. To be noted as well is his elegant style in long stretches of the book. Kingwell is in control of his prose. It is a hopeful sign of the times that books like this are being published, books that address central problems in our culture, are intellectually rigorous and yet appeal to a wide reading public. Kingwell has illustrated Aristotle's idea of virtue by writing an excellent book.

Shortly after I read *Better Living,* I had some conversation with Kingwell. What we talked about mostly were some of the political implications of what he had written. I began with a question about democracy. If from one end democracy is compromised in its very foundations by a thin utilitarianism that views people primarily as rational calculators of their self interest and from the other end by a passivity inducing consumerism, then how can it flourish as a political regime?

Kingwell took my point.

"We all have dark moments about democracy," he said, "when the forces arrayed against legitimacy seem overwhelming. I think the German thinker Jürgen Habermas was right when decades ago he saw legitimation crisis as endemic to modernity. But despite that I cannot believe there is no form of democratic participation available to us that would evade, if not avoid, such problems. I see a couple of points of light. First of all, democracy is not just a modern development. It goes back to the Greeks, and some of the (better) philosophy of Aristotle and the Stoics can be imported to shore it up—some of Aristotle's virtues, for example, like friendship, magnanimity, and civic commitment. Like the word *virtue* itself they may seem quaint and outdated. But we would do ourselves a favor by rehabilitating them. And secondly, I favor Habermas's kind of solution and have for a long time: legitimation through dialogic participation.

"Do you believe there is a legitimation crisis?"

"I do believe there is a legitimation crisis for roughly the same reasons given by Habermas but made more pressing and yet more shadowy by capitalist triumphalism, the global exporting of consumerism, and the replacement of political awareness with brand consciousness."

"What did Habermas mean by a legitimation crisis?"

"He meant that in post-war Europe there was a breakdown of the previously stable consensus regarding the foundations of the state. This was particularly acute for Germany but was wider than that because it was a function of modernity entering a late state. The old foundations of how we came to accept the rule of law—moral objectivity, social contract, even pragmatism—were no longer viable. Hence a crisis of legitimation. Habermas's theory of communicative action, and specifically his notion of dialogic participation, is an attempt to meet this crisis with a new form of legitimation—one that is part of modernity's rational legacy but is also participatory and democratic."

"Say a little more about what Habermas meant by dialogic participation."

"Habermas talked about an 'ideal speech situation' in which all participants in the political process would be able to make their views heard in conditions of equality and noncoercion. We will never reach that ideal situation. But we can use Habermas's insight as a regulative ideal on our actual political discourse. We fall far short of that ideal now when so many people have simply opted out of politics in favor of a narrow notion of private life. We must reinvigorate the notions of citizenship through dialogic participation so that we can see how much any aspect of private life depends on a vibrant public sphere."

"You are unusual among philosophers because you write a lot about popular culture. Do you take flak from your academic colleagues for this?"

Kingwell smiled. "They don't like it much," he said.

"You would probably see popular culture as part of what you have to study as a political philosopher?"

"Absolutely," Kingwell said. "And thank you for putting it that way because most people don't see that connection. Political theory cannot ignore its social and cultural contexts. I think that writing on popular culture is a natural extension of the teaching mission. And by that token I see cultural theory and criticism as branches of political theory. But it is not a view that is widely held."

"How did you come to that view?"

"I think in the first instance it was just a matter of being trained as a political theorist and then linking that with something that I have done all along in casual conversation, which is reflecting on my cultural experience. I think it is a natural thing to do. People do it all the time."

"Socrates would probably agree with you. He took philosophy to the agora and was a media star in his own right."

"It's always good to be in the company of Socrates."

"I gather from what you said that you teach about popular culture as well as write about it."

"Yes."

"Do you find it pedagogically effective, a good way to get the attention of your students?"

"Yes, but it is philosophically significant as well because it allows me to engage critically with popular culture, which is the material of everyday life for my students and for most people. To ignore so much seems to me simply irresponsible."

"But isn't a lot of popular culture just junk?"

"Sure but critical engagement with the bad stuff is part of doing philosophy, a way so to speak of making philosophical points. But don't think it's all bad. Some elements of popular culture have critical awareness built into them and it is important to isolate those."

"What would be an example of the latter?"

"A recent example is a television show that I really like called *Buffy the Vampire Slayer*, which seems like an absurd place to stake my claim. But when you watch it and observe the sophistication of the way it is presented and the kind of values that are actually just under the surface, it's actually much more critical and engaged that one might think. It is certainly the antithesis of the kind of banality you encounter in a show like *Baywatch*. Pop music is another example. One of the reasons it gets a bad rap is that people don't pay attention to the lyrics. But real listeners do. So my general point is that it is a mistake to fail to engage popular culture because if you don't you consign yourself to (at least in some cases) a well deserved irrelevancy."

"What for you is the big political problem of our time?"

"Justice. Without a question."

"How did you come to that view?"

"I think as usual for scholars there was a mixture of personal interests and obsessions and a kind of internal logic of one's readiness. I was interested in questions of social justice from the point of view of activism as an undergraduate. I don't think we can point to a single nation state right now and say it's a just society. The interest in justice persisted into graduate school. The publication of John Rawls's *Theory of Justice* in 1971 set the bar for all discussions on justice since then. As it turned out, I wrote my doctoral dissertation on justice and published it under the title *A Civil Tongue: Justice, Dialogue, and the Politics of Pluralism*. As I wrote there, the question of justice resolves itself to a vigorous debate about how a pluralistic society should be organized. This vigorous public debate is all the political meaning that the vexed word 'justice' should have for us. The desire for a public conversation that is challenging, lively, divisive, undistorted, and fruitful is widespread. Unfortunately, disagreement about what this conversation should be like is just as widespread. I think current theories of justice fail on two counts: the theory fails to find wide application in practice, and also the rational chooser model that dominates liberal justice theories fails to model real life commitments. So I tried to develop a dialogic model of justice following Habermas. This puts the focus on citizens and their forums of conversation and communication."

"Would you say then that the problem of justice reduces to a problem about citizenship?"

"Yes, I think there is a deep sense in which that is true. I am actually working on that connection for my next book."

"Would you also say that citizenship is as problematical as justice?"

"Yes. What we confront now are new realities about globalization. So we have to raise the question about citizenship for a transnational or postnational world. Our ideas of citizenship are to some extent obsolete because of our new situation."

"How is your thinking going?"

"I'm asking myself what it might be like to reinvigorate the cosmopolitan idea of citizenship which has been out of favor for two centuries. If you look at something like the Universal Declaration of Human Rights you'll get an idea of where I am going. The Kantian infusion there is obvious. Now I wouldn't want to be a full-blown Kantian. But I think cosmopolitanism is ripe for defense again. It's interesting that we have global markets and global information exchange but we don't have a globalization of political ideals. We don't have a globalization of peace or security. What we are perhaps seeing is that some of the virulent strains of Western culture have shot out into the world at large but our countervailing healthy strains have not. Paradoxically, we may have an opportunity to articulate a better ideal of citizenship in an inclusive, global context than we did at the national level."

I had to remind myself of what Immanuel Kant said about cosmopolitanism. I recalled that he wrote an essay on "Universal History with a Cosmopolitan Intent" in which he called for a universal civil society. Was that what Kingwell had in mind?

"That and his idea of the intrinsic worth of each individual human being. Against the old orders of privilege based on social hierarchy, bloodline, and salvational status, he offers the modern world a vision in which every human, regardless of station or wealth, must be treated as an end in himself or herself and not merely as a means to an end. Kant bequeaths to us a twinned vocabulary of individualism and universalism that runs deep in our reigning view of the moral and political self. An individual is worthy of respect simply by virtue of being alive. And that worthiness extends without borders to encompass every individual, ignoring all particularities."

I asked Kingwell if he found his students alienated from politics and the language of politics.

"Not quite that," he answered. "But I do find a great deal of cynicism. Cynicism is the baseline. When I was an undergraduate, which was not so long ago, cynicism was understood to be extreme. We were all political. We all thought that being politically engaged was part of what it meant to be a university student and a citizen. Today I find students noticeably different in that they don't see any reason why they should take politics seriously."

"What can be done about it?"

"Speaking for myself, I go back to the Socratic situation. Everyone he encountered whether citizens, students, or in many cases professional philosophers, he found in a prereflective state. That's the condition of students today. One reason for teaching philosophy is to overcome what I call reflective conservatism of various kinds in favor of a more reflective outlook. That is probably the only solution to political indifference and cynicism. And, of course, it is hard work."

"Is that what attracted you to philosophy in the first place?"

"Yes. Philosophy, at its best, digs deepest and pushes farthest."

"Does that make you an optimist, of sorts?"

"A lot of people think of me as a pessimist. Some of my friends tell me I am a cultural pessimist. And it's hard to avoid pessimistic conclusions about the way our culture is manufactured and consumed. But one can be optimistic too.

I learned from Jonathan Lear, one of my professors in graduate school, and one of the best philosophical interpreters of psychoanalysis, that we should take seriously Socrates' claim that the good poet should know both tragedy and comedy. The human condition is both tragic and comic."

"What is the basis of your optimism?"

"When we carry social analysis far enough we discover a basis of commonality. People want to be happy; they want to be fulfilled; and there is a lot of evidence that material comfort does not equal happiness. The utilitarian calculus is a broken happiness machine."

"People are resisting the dominant culture."

"They really are. They are not as much victims of their culture as some suppose. In my book I spoke of a strategy of individual acts of cultural resistance, what some call culture-jamming. This means the refusal to allow the messages of advertising, television, publishing, and conglomerated media to dominate our consciousness. In practice this means constant vigilance and the perpetual deconstruction of the taken-for-granted aspects of our culture."

"It sounds like good Stoicism to me."

"I think of Stoicism as the ethics of last resort. It crops up in critical times like our own and it signals a desire for meaning in our lives, an awakening to new possibilities of the spirit."

This tied back to a major theme in Kingwell's book and was a good moment to conclude our conversation.

PART THREE

Democracy as a Moral Vision

Headnotes

Democracy is an idea, supported by a sound body of theory. It is a practice, carried out in countless daily activities. It is also a vision, a dream, a moral ideal for a better world. This aspect has already been alluded to in several of our conversations, in fact in most of them. Those who struggled during the cold war period were sustained by this hope. Ben Barber says: "If people in Buchenwald could dream of a better day, then I can live in difficult times in America and dream of a richer democracy." Daniel Kemmis speaks movingly of a "city in grace." Elmer Johnson believes in the primacy of "a life of the spirit" and calls for a leadership that can "arouse and transform the many from their ignorance and apathy and self-indulgence that they are enabled to lead lives of freedom and dignity and moral worth." And through Arthur Kroker's grim analysis of technology shines a vision rooted in the moral tradition of the great religions and philosophies.

The conversations in Part III deal more amply with democracy as a moral vision. Christopher Lasch has pride of place in this group. His was a clear prophetic voice in our midst, speaking out against the idols of education, liberalism, and collectivism. He refers admiringly to Puritanism as "perhaps our strongest reservoir of moral idealism." Walt Whitman and Ralph Waldo Emerson "articulated a moral vision of democracy that bypassed liberalism altogether and bought into an older, more idealistic, even Platonic strain of thought." And then there were John Dewey, who never abandoned his idealistic roots, and William James, who saw life as "an arena of moral combat." Lasch speaks of civic republicanism and populism, traditions that agreed on the necessity of having virtuous citizens. Then there is the moral vision of Thomas Jefferson. All of this, Lasch says, we must import back into our thinking about democracy.

William Connolly is fascinated by the shifting distinction between the secular and the sacred in our society. He quotes Nietzsche who spoke of a non-theistic religiosity, "a sense of reverence and gratitude for the essential ambiguity of things and the abundance of life over the different kinds of identity we construct out of it." Connolly also finds things of interest in Augustine about whom he wrote a book. Like Augustine he talks of the will, belief, and evil, but in different terms, in modern terms of difference and otherness, of ambiguity and contingency. For Connolly how we cultivate an ethical sensibility is a central question of our times. And he does what many would consider impossible: he derives a theory of democracy from Nietzsche's philosophy. With Nietzsche's help he is able to rethink questions of justice, truth, the grounds of morality, religion and creativity.

Jean Bethke Elshtain tells us we suffer from "the politics of displacement," in which the private and the public have become hopelessly confused. "Politics," she says, "refers to what is in principle held in common. If there are no distinctions between public and private, it follows that there can be no differentiated activity or set of institutions that are genuinely political." Our therapeutic culture, where everything private becomes grist for the public mill and everything public is privatized and played out as a psychodrama, feeds on this confusion. So do some aspects of feminism, such as the claim that the personal is the political.

Like William Connolly, Elshtain finds inspiration in traditional thinkers like Augustine. Augustine, she says, is "one of the great undoers of Greek misogyny." She also likes Aristotle for what he says about the common good, associated living, friendship, and participation. Like Christopher Lasch, she turns to the puritan tradition for the convenantal model of politics. She uses the word *covenant* "because political theory has been overrun by social contract discourse, but a contract is not the same as a covenant. Contract says individualism, self-interest, privacy. Covenant points to community, civic identity, shared interests."

Overall, Elshtain remains cautiously optimistic about democracy. She reminds us that "we have witnessed astounding victories for democracy in the twentieth century." And although democracy may be in peril, "it remains vibrant and resilient, the great source of political hope in our troubled world."

On the Moral Vision
of Democracy

I first interviewed Christopher Lasch in the fall of 1980. He had just published his best-seller, *The Culture of Narcissism,* which remains the classic critique of the "me" generation. In it, he had some hard-hitting things to say about the state of higher learning in America. He wrote, for example:

"Not only does higher education destroy the students' minds; it incapacitates them emotionally as well, rendering them incapable of confronting experience without benefit of textbooks, grades, and pre-digested points of view." He also wrote: "The university remains a diffuse, shapeless, and permissive institution that has absorbed the major currents of cultural modernism and reduced them to a watery blend, a mind-emptying ideology of cultural revolution, personal fulfillment, and creative alienation."

Strong words! In fact, at the time, I thought them excessive. But what I understood from the interview was that Lasch's criticisms of higher education were part of a broader analysis of our political culture. The disintegration of our public life was the focus of his concerns. He spoke quite eloquently of our eroding liberties, the new paternalism of government, the Midgard-like grip of huge bureaucracies, and the substitution of therapeutic justice for retributive justice. In fact, he came down hard on the professions for their lack of civic concern. They, too, have become engulfed in the pursuit of narcissism.

Lasch's later writings contributed significantly to the literature, pointing a way out of our public philosophy impasse. His main argument is that our choices historically have been limited to some form of liberalism, on the one hand, and some form of collectivism on the other. Each has led to unacceptable social pathologies. Liberalism has emphasized individual rights and autonomy to the great detriment of community and the common good.

Collectivism has gone in the other direction and usually ended in authoritarian regimes and political repression. Lasch offered the communitarian compromise as a middle position. What we need, he said, is a political conception of community that can overcome the excesses of liberal individualism and the cloying, holistic conception of community that ends in a sentimental glorification of the past.

The last time I talked to Lasch was after the 1991 publication of *The True and Only Heaven: Progress and Its Critics*. I began this conversation by asking him why he was so hard on liberals.

"Because I think liberalism is an impoverished philosophy, and it is causing all kinds of problems in our society."

"Which liberalism is the villain? There are many varieties."

"Think of the kind of liberalism that is currently identified with the Democratic party."

"Of so recent a vintage?"

"As I interpret the history of liberalism it underwent a kind of sea change in the 1920s. Then liberals began increasingly to define their position in terms of a set of cultural values rather than any specific politics. H. L. Mencken was a leading figure in this change. He had nothing but contempt for the majority of Americans and developed the style of what I have called the civilized minority school of social criticism. It is a school that holds itself superior to the vast majority of Americans and is candidly elitist in outlook. Walter Lippmann called Mencken the most important thinker of his times. This elitist view came more and more to infect the liberalism of the Democratic Party, which hasn't given a hoot for workers in decades, and especially to infect academic liberalism."

"Presumably Lippmann himself was guilty of this elitism?"

"I think so."

"What about the classical liberalism we associate with John Locke and John Stuart Mill?"

"I am worried about that too because it substitutes efficient organizations for virtuous citizens. Liberals are inclined to think that democracy can dispense with civic virtue, that institutions not the character of the people, make democracy work. People are left free to pursue their private interests so long as government is there to referee things with some modicum of fairness."

"But you suspect that it is sometimes less than a modicum?"

"As it turns out, yes. It has become unmistakably clear that even a liberal social order requires a moral infrastructure—neighborhoods, families, churches and an array of institutions in which self-government actually works. No social order can get along without them."

"That was Tocqueville's point in the 1830s," I pointed out, "but you surely wouldn't want to deny all moral vision to classical liberalism. It wasn't, after all, only political nuts and bolts, procedures and institutions. What about the philosophy of rights? The emancipatory presuppositions of liberalism, a legacy of the Enlightenment, were what chiefly distinguished it from other political philosophies. Such a philosophy can properly be called a moral philosophy and is very much alive among us."

"Yes, it is a moral vision, but a very limited one. The enlightenment concept of reason was very abstract, and the liberalism that flows from it as a matter of fact is quite neutral and noncommittal about a whole range of moral issues. It assumes that if you eliminate impediments to free choice, all sorts of beneficent consequences will follow, including a well functioning society. Reason was seen as something self-regulating and axiomatic. Descartes said in future generations the ordinary peasant would know more than the philosophers of his day. This attitude is the source of the idea of progress that I criticize in my recent book. Moreover, what we don't often remember is that classical liberalism relied on the moral and cultural capital of earlier traditions to underwrite its vision of a liberal society much more heavily than it was willing to admit at the time. Adam Smith is a case in point. As a political economist he could speculate boldly about free markets, the acquisitive self, and invisible hands. But as a moral philosopher part of his being was firmly rooted in a restraining tradition."

"John Locke might be an even better example."

"Sure. Locke can no longer be held accountable for the 'possessive individualism' often attributed to him. Religion, more particularly Calvinism, was a major part of Locke's perspective."

"And not only religion," I said. "He was closely allied with a group called the Cambridge Platonists in much of his moral and political thinking. He seems to have accepted the ancient view of the universe as a cosmic harmony that exercises a strong moral and erotic pull upon us."

"Interesting."

"While all of this is very true, it still seems that the philosophy of rights today does not seem either neutral or minimalist but quite aggressive."

"It is aggressive when confronted with overtly oppressive institutions. I grant that. I don't say there is no moral value in the liberal tradition. But I do say it is limited. Liberals have a lot to say about rights. But on the whole they do not have much to say about responsibility—a lot less in any event."

"Is democracy in worse shape now than it has ever been?" I asked.

"I don't know about that. What I am saying is that it is not in very good shape."

"Can you point to a time when it was in better shape?"

"That would be futile."

"Maybe it is the case that democracy is not designed to work very well."

"That is one argument. Another is that democracy is better than any of its alternatives, even though it doesn't work very well."

"Do you buy that?"

"Well sure, who wouldn't? But that is not an argument that is going to get you very far."

"What is the essence of democracy for you?"

"What interests me is that in the early iterations of democratic theory, it was understood that you had to have certain preconditions in order to make democracy work, the most important of which was the wide distribution of property ownership. Democracy was based on small property and the responsibility that went along with that for the formation of certain habits of mind and character development. This was the necessary basis of democratic citizenship, a view clearly articulated, for example, in Jefferson. It comes out again in the suffrage debates in the middle of the nineteenth century. Suffrage qualifications were removed only because it was believed that property was sufficiently widely distributed to make restrictions on voting unnecessary. Now, what happens in a society where we have a permanent wage-earning class? This develops a servile rather than an independent state of mind. The central question now is: What is going to substitute for the small property owner in our democratic polity? That is a question that is not being addressed very well."

"Couldn't much the same be said of the habit-forming institutions in general?"

"Yes. They have all been seriously weakened."

"And you blame liberalism for this?"

"It would be much too simple to see liberalism as the evil genius behind all of our problems. What I am insisting on is that liberals haven't given this problem attention enough. They have assumed that if we democratize access to consumer goods and put in place a minimal welfare state together with certain governmental procedures, things would run pretty well. It is no longer possible to believe that. Through all the permutations and transformations of liberal ideology, two of its central features have persisted over the years—its commitment to progress and its belief that a liberal state could dispense with civic virtue. The commitment to progress alone generated many of the difficulties that now threaten to bury the liberal state, since progress meant large-scale production and the centralization of economic and political power. The belief in progress also contributed to the illusion that a society blessed with material abundance could dispense with the active participation of ordinary citizens in government."

"What we are talking about here is a lack of moral vision," I responded. "You argue well that the moral underpinnings that sustained earlier liberalism now no longer do so. So it has become, so to speak, an empty shell. But is that entirely true in America? When I teach my American thought course I try to impress upon students the enormous and still politically influential importance of the Puritans. Fred Greenstone at the University of Chicago proposes a middle theory between liberalism and the classical tradition which can be found in the convenantal tradition. He suggests that the American political tradition flows from two main currents of thought. One is liberalism and social contract theory. The other came down through Puritanism and was expressed in the image of a covenant which offers a quite different cluster of values."

"There is no doubt that Puritanism remains a strong moral force in American life. It is perhaps our strongest reservoir of moral idealism. Where moral vision is alive today it can be connected rather directly to the Puritan tradition. I believe that profoundly."

"It's interesting," I said, "that in the mid-nineteenth century, leading figures like Ralph Waldo Emerson and Walt Whitman articulated a moral vision of democracy that bypassed altogether liberalism and bought into an older, more idealistic, even Platonic strain of thought. They did not speak in the accents of a Locke or a Madison."

"That is precisely because they were concerned with the moral vision that sustains democracy and without which democracy would not work. They were interested in problems that couldn't be illuminated by political machinery. This is clear in Whitman's *Democratic Vistas;* it is full of misgivings and harsh criticisms about democracy. Whitman could be downright gloomy."

"So we agree liberalism hasn't entirely won the field?"

"No, not entirely. My criticism bears on the fact that liberals haven't given the cultural presuppositions of democracy enough thought. The moral tradition is alive but not well."

"Do you see a consensus on that point shaping in American society today?"

"Yes, I do."

"Where do we find it today? In feminism? In multiculturalism?"

"I don't see much there. That's politics as usual, different groups trying to get a bigger piece of the pie."

"In religion?"

"Not much. It is present in unarticulated form in the experience of many people. But it won't help us much if it remains unarticulated. One finds flashes of it in the Catholic tradition. The Catholic bishops' letter on social justice was very good. One might even say that the pope has some of the best insights into social questions."

"Writers like Whitman and Emerson effectively grounded their moral vision of democracy in a metaphysics of nature. That wouldn't get us very far today. So where do we turn for a convincing ground?"

"One hope may be a recovery of the American pragmatic tradition. I am thinking of William James who was such a compelling figure in American intellectual history and who forms a bridge of sorts between the earlier Puritan and the later pragmatic schools. And there is John Dewey. A colleague of mine, Robert Westbrook, wrote a very fine book on Dewey, and I sense a renewal of interest in him as the philosopher of democracy."

"Say a little more about James as a bridge."

"James saw life as an arena of moral combat. He entered into the debate begun by the Puritans about good and evil, heroism and conformity, hope and despair. The question for James was always: How are our moral energies to be distributed? Life, he said in a memorable phrase, must be conceived as the moral equivalent of war."

"In our present intellectual climate, I suspect moral equivalence arguments would be as futile as the earlier arguments based on nature mysticism."

"You are probably right. So I keep coming back to populism in some form as our best hope for a morally respirited democracy. It's an old tradition in America with lots of life left in it. Ronald Reagan with great political astuteness appealed to the still living elements of that tradition. That was one of the most extraordinary developments in American political history. And it all happened in something like four years. As late as 1976 the Republican Party was still the party of anticommunism, of wealth and privilege. Four years later it was the party of ordinary Americans with much grassroots attraction."

"And you credit Ronald Reagan with that turnaround?"

"Absolutely. Reagan was a political genius. His ability should never be underestimated as it is all the time. You simply cannot understand recent American history if you think Reagan was some kind of bumbler, a B-minus actor with little political savvy. His policies were quite disastrous in my mind, but he had an imagination that transformed the political landscape and a populist instinct to boot."

"Do you find it odd that the Democrats can't seem to connect to that tradition, which is after all their own? It is as though Reagan and the Republicans stole the crown jewels in broad daylight."

"I find it puzzling and deeply distressing. We can put our finger on some of the reasons for this. I mentioned the elitist factor earlier. Leadership is another problem—the party's captivity to certain interest and minority groups. You can't go to the mat on issues like pro-choice, affirmative action, gay rights, and the like and still tap into the older tradition without running into incompatibilities."

"We've been talking about civic virtue. I take it you mean the populist variety rather than the classical republican tradition."

"Yes, but I do see classical republicanism as one of the sources from which populism drew. I think of 19th century populism in America as a mix of classical republicanism, Lockean liberalism, Puritanism and other elements as well. They were all agreed upon and right on the central issue: we've got to have virtuous citizens."

"How much of this was in the Framers?"

"It was there to an extent. Jefferson had it but I doubt Madison did. Historian Gordon Wood claims that the Constitution represents a departure from republican thought rather than a continuation or fulfillment of it. Wood says republicanism died in America at the end of the eighteenth century. For one thing, those influenced by the republican tradition were uncomfortable with the whole idea of representative government. They conceived citizens as people who would not hand their civic duties over to hired representatives. So the adoption of representative government is already a defeat of sorts."

"Do you see anything in the current education debate of significance?"

"I think it draws away a lot of energy that might better be put to other issues."

"For example?"

"Well, what we were just talking about. Where in the debate do we hear anything about civic virtue?"

I agreed that it is a missing piece in the education debate.

"It certainly is," Lasch said. "That is why talk about canons, multiculturalism, political correctness, and so forth is so tedious. These are not central issues. They don't address the problems of standards, substance, vision. We can't isolate education from the moral vision of democracy and expect either to work."

"Where have we gone wrong in our thinking about education?"

"I think we took two wrong turns. At a certain point we began to think of education as the path to upward social mobility, a way of climbing the ladder of success, storming the doors of opportunity. This provided the key to middle-class hegemony. More recently, we have taken an even narrower view of education and come to see it as exposure to and the imposition of the culture of dominant groups like white European males. As a result we have lost to all intents and purposes any concept of liberal education."

"What would liberal education be for you?"

"I would hearken back to an older tradition that thought of education as a common achievement of humanity that is multicultural in the best sense of the word. Far from enclosing the mind in class-bound dogmas and ideologies, liberal education opens the mind to new horizons and calls every kind of dogma and ideology into criticism. It offers a critical perspective on every position. Liberal education is power and freedom, cogent analysis, orderly exposition, logical argumentation, the discipline of study and thought, the rich experience of the past, as well as the assimilation of past culture and the common sense of modern civilization. This is education conceived neither as upward mobility nor assimilation to regnant ideologies, but the acquisition of intellectual resources that make us free. I would want to argue that the notion of upward society mobility is pretty much what we mean by freedom today."

"How does that argument go?"

"Take the example of affirmative action. Social mobility is the cornerstone of liberal thinking on the issue of race. The gist of this thinking is that an educated, professional, upwardly mobile class of blacks will serve as role model for other blacks. But this is wrong-headed thinking because it assumes that the mobility of the few will benefit black people as a whole. It is now all too clear that it won't. Even as more and more blacks are assimilated to the money-getting classes, black neighborhoods and the cities in general tend to deteriorate. Enterprise and ambition emigrate to the suburbs, leadership is drained away, communities weaken. We are accustomed to thinking that the suburbs are the solution to the problem of the cities. We need to recognize that in the deepest sense they are the cause of the problems and not the solution. Suburbs institutionalize a false idea of freedom as social mobility, as climbing out of one's class. They dramatize the dangerous freedom that drains talent and wealth and imagination away. To say that our ideal of freedom is above all a suburban ideal is to give it palpable shape; it helps us understand more explicitly than any other image what's wrong with it. It is not only the underclass that is impoverished by this flight to the suburbs. In one way or another it diminishes all of us. The suburb organized around the shopping mall rather than the neighborhood eradicates the last vestiges of reciprocal obligation. It underscores the illusion that the good life consists of unlimited choices unconstrained by any sense that others are in the picture. No less than the drug culture of the ghetto, suburban culture rests on the phantasy of escape. So it is no accident that the suburbs have a drug problem too, or that young people in the suburbs find that nothing holds their attention, that sustained effort is beyond their powers and that nothing seems to justify sustained effort anyway."

"It cannot console you that the largest single voting block now resides in suburbia," I said.

"No consolation."

"If the suburbs are a problem, it is likely to be with us for a long time, mainly because they aren't perceived to be the problem as you describe it."

"True. I think in the long run that the best solution would be to have cities and suburbs under the same political jurisdiction. This isn't a panacea, but it is the best solution I can think of. It might do something to improve inner city schools and equalize the tax burden. I think busing would have taken on a very different complexion if in the 1970s the suburbs had been required to participate in that experiment in social engineering."

"You've always placed great stress on the educational value of neighborhoods."

"Public order is not just a function of the state, which can safely be entrusted with the responsibility for education and law enforcement while citizens go about their private affairs. A society in working order has to be largely self-policing and to a considerable extent self-schooling as well. City streets keep the peace and instruct the young in the principles of civic life. Neighborhoods recreate many features of the village life celebrated in American folklore, even as Americans reject the promiscuous sociability of the village in favor of 'life-style enclaves,' as Robert Bellah calls them, in which they can associate exclusively with those who share their own tastes and out-looks. Neighborhoods provide the informal substructure of social order, in the absence of which the everyday maintenance of life has to be turned over to professional bureaucrats."

"Let's conclude on a more personal note and talk a bit about your own intellectual development. By what paths have you come to your present views?"

"I grew up in the tradition of Midwest progressivism and New Deal liberalism. In the late 1960s I called myself a socialist and made a thorough study of socialist thought. Marx was very important to me."

"Why was Marx important?"

"As I read him through the interpretations of Frankfurt school thinkers like Herbert Marcuse and American socialists like Dwight Macdonald and Irving Howe, the main thing was the critique of mass culture, his insights into what Gramsci called the devastated realm of the spirit. The theme that began to preoccupy me was the powerlessness of individuals in a mass society of large agglomerations. That is why I was much more impressed by Eisenhower's farewell speech warning about the military-industrial complex than I was by Kennedy's inaugural address about getting the nation moving again. I feared the motion would be entirely in the direction of what Eisenhower warned against. It became increasingly evident to me that mass society no longer required the informed consent of citizens and was not in fact governed by a moral consensus."

"Would you now call yourself a Marxist or even a socialist?"

"No. My faith in the explanatory power of the old ideologies began to waver in the mid-1970s when my study of the family led me to question the Left's program of sexual liberation, careers for women, and professional child care. I saw a new form of socialization taking place as children were less subject to parental authority and more subject to the tutelage of the mass media and the so-called helping professions. I saw this inducing important changes in our understanding of personality and character, especially the decreased capacity for independent judgment, initiative, and self-discipline upon which democracy had always been understood to depend. It was, broadly speaking, a crisis of authority, but it included the degradation of work and the substitution of careerism for vocation, addiction for commitment, and training for education. My experience as a parent exposed me to our society's indifference to everything that makes it possible for children to flourish and grow up to be responsible adults."

"Have you then become a man of the Right?"

"People sometimes say I have. And there are obviously some forms of con-servatism I espouse. But if I have to be labeled I would prefer to be called a populist. That is an ambiguous term to be sure and can give rise to all sorts of misunderstandings. I readily admit populism can be reactionary. Nor has it been successful at countering bad economic programs with good ones of its own. I use the term primarily to recapture a moral vision that has been largely lost in modern society. It is, first of all, a useful way of criticizing the preten-sions of progress and also a way of setting in relief certain values I cherish: a sense of limits, a respect for the accomplishments and aspirations of ordinary people, a realistic appraisal of life's possibilities, genuine hope without utopi-anism which trusts life without denying its tragic character. Populism, however ideally we might want to reconstruct it, does not offer a ready-made solution to our multiple ills. I think, however, it asks the right questions. And it comes clos-est to answering the question about civic virtue. Above all, it is connected to a moral tradition. For this reason alone we cannot let it go out of fashion."

I recently read Lasch's posthumously published *Revolt of the Elites and the Betrayal of Democracy*. There many of his familiar themes were reprised. There he raises once again, although more pointedly this time, the question that is at the heart of his work: Does democracy have a future? And there again he tabulates the principal obstacles to a flourishing democracy: the de-cline of community and self-reliance, the disappearance of public forums where a vigorous and free exchange of ideas can take place, the abstraction in-sularity and aridity of the symbolic universes inhabited by our elites and, here more strongly than before, a lament for the loss of religion as a formative in-fluence on the democratic temperament.

With regard to the question of democracy's future, Lasch states bluntly that today democracy has to prove itself all over again. The picture of our so-ciety he draws is an essentially Hobbesian one. Like all political thinkers, Hobbes began by making a judgment about human nature. As recalled in the introduction, Hobbes did not form a high estimate of human potential. We are, he reasoned, frail and paltry creatures, with only intermittent glimpses of the truth of things, driven by self-interest and destined for a life that is, in his famous words, "solitary, nasty, poor, brutish, and short." He has an answer to the question, What sort of government will work for so benighted a species? He says that what is required is a powerful and fearsome Sovereign, a great Leviathan, to impose an intricate web of laws and restraints. The weaker human nature, so the logic goes, the stronger must be the political authority to threaten punishment and exact obedience.

We are today, in the opinion of many, living in a Hobbes-like society of minimal freedoms and maximal authority. A new Leviathan has arisen in our midst in the form of powerful social agencies that multiply laws, regulations, statutes, decrees, taxes, and penalties which are neither clear nor consistent nor, truth be told, very useful. They cannot be understood without the help of a cadre of experts nor enforced without the heavy hand of large bureaucracies. Regulatory agencies maintain a constant surveillance over the lives and assets of American citizens. Our rights and freedoms are less what is by nature ours than, as with Hobbes's Leviathan, what the elites choose to bestow.

People argue about when what has been called the "totalitarian turn" in democracy occurred. Some say, as Lasch seems to, that it set in at the time of the founding when the Framers opted for a representative rather than a participatory model of democracy and that their underlying fear of unregulated masses motivated that option. Others think the turning point came when government sought to guarantee positive as well as negative rights. This led to the slippery slope of politicians swapping votes for promises to satisfy particular wants, interests, and discontents. The list of the latter is, of course, infinite, and any politician seeking to satisfy them can only cut a comic figure. Still others see the problem stemming from the command economies of two world wars and the interim period. This opened the door for the bureaucratic elites who preside over our society with a power that citizens can only dream of. This is essentially Lasch's answer. At the heart of our present predicament is a misunderstanding of the nature of political power. Political power is not generated by governments but by people. This is the deep meaning of the sovereignty of the people principle that informed the Constitution. As Madison put it, the Constitution derived its entire authority from the subordinate authority of the people. Hannah Arendt offers this thought on political power. "It comes into being," she says, "whenever we join together for the purpose of action and it will disappear when we disperse and desert one another." The elements that create and sustain political power are here laid bare: to come together, to make choices, to pledge ourselves in common action, and to remain together.

So Americans are rightly worried about the state of their democracy and the erosion of their freedoms. More and more they are wondering what is happening to them and what can be done about it. In 1768 Thomas Paine wrote: "As the total subjection of a people arises generally from gradual encroachments, it will be our indispensable duty to oppose every invasion of our freedom from the beginning." The point of Paine's reflection is that in the final analysis people are responsible for their freedoms. If we let them be usurped, we will lose them; if we fight off untoward invasions, we will keep them; if we are indifferent to them, we will have opted out of the democratic condition. Democracy is a matter of choice.

The Democratic Imagination

William Connolly argues that we can't understand the political tendencies of our time unless we elaborate a generous context that brings in considerations of divinity, nature, sources of self-formation in modern society, language, gender, class, epistemology, the common good, history, the past and future, and, of course, politics itself. What he attends to especially are the sources of self-formation in modern society. He asks questions like: Who are we, we human beings living in late modernity? How did we get that way? And what might we do to improve our condition? We can't think politically unless we understand the existential grounds upon which politics builds, unless we gain some purchase on the broad issues, problems, and possibilities of the age in which we live. Philosophy, said Hegel, is our times comprehended in thought. Connolly seems to adopt a similar notion of political philosophy.

He identifies three characteristics of contemporary life that he deems highly relevant to our political condition. The first is the power of bureaucratic forces in our lives. We are more and more dependent on the social institutions of modern life but less and less certain of the benefits they claim to offer, a condition that Connolly calls "dependent uncertainty." The second is a growing sense of malaise. Because we are born incomplete and cannot survive in a state of nature we form societies to provide mutual aid. But society exacts large psychic costs in conformity and repression. Gradually we come to resent the costs exacted, and a profound sense of dissatisfaction grows within us. This condition Connolly calls a mood of "generalized resentment." It refers to those in the white middle class who are officially in independent positions but who experience acute uncertainty and a sense of dependence. They respond to their ambivalence by projecting resentment against target populations who call upon them to make new sacrifices or to increase their level of tolerance. Connolly's lengthy list of these target constituencies includes third world countries, criminals, mental patients, welfare claimants, affirmative action candidates, coddled athletes, minorities, teenagers, illegal aliens, and college students. The third characteristic of contemporary life, what Connolly calls the defining mark of late modernity, is "the globalization of contingency," a rubric that covers the decline of the power of the nation-state, the speeding up of transnational relations, an electronic technology that follows its own imperatives, the fragility of institutions, and our overburdened psyches—all of which add up to "an ominous set of future possibilities."

"It is profoundly important to engage our traditional political categories under these new conditions of possibility," Connolly told me when I talked to him in his office on the campus of Johns Hopkins University. "We have to especially rethink pluralism. What I find is that the existing models of political thought, and I guess they are all in one way or another liberal models, are pretty much built around a preexisting pattern of diversity that is already congealed and set in place and in which our ideas of human diversity are coded into fairly well accepted notions of justice and morality. The key to pluralism for me is the constitutive tension between existing pluralism and the politics of pluralization by which new identities push themselves from a position of marginality onto existing pluralities and change their terms."

One of Connolly's major concerns is the limited way in which traditional liberalism has dealt with pluralism and diversity. It has most often shown itself too ready to establish sameness at the price of excluding large numbers of people. In an incisive passage in his 1991 book *Identity/Difference*, he makes the point in these words: "One must now program one's life meticulously to meet a more detailed array of institutional standards of normality and entitlement. If one fails to measure up to one (or more) of these disciplines, one runs a high risk of entrapment in one of the categories of otherness derived from it: one becomes defined through a reciprocal category of delinquency, irresponsibility, dependency, criminality, instability, abnormality, retardation, unemployability, incapacity, obsolescence, credit risk, security risk, perversity, evil, illness, or contagion. And these latter categories of abnormality license bureaucratic correction, discipline, regulation, exclusion, conquest, help, conversion, incentives, or punishment. The more tight and extensive the disciplines become, the more deep and widely distributed become the deviations to be dealt with. This is the irony: the intensification of social discipline fosters the proliferation of differences defined through multiple categories of subordination, inferiority, incapacity, and degradation."

"Are we due for a paradigm shift in our political thinking?" I asked.

"That shift has already taken place," Connolly said. "What we have to do now is demarcate its character. My general principle is that contemporary politics should seek to mitigate generalized resentment and respond to historical contingency. On a more specific level we note so many things that have changed in terms of the territorial presuppositions of democracy, populations across borders, the speed of communications, and so forth. The old debates between liberals and conservatives are changing, where they are not actually obsolete, and political parties and effective politicians and, indeed, all of us, will be categorized in the future by those who respond to the new conditions of contingency or by those who try to restore a fundamentalism of some sort—religion, gender, nationalism—whatever."

"Who's responding best?"

"It always tends to be a grass-roots sort of thing. There have been some amazing shifts in our society. A dramatic one is how homosexuality has been redefined as gay-lesbian rights and entered into our mainstream political vocabulary. Our understanding of the issue has changed as has our attitude of acceptance. This success has been the result of a critical receptiveness on the part of a large minority of heterosexuals. We now tend to think of sexuality as an entrenched contingency rather than something ordained in the nature of things. This is a good example of what I call the politics of pluralization. Feminism, of course, was an earlier shift of equally dramatic proportions."

"Where do you see the next breakthrough?"

"Maybe crime. The prison system in the United States neither prevents crime nor corrects criminals. It reflects more than anything else generalized resentment aimed at socially legitimate targets. If and when the connection between this resentment and the self-defeating character of the prison system becomes visible, we may see an important shift in public sentiment in this domain. I would also hope for ways in which we can reduce inequality. These are issues that cry out for attention but are not part of our public debate today. Of course, it's hard to put a finger on where the next breakthrough will come because we can only define ourselves towards an issue after it has become congealed in normal discourse. It is hard to take up a position or even understand an issue that hasn't yet emerged with some clarity."

Connolly dwelt at some length on an issue he thinks might be in the works and which fascinates him very much. That is what's happening to the distinction between the secular and the sacred in our culture.

"It may not go anywhere," he said, "but I see interesting things happening. There is, of course, the obvious response to polarize and fundamentalize. But thinkers I draw sustenance from can't be readily situated on the spectrum of the sacred-profane. They are not monotheists or even theists; but they are not secularists in any ordinary Enlightenment sense of that word. They don't, for example, talk about justice under the veil of ignorance, or a social contract basis of morality, or an instrumental sense of the self or a fixed identity. I think what's going on here is a nontheistic reverence for the ambiguity and diversity of being, and it doesn't fit into the paradigm. This is a possible moment of change in our culture. It may not succeed, but it opens up new possibilities of communication across the polarities. We are seeing some interesting affinities between the sacred and secular that people on both sides of the divide are uneasy about."

I wondered if we could speak of a new birth of religion in this context. Connolly quoted Nietzsche who said: "I sense that the need for theistic gratification is declining but the pursuit of religiosity is growing."

I asked him what he supposed Nietzsche's sense of religiosity was.

"I would call it an ethic of cultivation," he answered, "that is not grounded in an ethic of command, which justifies ethics on some external criterion, or a teleological ethic according to which we are presumed to follow certain purposes by nature. Nietzsche's religion is a nontheistic sense of reverence and gratitude for the essential ambiguity of things and the abundance of life over the different kinds of identity we construct out of it. In a word, Nietzsche's is a life-affirming ethic. I read the will to power in Nietzsche not as the will to dominate but rather the energy through which new possibilities are propelled into being and the energy through which established forms jostle with and against these new possibilities for space to be."

The prospects of a secular postmodern religiosity intrigued me. I asked Connolly if he was religious.

"Not traditionally or in any traditional sense," he said. "But the more I became critical of certain strains in secularism to naturalize existing ways of being and identity and certain conceptions of communal morality, the more interested I became in religious orientations without the support of an identifiable God. That's why I went back to study Augustine and eventually wrote a book on him. As I thought about the undercurrents in moral perspectives advanced by such leading figures as Charles Taylor, Immanuel Kant, John Rawls, and Jürgen Habermas, I suspected Augustine behind a lot of what they were saying. So I read Augustine to try to understand some contemporary currents of culture."

We digressed for a moment on the importance of Augustine in modern and postmodern thought. Both Hannah Arendt and Albert Camus wrote dissertations on him. Deconstructionists are interested in his attempt to represent the otherness of the divine in language. Neo-McLuhanites like Arthur Kroker lay the technological will at his doorstep. Those into alienation theory find a treasure trove in his ideas of exile and the divided self. He was a principal source for modern existentialists. Narrative theory is indebted to him. And of course, religionists of many persuasions, including fundamentalists, find inspiration in him.

Connolly is interested in Augustine's conception of the will. Before Augustine's time the will was not a major philosophical category; he elevated it to primacy and made it the source not only of freedom but of evil as well.

"Our political tradition is a variety of themes on Augustine," Connolly explains. "For Augustine the divided will is healed through faith, which is to say obedience to another will. We find traces of this legacy in the thinkers I mentioned earlier, but also in the mainstream political tradition that includes Machiavelli, Hobbes, Rousseau, and Hegel. The will is a highly problematic notion for all political thinkers. They can't save it in and of itself but only through its supplements. These vary but are consistently recognizable as Augustinian. Take Rousseau, for example. For Rousseau, the locus of freedom is also within the will. Listen to the Augustinian echo within this political formula: 'For the impulse of appetite alone is slavery, and obedience to the law one has prescribed for oneself is freedom.' Freedom remains bound up with the will, and freedom of will remains tied to obedience, even though the agent to be obeyed has now changed. Rousseau, like Augustine, gives primacy to the will—a concept that remains crucial and problematic from Augustine through Rousseau and beyond. He also, like Augustine, inevitably seeks a supplement through which to heal it. But he shifts the locus of the supplement from obedience to the will of a god to obedience to oneself, an obedience made possible only by a new form of political organization."

On the one hand, Augustine is the origin of, or at least an early and influential proponent of the view that evil is located in a divided will, in the interior of the person. On the other, he espoused the position that there is an objective moral order which we must not only pursue on a subjective level but strive to embody in our politics and social morality as well.

Connolly challenges both of these views. The notion of an intrinsic moral order has had the deplorable effect of casting into otherness those who do not conform to it—the heretic, the sinner, the deviant, the enemy—in short, a large population of the demonized. Connolly recommends instead what he calls "agonistic respect" for those who differ from us, for those who fall outside of normalizing categories. For the objective moral order of Augustine he would emphasize the contingent, constructed, and relational character of social norms.

Connolly also wants to relocate the source of evil from the divided will to social relations themselves. As he wrote in *Political Theory and Modernity:* "Evil—as fundamental and undeserved human suffering flowing through social relations—is located above all in the structure of identity / difference relations themselves. It is lodged in the cultural demand to promote self-sufficient, secure, personal, group, and collective identities in a world in which that demand is never attainable. It is located in a 'paradox of difference' that, on my reading, reaches deeply into social relations, a paradox in which every identity specifies itself through presentation of a set of differences and in which this very crystallization of identity through difference signifies the incompleteness, insufficiency, or element of arbitrariness in the identity in question."

Traditional concepts of identity too readily cast difference into otherness, which in turn is either negated or marginalized. Then we have foreshortened the conditions of human flourishing. But there is another way of looking at the matter. Difference can be looked upon as an opportunity for political negotiation, for creative coexistence. "A democratic culture," Connolly says, "now becomes one in which productive tension is maintained between political governance through electoral accountability and political disturbance of closures in conventions and identities that have become fixed or naturalized. The politics of disturbance, so little appreciated by Hobbes, Rousseau, or Hegel, creates spaces through which to address concealed violence and enable new enactments."

I couldn't suppress the thought that there must be something deep in human nature that undergirds the views we have traditionally bought into. We want grounds for our choices, we want to ward off the alienation that comes with being born, we want in short a measure of security in an insecure world. So I asked Connolly where he would place the limits. How much ambiguity and contingency can we take?

"That is a good question," he said, "perhaps the important question. Everything has limits and exclusions. But I don't want to move prematurely to those limits and exclusions. When we respond to shifts in our culture and re-think the social forces of identity and the differences of which it is constituted and which threaten it, it may well turn out that we don't have to ask for a natural grounding, a sense of completion. We don't have to worry about the truth of our identity nearly as much as traditional culture would demand. In this perspective, of course, ambiguity, tolerance, and uncertainty grows. How much can we take? We don't know. There are limits determined by what is happening in the culture. What I referred to earlier as constitutive tension has to be negotiated. Tensions determine where we stand. I see myself on both sides of the division. Depending. So my answer is: I don't know. We can take more ambiguity than our culture allows for. But how much is relative to the situation. I think the far greater danger today is the fundamentalization of our lives as a response to cultural conditions."

Connolly makes a distinction between morality as a code and as an ethos. An ethos is the reserve we draw on in rethinking the code, somewhat analogous to the distinction between pluralism and pluralization. Pluralism is the existing patterns of plurality which are both the condition of and the barrier to the process of pluralization. Both are implicated in a dialectic of conformity and resistance, of stasis and creativity. Pluralization is the politics by which something new is brought into being, and this new entity changes the terms of discussion, elaboration, moral judgment, and justice. This is an ambiguous process, but it goes on all the time.

It is not hard to detect the long shadow of Nietzsche in Connolly's remarks. It was indeed Nietzsche, arguably the greatest philosopher of the twentieth century (even though he died in 1900), who broke our settled ways of thinking and doing wide open, who launched the first effective attack on the Augustinian tradition, and set in motion the whole adventure of modernity. Connolly admits that his engagement with Nietzsche was crucial and pivotal.

"How did you come to Nietzsche?" I asked.

"By thinking about the question of ethics," Connolly responded. "In the 1970s I was asking myself the question: How is the ground of morality and identity produced? Where does it come from? When I read Nietzsche on the injustice of justice and the immorality of morality and the untruth of truth, things started to click for me. I read Michel Foucault first. Then I started playing one off against the other and eventually came up with some space I could call my own. Nietzsche and Foucault both oppose skepticism and absolutism. They resist the question: 'Why be moral?' as childish and moreover pernicious because it can only lead to nihilism, to postulating a foundation that isn't there and can't be sustained. The question is rather: How do you cultivate an ethical sensibility? Everyone is moral. The interesting question is how we get that way. Nietzsche's *Genealogy of Morals* is a central text for our times."

Connolly gets more than a way of thinking about ethics from Nietzsche. He derives the elements of a strong theory of democracy. As he puts it, "Despite Nietzsche's own proclivities, a democratic culture is crucial to the actualization of some of the most compelling themes in his philosophy." This is a bold and somewhat unusual claim, given that Nietzsche can also furnish elements for a quite undemocratic politics. We have to read Nietzsche creatively. Let's break Connolly's claim into some of its constituent elements. To begin with, Nietzsche sees new possibilities in the human condition and offers a language to explicate them. The gist of Connolly's thesis is that democracy today stands in need of a legitimizing theory. The varieties of liberalism that have shored up democracy since the seventeenth century have worn thin, and been rendered impotent in the late modern state which has to resort increasingly to external and internal modes of repression to legitimize itself.

One element is the notion of justice. Nietzsche raises the question of whether or not justice must always be an expression of resentment. "If we cultivate an appreciation for the diversity of life," Connolly comments, "we can fend off the desire for revenge and affirm a plurality of partial, incomplete identities that can affirm themselves without fear of reprisal." Resentment, Nietzsche said, flows from two sources: rage against the human condition which gives no transcendental purpose to suffering or death, and, second, from social institutions which impose suffering and injury on some for the benefit of others. This resentment drives the urge for fundamentalist solutions and poisons our relationships with one another, including our political relationships.

The justice question is related to the truth question. How one punishes in a society is an important clue to our self-understanding as moral beings and to the ways in which we make judgments about truth and falsehood. To label a certain action good or bad, or a certain proposition true or false, is an important political act, decisive for the ways in which we constitute ourselves as political subjects. Similarly for the question of sexuality. Nietzsche was the first modern thinker to say anything interesting about sexuality. How sexual behavior is formed in the first place and then translated into discourses of approbation or disapproval, and how these discourses in turn inform our modes of justice and politics, are highly original contributions from Nietzsche, and later elaborated upon by Foucault and others. Nothing is more political than how we distribute our libidinal energies. And so on to the question of power and other key political concepts.

Nietzsche's constant message is to overcome the temptation to rage against ambiguity and contingency and celebrate life's rich diversity. Reading him expands the democratic imagination along several fronts that include difference, the tragic, the noble, the religious, creativity, and generosity. We end with the knowledge that we must build our political houses on an "ontology of discordance," that what we think about the self, justice, or the common good or any other subject must take full account of those discordances that pry us loose from Platonic paradigms of resolution and quietude.

I asked Connolly how his thinking was reflected in his discipline. "Well, in my field," he said, "we have two camps. There are political theorists who deal with domestic issues of belonging, community, justice, and morality. And then there are international theorists who deal with the relationship between states in a more amoral setting. But that is no longer a valid distinction. The nation-state is no longer a self-sufficient entity. We can't think of justice and morality and political activity simply within the context of the state. Fundamentalists try to do just that in a reaction against global contingency; they try to reassert the state as a self-subsistent entity when it can't be. An important part of political activism and education is to convince people that any effort in this direction will simply turn a democratic state into an authoritarian state."

Connolly said that even though he wasn't technically an international theorist, his thinking takes a decided internationalist bent. It is important to pursue non-statist or cross-national issues. Political parties as they are presently constituted don't do this very well. Corporations do it. Criminal rings do it. Scholarship does it. Popular culture spans nations, but citizens don't. Citizenship still remains imprisoned behind the bars of the state.

I was interested in what he was saying about citizenship. Connolly summed up his position: "If you want to think creatively about democracy and citizenship today, you have to multiply the sites of political allegiance and activity to include the global. The sites of citizenship are changing. Amnesty International. Greenpeace. These are examples of new citizen activity. Think of the divestment movement. It had the effect of changing the political face of South Africa. Ecological concerns is another example. Ecological systems like the open seas don't correspond to national boundaries."

I asked Connolly if he was an activist.

"I have been through various stages of activism including the conventional ones," he said. "Now I consider myself an intellectual activist."

I liked that expression. We too often forget that thinking is an activity, a mode of action, indeed a mode of political action.

"So," Connolly continued, "if we want to reinvigorate the notion of citizenship, we have to link local and national issues to international ones. The idea of participatory democracy at the local level is fine. But all too often the local level has an international dimension. The factory you are picketing may have its headquarters in Japan. McDonald's is an international corporation. So the cliche 'think globally, act locally' has to be revised. We don't know in advance where the target of our activity is going to be."

What kind of America does Connolly the political theorist see at the present moment?

"There is a heavy load of resentment and normalization," he said. "Too heavy. Things are not looking wonderful at the moment. The forces of fundamentalization are having a field day. This goes back to Nietzsche and my thinking in the 1970s. I was aware then that the politics of resentment was growing. So I asked: What are the deepest sources of resentment and how do they function? One of the things I noted then was that the politics of the New Left, and liberal politics generally, had a sharp exclusionary edge to it. One legacy of that period was the marginalization of white male members of the working class. Even then I was arguing against this. I said we had to find ways of advancing the agendas of feminism, ecology, and so forth without driving white workers into deeper wells of resentment. One suggestion I made was to add an income dimension to affirmative action programs, educational opportunities, and elsewhere. A good rule of thumb is that no policy is sound which is divisive. We are now paying the price of the policies of the early 1960s and early '70s."

Connolly explained that resentment conspicuously breeds two "isms" on our political landscape: fundamentalism and cynicism. And there is a close relationship between the two. Both demand an authoritative, final ground for what they believe. The cynic can't find such grounds, so concludes everyone is hypocritical; the fundamentalists think they have the answer and want to impose them on everyone. "The politics of our time has to find ways to address both phenomena," said Connolly.

I told him that although he was aggressively critical of the liberal paradigm, his own thinking still seemed to fall within that paradigm. "I'd say you are an old-fashioned liberal at heart," I said.

"That's all right," he agreed. "I don't think of my position as the enemy of liberalism—rather, its best ally. We have to reconstitute liberalism along the several dimensions I have been talking about. As a matter of fact, I have characterized my philosophy as a radicalized liberalism."

That called my attention to the conclusion of *Political Theory and Modernity:*

"Perhaps a reconstituted, radicalized liberalism is needed today; one which reaches into the subject itself rather than taking it as the starting point for reflection; one which challenges the hegemony of economic expansion rather than making it a precondition of liberty; one which treats nature as a locus of difference and resistances essential to life as well as a shelter and set of resources for human use; one which copes politically with the tension between the human need for a common life and the inevitable points of subjugation in any set of common norms; one which relaxes the hegemony of normalization to enable some things to be which its predecessors found to be irrational or perverse or sick; one which restrains the drive to comprehend and cure various forms of otherness by confronting first the way its own contestable standards of normality and realization help to constitute these phenomena; one which measures the legitimacy of its state's foreign policies by the degree to which they foster its ability to co-exist peacefully with the rest of the world; one which idealizes politics over administration, economic rationality or welfare dependency."

"Is that what you teach your students?" I asked.

He answered, "I tell my students that politics resides in the ambiguous space between the rewards of commonality and the worlds of possibility before them. I urge them to act always on the presumption of possibility. Things are changing all the time, often with stunning rapidity. My radical liberalism invites me to examine honestly and squarely issues in our life today and to be ready to dissent, vigorously if necessary, from the settled frames in which those issues today are all too often debated."

I left Connolly's office to catch an Amtrak train to New York City. I rode into the evening, as the last rays of sunlight struggled through the East Coast smog, and reflected on what I heard, trying to match Connolly's insights with some of my own thinking about democracy and citizenship or, more broadly, about the kind of creatures we are and the kind of world we live in.

Connolly serves up more ambiguity and contingency that I am comfortable with. Still, no one can deny that democracy is a difficult project, a highly fluid concept, always changing, always more possibility than reality, an ideal we strive for through many brute experiments. Democracy is always a politics of hope and, like old age, not for the fainthearted. This is a perspective congruent with pragmatic thought which holds life to be largely an improvisation, democracy our provisory arrangements with the unstructured rush of experience, and our identities loose-fitting social garb.

Much of what Connolly discusses under the rubric of resentment I think of in terms of pervasive alienation. The incredible events of our time testify that large numbers of people have felt lost, decentered, and out of place in the twentieth century. The metaphors of disconnection are the most powerful of our literature. And Nietzsche, with whom I have an ongoing love-hate relationship, is the source of many of them.

In my struggle with the problem of how to educate young people for practicing the art of democratic politics, I have gone back time and again to a reexamination of dialectical thinking as it was first illustrated by Socrates in his attempt to devise a language with which to talk about justice and other political ideas. Such language begins in confusion and puzzlement rather than clarity, relies primarily on dialogue rather than logical demonstration, and yields a moral or political outcome. In my opinion, the best thing that colleges could do to make good on their promises of political education is to educate students in the dialectical tradition.

What I heard Connolly saying, finally, is that today we must stretch that tradition to meet the new challenges of a far more complex society in far more perilous times than Socrates ever knew.

Democracy on Trial

As I was driving out to the Green Hills section of Nashville, Tennessee, on a clear morning in early September for an interview with Jean Bethke Elshtain, I listened to yet one more program on the death of Princess Diana. It was the sixth day of "Diamania." Never had there been such a media blitz, and I felt something must be stirring in the zeitgeist. I asked Professor Elshtain, one of the leading political theorists in the country and a shrewd commentator on current affairs, what she thought. She said she had just finished her "Hard Questions" column for the *New Republic* on the very subject and showed me a rough draft. I read it over while she made some tea. Elshtain called the Diana phenomenon "a sign of our pop-therapeutic, celebrity-drenched times" and a spectacle of "besotted grief feeding on itself." She thought the Diana story marked the "final merger of politics into celebrity and the conversion of news into a kind of ersatz spirituality of feeling and self-indulgence." Diana, Elshtain declared, was "the New Age Princess who shared the voracious appetites and shallow urgencies of a huge public who could not get enough of her or of itself ingesting her."

The Diana phenomenon illustrates what Elshtain thinks is one of the principal weaknesses of our modern democracy, what she calls "the politics of displacement." The politics of displacement, she explained in her 1995 book *Democracy on Trial*, ". . . involves two trajectories: In the first, everything private—from one's sexual practices to blaming one's parents for one's lack of self-esteem—becomes grist for the public mill. In the second, everything public—from the grounds on which politicians are judged to health policies to gun regulations—is privatized and played out in a psychodrama on a grand scale. . . . The complete collapse of a distinction between public and private is anathema to democratic thinking, which holds that the differences between public and private identities, commitments and activities are of vital importance."

We now find it natural to make a public display of our most private experiences—our sex lives, our childhood beatings, our deepest fears. Our public language is coated in a fuzzy emotional glow of caring, reaching out, feeling the pain. It is considered cool to reveal personal vulnerability and adopt the self-confessional vocabulary of the talk shows. But this theatrical display of emotion does not bring us together in a republic but rather isolates us from one another, reducing us to a society of windowless monads. What is truly private cannot be shared publicly, and what is truly public cannot be dissolved into the private. That is a problem with some versions of multiculturalism, those that privilege only the interests of particular individuals and groups over against common interests, or even the possibility of such.

Politics, Elshtain says, refers to what is, in principle, held in common and what is, in principle, open to public scrutiny and judgment. "If there are no distinctions between public and private, personal and political, it follows that there can be no differentiated activity or set of institutions that are genuinely political, the purview of citizens, and the bases of order, legitimacy, and purpose in a democratic community. If genuine politics ceases to exist, what rushes in to take its place is pervasive force, coercion, and manipulation; power of the crassest sort suffusing the entire social landscape, creating a world ripe for antidemocratic solutions."

I asked Elshtain how she saw the relationship between Diana and feminism. She thought it was complex, and it would take a while to work out.

"Did Diana do anything for feminism?"

"I don't think so. She is an example of the very collapse of the private and public that I decry. And it bothers me that women are the primary consumers and transmitters of this tabloid culture. When I went out to get the papers this morning I overheard someone at the newsstand say "Oh, that poor little girl!" Well, Diana, whatever she was, was not a poor little girl. And after fifty years of feminism, we should not be treated to that kind of patronizing language."

"But surely the feminist movement can't be held responsible for Diana," I objected.

"In a sense it can," Elshtain replied. "Take the 1970s feminist slogan 'the personal is the political.' In its give-no-quarter form in radical feminist argument, any distinction between the personal and the political was disdained.

The claim was not that the personal and political are interrelated in ways previously hidden by male-dominated political ideology and practice, or that the personal and political might be analogous to each other along certain axes of power and privilege. Rather, there was a collapse of one into the other: the personal *is* political. The private sphere fell under a thoroughgoing politicized definition. Everything was grist for a voracious publicity mill; nothing was exempt. There was nowhere to hide. There are few alternatives in such a world. One is either victim or victimizer, oppressed or oppressor, abject or triumphant. That kind of feminism did a lot of damage."

"What kind of damage?" I asked.

"Take the example of battered women," Elshtain answered. "Clearly domestic abuse is wrong. And it is not just a private affair. Something must be done about it. But notice how solutions to this problem tend to work in practice. Almost always the first step is to expand the powers of police and the courts. But the abuses inherent in extending the therapeutic powers of the state are commonly ignored. This is the first step on the slippery slope of reliance on a society of scrutiny. In such a society the social space for difference, dissent, refusal, and indifference is squeezed out. Such an approach promotes the view that women are society's prototypical victims. But an ideology of victimhood diverts attention from concrete and specific instances of female victimization in favor of pushing a relentless worldview structured around the victim-victimizer dichotomy. This gives rise to moral panic and fuels women's fear and, paradoxically, disempowers them; it does not enable them to see themselves at citizens with both rights and responsibilities."

I said this line of argument probably wouldn't be too popular in feminist circles.

"Certainly not in some feminist circles," Elshtain said.

"Do you call yourself a feminist?"

"Yes, I do, though 'feminist' is just one dimension."

"What kind of feminist are you?"

"I would like to think a sensible feminist, someone concerned with the dignity and standing of women. I am not a radical or ideological feminist. Rather I think of feminism as a way of naming concerns. Feminism is at bottom about rights and responsibilities, it is about responsible citizenship."

"Have women's studies programs helped name these concerns?"

"Yes, in many institutions. They have been important in raising certain legitimate scholarly concerns. I think they have probably peaked as freestanding programs and can now better achieve their objectives when feminist concerns are integrated into broader ethical and political forms of inquiry."

"Would you say that the majority of feminists are now of the sensible rather than the ideological type?"

"I am not sure that is the case in academia. Much feminism there remains very antifamily, very concerned with power narrowly defined."

Elshtain has written extensively on the Western political and philosophical tradition from a feminist perspective. Most feminists I talk to find that a pretty dry well, with a heavy bias of patriarchy, misogyny, logocentrism, and the like. I asked her what she had found.

"Of course, one finds some of this."

"Isn't it too easy to blame the dead white males?" I asked, raising an objection that often draws blood in conversations of this sort. "After all," I went on, "given the state of human evolution and the conditions of the times, the way people defined social reality and lived out their lives could hardly have been otherwise. And if things could not have been otherwise, then our ancestors ought not be blamed for views they held in light of more recent, shall we say more enlightened, opinion."

Elshtain thought my point might be a little too deterministic.

"People always have choices," she said."I agree that it is not very profitable to rake over the Western tradition to dig up every damning reference to women. In my *Public Man, Private Woman* I say that would be a tedious and depressing exercise. One can find those references and in abundance. History always has a dark side. But I also discovered thinkers who were troubled, puzzled, even angered at received notions about men and women, about public and private. I discovered a usable past."

"Future generations will no doubt look back on us and find plenty to complain about."

"Yes. They will say we abandoned our children, sometimes physically, all too often emotionally."

"Maybe a little Greek patriarchy won't look so bad by comparison."

"I don't think anything could be as bad as abandoning our children."

"What thinkers from the past have you found helpful?"

"Aristotle, for example. His reputation among contemporary feminists is not great because he reached conclusions that absorbed women completely within the household and denied them any possibility of a public voice or role. But there are other dimensions of his thought that are highly relevant to our contemporary efforts to create and sustain a participatory, normative ideal of political life. It is easy to categorize Aristotle as a misogynist who thought women were inferior by nature, but if we let it rest there we miss other more positive aspects of his thought, particularly in his books on politics and ethics—what he has to say there about the common good, associated living, friendship, participation, and the like. Here he has a vision which remains alive, and he can instruct feminism, which I think lacks a viable vision of either politics or the political community and has thus far failed to create an ideal of citizenship."

Elshtain finds other major thinkers, despite their cultural limitations, fruitful sources for contemporary efforts to think about feminism, democracy and citizenship. She particularly likes Augustine on whom she is currently offering a seminar at the University of Chicago. Since I frequently offer a seminar on Augustine myself I asked Elshtain to share some thoughts on that most colorful and most tortured of thinkers from our past.

This is the essence of what she said:

Like Aristotle, Augustine, together with the Catholic tradition he did so much to structure, frequently finds himself on the dead white male list of feminist targets. But there is another reading, and that is to see Christianity ushering a moral revolution into the world which dramatically and for the better transformed the prevailing images of male and female, public and private, and offered a new way of seeing social reality, created a new vocabulary of moral agency and gave new answers to the Socratic question: How might we live a just life? The enduring contributions of Christianity were its emphasis on the sanctity of human life and daily activity (thus effectively ending slavery), the notion of principled resistance to secular power, and above all the ideal that we are all endowed with freedom and therefore responsible for our destinies. Women, as indeed all persons, had an honored place in this scheme of values. They discovered that the qualities most often associated with motherhood—giving birth and sustaining human life; an ethic of responsibility toward the helpless, the vulnerable and the weak; gentleness, mercy, compassion—were all to be celebrated.

It was Augustine's genius to locate the problem of language at the root of inequality and our inability to achieve a good and just society. Because we are divided by language we can't communicate well, we are always talking past one another. Whence the importance of voices—of finding one's voice, of giving expression to a voice, of hearing a voice, especially the voices of different others. Christianity was an experiment in giving everyone an identifying language, and thereby greatly expanded the definition of what it means to be human. Augustine placed the speaking subject at the center of his political and religious probing and turned up fresh insights into the relationship between public and private, freedom and necessity, politics and the family, between *cupiditas* and *caritas*.

Augustine, Elshtain concluded, "is one of the great undoers of Greek misogyny."

At this point Princess Diana and Augustine were coming together in my mind: Diana, the image of victimhood, and Augustine, the great spokesman for a tradition that gives voice to victims. It occurred to me that victimization is not something experienced only by some feminists and minorities, not something merely idiosyncratic and aberrant, but rather a generic affliction, something in the nature of a metaphor for the human condition at century's end. Most of us in one way or another are victims. We experience the moral impotence and intellectual confusion brought by a mystifying political order, by the juggernaut of technology, by a feverish economy cartwheeling across the face of the globe. We lack a language capable of properly naming our concerns, moral resources commensurate with the problems we face. We don't have a matching concept of duties and rights adequate to our situation. All our notions of right and wrong have been thrown off balance by the genuinely new circumstances in which we find ourselves. How very Augustinian is our modern predicament. I asked Elshtain what hope she saw for democracy, given such circumstances.

She cautioned me against taking the easy road of cynicism. Democracy, she said, is not reducible to either images or the market. "We have witnessed astounding victories for democracy in the twentieth century. World War II was a victory. The end of the cold war was a victory. The dissidents in Eastern Europe won basic freedoms and rights for public space and a concept of human dignity that cannot be gainsaid. Think of the achievement of Martin Luther King Jr. Remember the strong voices of other moral leaders like Deitrich Bonhoeffer in Germany, Albert Camus in France, Nelson Mandela in South Africa, Rienhold Niebuhr in America, and the group Las Madras in Latin America. Throughout there have been palpable social and political gains for women, for the poor, and democratic victories in third world countries that remain exemplary."

"Yours is a voice of hope."

"A cautious one. Democracy may be in peril but it remains vibrant and resilient, the great source of political hope in our troubled world."

In *Democracy on Trial*, Elshtain called for a new social covenant "to break the spiral of mistrust and cynicism."

I asked her what was involved in this proposal.

"I use the word covenant because political theory has been overrun by social contract discourse. But a contract is not the same as a covenant. Contract says individualism, self-interest, privacy. Covenant points to community, civic identity, shared interests. The emphasis on contract has given rise to a democracy that too often pits citizen against citizen in a zero-sum game, the I-win-you-lose juridical model of politics I criticize. The social covenant is the name given to a hope that we can draw on what we hold in common, even as we disagree, a name for releasing the vibrancy of a tradition, a name for constructing an ethical polity and dwelling in hope."

I recalled the great covenantal model drawn up by John Winthrop in 1630 as the pilgrim ship *Arbella* approached the shores of the new world. Winthrop said on that occasion: "We must entertain each other in brotherly affection, we must be willing to abridge ourselves of our superficialities, for the supply of others' necessities. We must uphold a familiar commerce together in all meekness, gentleness, patience, and liberality. We must delight in each other, make others' conditions our own, rejoice together, mourn together, labor and suffer together, always having before our eyes our community as members of the same body. So shall we keep the unity of the spirit in the bond of peace."

"That is very powerful," Elshtain said.

"But a hard sell these days."

"That's because we don't want to be serious. We want to be trendy. We want to pretend to be serious and we think that projecting a lofty sounding, abstract vocabulary makes us serious."

I asked Elshtain what connection she saw between religion and democracy.

"A very deep one," she said. "And in a double sense. As an empirical matter democracy arose out of the matrix of the Judeo-Christian tradition. Ideas of equality, freedom, rights, the dignity of the human person, and covenanted relationships that issue into membership spring rather directly from that tradition. It is impossible to explain them otherwise. I challenge anyone to try. And, secondly, democracy cannot be sustained without institutions of moral formation of which religions are preeminent."

"What does religion mean to you?"

"It is finally about what has been called a harsh and dreadful love."

"Can you conceive of democracy without religion?"

"I suppose you could imagine as a thought experiment a functioning democracy without religion. But then the question becomes: Where do ethical commitments and ethical restraints come from? How do these emerge? How are they structured and sustained? Come up with a sturdy set of substitutes, and then you might persuade me. There has been some recent social science research that shows people who are actively involved in their churches are also more committed to democracy and civil society, more involved in political things, in responsible commitment to others, the brotherhood and sisterhood issues that are so essential to democratic life. It seems to be the case, for example, that to the extent anything is being done to stem civic decline in the inner cities, it is being done by the churches. This is no surprise really. We can imagine some kind of procedural republic without religion. But that isn't democracy. So the question is: Where are the sites for the formation of moral persons? Looked at empirically, the weight of evidence, I think, would be on my side. We are beginning a civil society study at the University of Chicago that will examine this question more deeply."

"Are we talking here about a rebirth of civil religion?"

"I am a little leery of that expression because it draws the knot between religion and politics too tightly. There is a connection. The question is: How tight? But however we define the connection, I do not believe that there is any substitute for membership that calls us to stewardship. Everywhere else we are told to maximize self-interest. Where else will we get this message? The new covenant as I understand it is not explicitly lodged in religion. It has to be much more inclusive than the covenant envisaged by John Winthrop. It has to meet the challenges of a mass society, of multiculturalism, of cybernetics. And it has to set itself squarely against the econometrics and marketization of identity, the fragmentation of personality into ever finer slivers of identity. This is what identity politics is coming to: the notion that we can only associate with people who are just like us. The new covenant has to take up the challenge of social isolation in modern society."

On reflection it seemed to me that Elshtain's reconceptualization of democracy was more in the spirit of Alexis de Tocqueville, perhaps the best theorist of democracy we have. Tocqueville proposed to overcome egoism and individualism, the twin enemies of democracy, by emphasizing the role of voluntary associations. These were the workshops of civic life in which different groups were brought together around some common purpose, where the skills of deliberation and an ethic of reciprocity without which democracy is not possible were taught. In Tocqueville's words: "It is through political associations that Americans of every station, outlook, and age day by day acquire a general taste for association and get familiar with the way to use the same. Through them large numbers see, speak, listen, and stimulate each other to carry out all sorts of undertakings in common. Then they carry these conceptions with them into the affairs of civil life and put them to a thousand uses."

Civil society so conceived is the great moral shaper in a democracy.

I asked Elshtain if there were other sources of moral formation besides the churches.

"One would hope the family. But that is a much battered institution these days."

"It's not a perfect world."

"No. The good, the bad, and the ugly are always with us. We can't get anywhere without a keen sense of the conflict and ambivalence at the heart of the human condition. That's one of the reasons I love Albert Camus so much. Like Augustine before him, he had that sense."

In Camus, Elshtain and I found a common interest, and we concluded the interview with some conversation about him.

PART FOUR

The Long Shadow of
the Cold War

Headnotes

The cold war was the moral center of the twentieth century. Together with the two world wars from which it sprang, it defined political life and the horizon of human possibility. It was the great metaphor for both good and evil in our time.

Erazim Kohák agrees on the centrality of the cold war in our twentieth century experience. "After forty years of communist rule," he says in reference to those countries in Central Europe that are trying to establish democracy, "we have developed habits and attitudes that were adaptive under communism but have become maladaptive now that we have the responsibility of governing ourselves." Drawing upon the thought of Edmund Husserl and the Czech martyr and philosopher Jan Patočka, Kohák shows a way beyond the cold war mentality.

"I came to see," he says in what is to me a startling insight, "that in so many ways the struggle for democracy in Central Europe is the cold war carried on by other means. The basic drama of the century was pitched as a politics of confrontation, a battle of good and evil, and framed in terms of an agenda of crushing the enemy." We have got democracy wrong from the start, assuming that if we defeat its enemies democracy will blossom forth as though by spontaneous combustion. Furthermore, the face the democratic West presented to the former communist countries is that of the free market and consumption, "a dream of irresponsibility, unreality, and instantly gratified greed." This is particularly true of America. Kohák is ruthless in his analysis: "It is difficult not to note that the consideration of the public good appears to have virtually vanished from American political rationality. Americans value democracy, but it is hard to avoid the impression that in great part they do so because it offers ever higher rates of personal consumption and makes ever fewer demands." And these measured words: "The future of democracy depends on our ability to break free of the heritage of the cold war. Our task now is no longer to fight for democracy but to rethink what democracy means, to rediscover all that was generous, all that was noble, all that was idealistic. Then democracy might have a future. Otherwise, I am not sure that it will and I am not sure that it should."

Martin Matustik grew up in Czechoslovakia as a member of a dissident community. He remembers the years of his youth as "intense." In addition to Czech thinkers and writers like Husserl, Kafka, Milan Kundera, Václav Havel and Jan Patočka, he was particularly influenced by Søren Kierkegaard, who put forth a theory of radical individualism that Matustik considers vital to democracy. Kierkegaard, he says, "was a fierce critic of the truncated instrumental rationality and atomistic individualism found in modern politics and economics. The demise of the individual is at the root of our political problems. Kierkegaard's point is that unless individuals are capable of radical self-choice in the first place, then social choices will be ungrounded. Deliberative democracy presupposes Kierkegaard's individual in order to sustain itself against cultural homogenization."

Matustik has done brilliant work in bringing the insights of existentialism and critical theory to bear on his analysis of politics and elaborating a theory of existential democracy. What is implied by existential democracy? The answer: a conception of the individual as capable of self-choice; a theory of communication that gets at how language works to transform personality; and third, the transgressive power of self-choice which enables us to go against the grain and get beneath the congenial definitions of such social values as honesty, responsibility, justice, action, community, and love.

Merab Mamardashvili lived in the eye of the cold war for most of his life, on the existential edge, in the lonely land between the forbidden and the unthinkable. From this perspective he viewed the events of the century and took the measure of the human situation. He is an outstanding example of one individual thinking his way through the worst our century has served up. By reflecting on history, consciousness, freedom, and the nature of civil society, by appropriating the works of Plato, Kant, and Marx, he learned the oldest lesson of life: when the chips are down we have to rely on our inner strengths and, like the Stoics of old, resolutely hold to our course in the face of unspeakable adversity. "What attracted me to Plato," Mamardashvili says, "was his metaphor of the cave in which he depicts people struggling with the shadows. That was my problem, too. All my life I worked in the shadows. And Plato showed a way out; he showed that the shadows can be transcended by consciousness, by thought. Communism was essentially a failure of thought, an inability to distinguish between reality and unreality. What Russia did was jump out of history and commit metaphysical suicide by trying to bypass the real for the ideal. What we have to do now is jump back into history."

All of the interviews in this book were conducted during the decade of the 1990s. Mamardashvili was the only one I interviewed before the fall of the Soviet Union.

Democracy in the Post-Communist World

As this discussion was getting under way, Erazim Kohák told me a story. A listener asks Radio Yerevan: "Is it true that on May 1 in Red Square comrade Ivan Ivanich was given a Volga automobile?" Radio Yerevan replies: "In principle the story is true. However it didn't happen on May 1 but on Lenin's birthday; and it was not in Red Square but in Pushkin Square; the person in question was not Ivan Ivanich but Petr Petrovich; the vehicle in question was not a Volga automobile but a bicycle; and it was not given to Petr Petrovich but stolen from him. Other than that the story is correct."

Kohák tells the story to illustrate the duplicitous nature of life under the communist regime, the challenge of always making one's way through a tissue of lies. But now that the communist regime has collapsed there is another challenge: the daunting task of choosing a form of government under which to live. We in the West, indeed many in the former Soviet bloc, assumed that the favored option was democracy. But matters are not so simple. Democracy is perhaps not so much something we choose as something we grow into. Kohák has been writing and speaking lately about the difficulties of establishing democracy in countries that have never known it. Throughout Central Europe there is general confusion about what political direction to take. The dilemma, says Kohák, is that the "morally pure are hopelessly inexperienced, while the expert and experienced are morally tainted by ties with the old regime. The fall of communism happened so quickly that there was no time to educate a new leadership." Another problem is the attitudes of the people themselves. "After forty years of communist rule," Kohák told me, "we have developed habits and attitudes that were adaptive under communism but have become maladaptive now that we have the responsibility of governing ourselves."

Kohák was exiled from Czechoslovakia in 1948 and came to the United States. He received his higher education at Colgate and Yale and has been a longtime professor of philosophy at Boston University. After the Velvet Revolution in 1989 he returned to his homeland and is now retired from Charles University in Prague. Kohák is a kind and energetic man with a keen sense of life as performance. He is also a delightful conversationalist who speaks English with a faint, brogue-like accent and the sensitivity to nuance and range of one who has learned it well, from the ground up, so to speak. The fate of democracy in the postcommunist world was the focus of our conversation but beyond this central theme there were other questions I wanted to ask—about his homestead in New Hampshire which he built with his own hands, about his philosophical views, about education and other matters. So our conversation meandered, as all good conversations must, but never strayed far from the main topic.

In addition to his political and more technical philosophical works, Kohák has written a memoir of his life in New Hampshire entitled *The Embers and the Stars: A Philosophical Inquiry into the Moral Sense of Nature*. It is a beautiful volume, part prose, part poem and in my mind one of the best books on ecology in this century. The evocative opening lines read: "There still is night, down where the long-abandoned wagon road disappears amid the new growth beneath the tumbled dam, deep, virgin darkness as humans had known it through the millennia, between the glowing embers and the stars. Here dusk comes softly, gathering beneath the hemlocks and spreading out over the clearing, muting the harsh outlines of the day."

I told Kohák that *The Embers and the Stars* reminded me of Thoreau, especially the Thoreau of *Walden*. He said Thoreau and the American transcendentalists didn't have much influence on him. "Robert Frost is my American writer of preference," he said.

I asked him when he discovered Frost.

"When I came to America, I read three books to learn English. And I read them over and over again: the King James Bible, the Episcopalian Prayer Book, and the collected works of Robert Frost. But I learned more from Frost than English. I learned a way of looking at nature, of seeing nature. I remember one poem in which he spoke of the ocean hurling itself with fury against a virgin continent. I saw in those lines an image of my own exile from a violent background to a new life."

"What did Frost teach you about nature?"

"Perhaps it would be better to say he confirmed in me attitudes I already had. In Czechoslovakia we were in a situation comparable to America in the late nineteenth century, only a first or second generation from the land. Everybody still had a grandmother who lived in the country, so there was a strong sense of nostalgia, a strong sense of returning to the land. The land has always been a point of stability for the Czechs in their turbulent history. People and governments change but the land remains constant."

"What was it Frost saw in nature that you see?"

"Frost saw that the world was value laden and meaningfully ordered, that nature was a world of meaningful wholes."

That way of putting it reminded me of a long tradition of nature mysticism. I asked Kohák if he considered himself a nature mystic.

"No," he said emphatically. "Perish the thought! Leave mysticism to the Nazis. Hitler was a mystic. Like Husserl I am committed to reason. Like him, I want a broader conception than reason conceived in narrow and technical terms. Our culture has reduced reason to so narrow a segment of experience that it has to declare most of our experience irrational. I do not believe, for example, that moral judgments are irrational or that the practice of religion is irrational."

I quoted a passage from his book that suggested a mystic strain to me. Kohák had written:

"So I have sought to see clearly and to articulate faithfully the moral sense of nature and of being human therein through the seasons lived in the solitude of the forest, beyond the powerline and paved road, where the dusk comes softly and there still is night."

"Sounds mystical to me," I said. "What do you mean by the moral sense of nature?"

"The ancients spoke of *logos* in nature. By that they meant not only that things exist but that they have a meaning, an order that inheres in them independently of any human interpretation. Nature has a sense of its own, its own way of being in the world. To have a moral sense of nature is then to see nature as a meaningful presence. It means also to say that nature includes a dimension of value, an integrity, a beauty, a rightness, a goodness that we humans do not impute to nature but discover in nature."

"Is that Frost's understanding of nature?"

"So I read him."

"Could it also be said that this is the leitmotif of your whole philosophy? You work in the field of phenomenology and have written books on Edmund Husserl and the Czech philosopher Jan Patočka and a leading emphasis of phenomenology is on values and meaningful wholes."

"The key word is lived experience, what in German is called the *Lebenswelt*, life's world. The root question of philosophy is: Does the world present itself as confusion and disorganization which we then organize with our concepts, or does the world present itself as prestructured and meaningfully ordered? Either we start out with an arbitrary world, a world in process, that has to be put together like a puzzle, or we start out on the assumption that the world and its meaning is something already there, given in time, which we discover in such fashion that the world and our knowledge of it form a seamless web of lived experience. Unfortunately, since Descartes we tend to think all of reality comes in two sizes: mind and matter, unreal but meaningful ideas or real but meaningless things. Husserl took up cudgels against this kind of dualism and abstraction and I follow him. The initial given is neither a mind nor an object but rather lived experience. I do not live in a world of ideas nor in a world of physical things. These are abstractions from experience. I once had a physics teacher who would bang his fist on the table and say: 'You students may think this is a table but it is really atoms and molecules.' But tables are neither physical objects nor mental abstractions. They are experienced wholes on the basis of which we form a notion of a physical table with properties like hard, spatial, square, and so forth. Students are told every day that their real life is not really real. The academic disciplines have mystified experience and perpetuated the impression that reality is not really real."

"All of higher education would appear to be an induction into abstractions that are less than the 'really real,' as you put it."

"All education is a drive to *theoría*, to reflection. I have no problem with that. My question is: What do you consider the basis, the reality about which you reflect? My quarrel with much academic philosophy is that it takes the abstraction for the basic reality."

"Were Husserl and Patočka of one mind in opposing this mentality?"

"Basically, yes. For Patočka, the starting point is Husserl's diagnosis of the crisis of the sciences. Patočka was one of the small circle to whom Husserl sent his typescript of *The Crisis of European Sciences* and had been his host in Prague when Husserl first presented that theme in a lecture. Husserl's basic thesis is that Western science, in the process of formalizing lived experience for the purposes of precise explanation and prediction, excised from its reality-construct a whole range of characteristics which render that experience humanly meaningful. Husserl, as well as Patočka, regards this procedure as in itself legitimate. What is problematic is the next step: taking this reduced reality-construct for reality itself, effectively forgetting or 'stepping over' the ground on which that construct is based. Western science, and Western rationality in its present mode, have lost the ability of providing an orientation for human activity because they have lost touch with their human grounding."

"What accounts for the fact that these philosophers had an enormous influence on the Czech dissidents?"

"In Central Europe, Descartes's great counterpart was Comenius. Now all but forgotten, he was one of the most acclaimed men of his age. Harvard wanted him for its president, the English Parliament hoped he would mediate between itself and the king, Sweden wanted him to reform its school system. Comenius bequeathed to Central Europe a very different vision of reality, one that was value laden and meaningfully ordered. Truth, beauty, and goodness appeared to him not as 'subjective' impositions on a value-free, meaningless, and 'objective' reality but as the intrinsic structure of reality itself.

"In the Franco-English West, a rising natural science, operating with a Cartesian conception of reality, largely crowded out all vestiges of the Comenian vision of a meaningful, value-laden world. In Central Europe, however, that vision has remained. It reemerged in Goethe, in Schelling, and for that matter, in a very different guise in Thomas Masaryk, famous for his statement: 'Values, too, are facts.' When in 1935 the Moravian-born philosopher Edmund Husserl wrote his *Crisis,* he located its roots precisely in the Cartesian notion of 'objective,' meaningless, and value-free reality. He proposed instead a Comenian solution, and the dissident Czech philosophers of today, committed to life in truth and to the reality of truth, goodness, beauty, are very much his heirs."

"The thrust of my earlier question about higher education was that much theorizing we do in academia is of the sort that leads us away from this understanding of experience in all its fullness."

"I would caution against hasty generalization. Some of it is. Some of it isn't. I am an academic and I hope I am not guilty of doing that."

"I suspect you are in the minority."

"That's possible. Again, the relevant text is Husserl's *Crisis.* He deals at length with this very problem. Heidegger had argued that humans fail to live up to their authentic possibilities. That has a nice therapeutic ring to it. But it is very elitist. Husserl and Heidegger define the trajectory of modern European philosophy. But they define it in different directions. Against Heidegger, Husserl would argue that the fault is not with people assumed to be too trivial for words. The problem is in the whole orientation of our culture, which has generated a set of categories in which we think and which lead to disastrous results. It is not that people are any greedier than they have ever been. Or that the American middle class is somehow venal in an exceptional way. The problem is rather that we have built up a social system which rewards greed and blocks other forms of social organization."

"This prompts a turn to your thinking about democracy. There is clearly a connection between your philosophy and your attitude toward nature. It seems to be the case that there is also a parallel between your philosophy and your views of democracy. A trinity of ideas seems to come together here."

"Phenomenology as I have described it is the base; it provides the tools with which I work. Conceptions of nature, democracy, and morality are three topics on which I work."

"One gathers from the different things you have written that you are not too sanguine about the prospects for democracy in the Central European countries."

"Two years ago I would have been very optimistic. Today the grounds for optimism are less. I am now more realistic."

"What caused you to change your mind?"

"I came to see more clearly that in so many ways the struggle for democracy in Eastern Europe is the cold war carried on by other means."

"How so?"

"Let's go back in history for a moment. This century has clung tenaciously to the notion that democracy was written in the stars, that it was our destiny. As we fought one war after another to make the world safe for democracy, we remained confident that once we had at last defeated its enemies, democracy would blossom forth, ushering in an age of peace, justice, and good will.

"The apocalyptic war with which our century opened was supposed to accomplish all of that. When the weary victors met at Versailles, they showed a great concern to punish Germany and Austria for their war crimes, but surprisingly little concern to create the conditions for democracy. That, they were confident, would take care of itself. Yet it was not democracy that grew on the wreckage of the old order but rather communism, several varieties of fascism, and national socialism that sprouted like weeds among rubble. Twenty years after the war to make the world safe for democracy, the world was locked in another world war and democracy was on a precarious defensive.

"Still, we kept the faith. In retrospect, perhaps the most puzzling aspect of the second World War was the conviction of the Allies that if only we could defeat Hitler and his clique, democracy would blossom forth, bringing in the promised age. The grand alliance, which included Stalin's Soviet Union as well as the United States and Britain, had no common program beyond defeating 'the fascist,' and that seemed enough. Given a chance, democracy, we assumed, would emerge spontaneously from the wreckage.

"It did not happen that way. 'Antifascism' proved far more fertile ground for communism than for democracy. Three years after the second war to end all wars, democracy was once again on the defensive, locked in another global war, no less bitter for being mostly of the cold variety. Yet the rhetoric of the cold war suggests that we learned little from the first two rounds. That rhetoric produced little critical reflection about the conditions that make for democracy, about what democracy is, what makes it work and what makes it fail. The emphasis was again on defeating the enemies of democracy, this time atheistic communism and its evil empire. Once that was accomplished, democracy would blossom spontaneously, bringing in the promised age of freedom, good will, and prosperity at long last.

"So you see the basic drama of the century was pitched as a politics of confrontation, a battle of good and evil, and framed in terms of an agenda of crushing the enemy. It was John Dulles who said that neutrality is treason, echoing the revolutionary St. Just who said '*pas de liberté pour les enemis de la liberté.*' Whether from the side of the communists or from the side of democracy, the dynamic of crushing remained the same."

I pointed out that this is not a view of democracy that would be recognized by the classical framers of democratic theory.

"Surely not," Kohák responded. "It was the Enlightenment conviction that all humans are capable of freedom and responsibility and so of sharing the prerogatives and burdens of power. Democracy is possible because all humans are capable of rationality, of grasping and pursuing the common good. But while the thinkers of the Enlightenment believed that this ability must be carefully nurtured, the twentieth century added a much more problematic Romantic belief that the maturing of humans and societies to the responsibility of freedom would happen spontaneously, that humans are 'naturally good' and therefore also 'naturally' democratic, as long as they are not corrupted and / or constrained by democracy's enemies, the communists, the fascists, the militarists, and perhaps others, like religious fanatics or nationalists. Hence our strategy. While the great philosophers of democracy, a T. G. Masaryk or a John Dewey, taught us that democracy must be first carefully nurtured in every one of us and in our society at large and only then can be expected to work as a political system, we preferred to believe that we could just fight the enemies of democracy and trust that democracy would simply happen. Democracy is an achievement, not a spontaneous growth. It takes an active and informed effort."

"Hasn't Václav Havel done much to promote just that idea of democracy?" I asked. "It seems to many of us in the West that Havel did much to reverse the legacy of the cold war and has appealed to many as a man possessed of a strong moral sense and leader of a new kind of politics that goes beyond the agenda of crushing."

Kohák agreed, in part. "When Václav Havel attempted to head a government of national reconciliation, he was trying, however ineffectually, to leave behind the cold war mentality of politics as war. The model he sought to introduce was one of democracy in Masaryk's prewar sense—and the Western sense—of cooperation in diversity and respect. For a people long conditioned to thinking in polar terms, however, that fell short of the victory over communism they expected. Supporters of the present right-wing regime dismiss the Velvet Revolution as an attempt by excommunists to shield the communists from the full consequences of their defeat and so as not yet democratic. To them, democracy can mean nothing less than a 'defeat' of the Left and a 'victory' of the Right. Building democracy then means making the 'victory of the Right' irreversible, much as the old regime interpreted 'building socialism' as making the 'victory of the proletariat' irreversible. To a Western observer, the idea of democracy as the irreversible rule of 'the Right,' even at the cost of breaking up the country to avoid any need for compromises, may appear nothing short of bizarre, and with good reason. However, after decades of confrontational politics, the binary habits are deeply ingrained and that idea of democracy, however counterproductive, seems only natural."

"Havel has nonetheless been reelected president."

"It is not a powerful position. Havel is completely subordinate to Prime Minister Václav Klaus. The government which took over from Havel's idealistic dissidents, now contemptuously dismissed as 'crypto-commies,' stridently identifies itself as 'right wing' and vilifies anyone dissenting from it as 'leftist.' The polar mentality remains, and as a basis for building democracy, is utterly deadly because it equates dissent, or for that matter, any critical inquiry, with treason."

"The story, as I understand it thus far, is that the struggle for democracy in Central Europe is vitiated by bad attitudes and mental states held over from communism and the cold war."

"On the one side. But it is also vitiated by the face democracy presents to us. To the dissidents during the cold war democracy meant anticommunism;

now it means consumption. What Central Europeans see in the West is primarily the glitter and glamour of an unrestricted market economy. A popular Czech cartoonist depicts freedom as a man on a sofa surrounded by an outboard motor, a television, a VCR, a computer, a portable bar and like commodities. I believe most people in my country unthinkingly assume that is the dream of freedom, not realizing that it is a dream of irresponsibility, unreality, and instantly gratified greed. I heard a man in one of the stand-up buffets in Prague say one day: '*Demogracie, to je mít meďoury, pivo v plechu a nic nemuset.*' Roughly translated that means that 'democracy means big cars, canned beer, and no obligations.'"

"Would it be rude to suggest that Cenetral Europeans are rather naive in taking that view of democracy?"

"Again, you have to remember the cold war context. For decades, both the communist government propaganda and Western counterpropaganda identified democracy with free enterprise. Prague's Radio Star and America's Radio Free Europe fully concurred that the cold war was a conflict between communism and capitalism. To the end, Mr. Bush spoke of the collapse of Soviet rule as a victory not of freedom or democracy but of 'democratic capitalism.' To a Western observer that assertion might well sound rather farfetched, but to populations conditioned by years of cold war propaganda it can sound entirely believable. After all, for years the communists had insisted that it was American capitalists who conspired to bring down the Soviet Union. When the Soviet Union did collapse under the weight of its own iniquities, the Czech listener was quite ready to give the credit to the Pentagon and Wall Street. Hence the somewhat surprising conclusion that the way to the twenty-first century leads through the nineteenth."

Kohák painted a pretty grim picture. One would surely want to make a better argument for democracy than consumerism.

"One would," Kohák said, "But as a good phenomenologist I am describing the reality as it is. For me, as an observer who loves America, it is difficult not to note that the consideration of the public good appears to have virtually vanished from American political rationality. Americans value democracy, but it is hard to avoid the impression that in great part they do so because it offers ever higher rates of personal consumption and makes ever fewer demands. John Fitzgerald Kennedy could still inspire his fellow Americans and the world by telling them to ask not what their country could do for them but what they could do for their country. Twenty years later, a mere hint of such an appeal proved deadly to Jimmy Carter's political career. It seems unlikely that a politician in America today could ask his countrymen to defer private gratification for the sake of the common good. In the down-at-the-heels post communist world, he would be cast out as a crypto-commie; here, the primacy of private gratification has become the synonym for democracy.

"That, finally, is another damning impact of communism and the cold war on our conception of democracy. Democracy had long built on toleration and good will, on generosity and responsibility for the common good and on a willingness to sacrifice for its sake. The cold war taught us instead the attitudes of confrontation and intolerance, the posture of greed and irresponsibility. We might, of course, argue that the attitudes of the 'me' generation are a product of the conditions under which we live and so appropriate to the world we seek to imitate. That, though, leads to a wider question: are the problems of democracy in the postcommunist world really unique to its special conditions or are they continuous with the problems democracy faces globally as it seeks to address the problems of the twenty-first century?"

Shortly after I talked to Kohák I visited Central Europe for a first-hand look at democratic developments there. In the spring of 1995 I returned to Prague as a scholar in residence at the Center for Theoretical Studies which is part of Charles University. I was able to confirm many of Kohák's insights on an empirical basis.

Of all the Central European countries, the Czech Republic seems to have rebounded most successfully from the communist era. There is nearly full employment, prices are still reasonably low, consumer goods abound, and the streets are teeming with energetic and purposeful people, including many tourists. Tourism is in fact the country's biggest business through a season that begins in February and runs into November.

There is a good deal of intellectual ferment as well. The Czech dissidents who for so long worked underground, meeting furtively in obscure bars and apartment seminars and pouring over their samizdat publications, now occupy prominent positions in universities, government, and the media. Somewhat comparable to the existentialists who emerged from the Resistance Movement of World War II, the Czech dissidents have infused political and cultural thought with new insights and intellectual energy. I talked with a number of these thinkers, sounding out their views on society and history, freedom and responsibility and, above all, on the developing democracy in their country. What they told me does not by any means add up to an unclouded picture. On the one hand, they value democracy highly. On the other, they find it hard going, and the temptation to impatience is strong.

So there is a good measure of anxiety and uncertainty in the air. One reason for this is historical. During most of their history, the Czechs have lived under some kind of domination. Their freedom and identity have come at a high cost. A second reason involves the changes in social status that followed the defeat of the communists in 1989. As Jirina Siklova, a sociologist at Charles University, put it: "The hierarchy of social groups and the values imposed by the totalitarian regime no longer hold. New relationships among the social strata are just now forming; no one knows who will be poor tomorrow and who rich. We are all suffering from the loss of our former identity."

My landlady told me the only difference between now and the communists is that now things are more expensive. She illustrates her point with an anecdote. If people wanted bread under the communists all they had to do was ask for a kilo of bread. Now they are asked: What kind of bread would you like? The burdens of choice are felt in even small ways. And it is an existential truism that choice breeds anxiety for we can never be sure that we have made the right choice.

It seems to me that the principal cause of uncertainty among the Czechs is anxiety about democracy itself. It is a heady experience for them. When I asked Ivan Chvatik, who runs a research institute in Prague, how democracy was working in the Czech Republic, he said there are two questions he wants to distinguish. The first concerns the meaning of democracy. The second asks whether democracy, whatever it is, is good for the Czech Republic in this transitional period. Many people think the first task ought to be to fix the economy, and then democracy will follow.

But this approach has its drawbacks. It is true that economic concerns are topmost in the minds of most Czechs. Polls indicate that around 90 percent of Czechs want to be part of Europe, that they want democracy. But the young aspire to become rich. So there is a fuzzy connection between economic values and democratic values, a confusion compounded by the fact that with the first wave of Western values came pornography and gambling.

The train that ran by my hotel carried a large ad for *Penthouse Magazine*, complete with a 25-foot likeness of a naked woman. Thus Czechs are understandably ambivalent about Western values and capitalism—and even democracy itself. The thought that freedom means Hugh Hefner and Las Vegas should give us all pause. What is even worse for the Czechs is the Russian mafia which is conspicuous in the burgeoning Czech economy. A friend warned me never to take newer model cabs. "They're all run by the mafia," he said. The shabby cabs were a rougher ride, but considerably cheaper.

I had a long interview with Petr Pithart, who was Prime Minister of Czechoslovakia in Václav Havel's government. What disappoints us, he told me, "is the West we thought we were catching up with is itself changing." By that he meant that nations like the Czech Republic expected firmer moral guidance from the West. When I asked him how democracy is working in the Czech Republic, he answered that now the question of civil society is more important than the question of democracy. "Democracy is working in a mechanical sense," he said, "but unless we strengthen those intermediary institutions, that range of what Tocqueville called voluntary associations between the private and public realms, it will not flourish. It will not take root in the minds and hearts of the people."

I told him that the question is an important one in America as well. He said that was not surprising: "During the cold war everybody put democracy on hold and now everybody has to reexamine it, rediscover it anew. We are all to a degree confused. We are all searching."

This uncertainty was reflected in an on-going debate between President Václav Havel and the then Prime Minister Václav Klaus—the battle of the two Václavs as it was sometimes referred to. Both were leaders in the Civic Forum, both were widely published intellectuals, both were in positions of power. But they were poles apart ideologically, and their respective positions dramatized the ambiguity of democracy in the Czech Republic and, for that matter, in much of the world. Havel spoke in a moral voice. He used expressions like "living in truth," "the care of the soul," and the "power of the spirit." Klaus was a follower of Margaret Thatcher and more or less identified democracy with free market economics. Many Czechs have gone from anti-communism to consumerism without the intermediary step of democracy. This is the point that Kohák had made so emphatically when we first talked.

Havel is nourished by the tradition of democracy as a moral ideal rather than the narrower sense of an economic system. He is particularly indebted to Tomas Masaryk, one of the founders and the first president of Czechoslovakia from 1918 to 1935, who based his political philosophy on the tradition of civic humanism, especially as this manifested itself in Czech humanists like Jan Hus, Comenius, and more recently, Jan Patočka. Masaryk summed up his philosophy. Masaryk had a doctorate in philosophy, wrote several books, and was elected to the Austrian Reichstrat in 1891 before founding his own party in 1900 after which he became the leader of young progressives who played a decisive role in the fight for Czech and Slovak independence. Masaryk was a dissident before his time whose notions of equality, freedom, and justice remain exemplary. He resigned the presidency in 1935, partly to protest the rise of Nazi power, and died two years later.

On a warm Sunday afternoon I visited Masaryk's grave in Lany, a quiet village some thirty miles west of Prague, where he lies beside his wife and son Jan. The latter died in 1948, presumably murdered by the communists who had in that year taken over the government of Czechoslovakia. The gravesite is beautifully kept, and fresh flowers are brought daily by the villagers. It is in effect a national shrine. I thought of it as a kind of eternal flame to the spirit of democracy in a land that has not known much of it in its brief and tragic history.

I continued my conversation with Kohák while in Prague. I caught up with him one Sunday morning after church services in the little Church of the Common Brethren. We walked around the city he had known so well in his youth. He pointed with pride to beautiful buildings that date from the middle ages and, with great sadness, to others that were falling beneath the developer's ball. Over a long lunch the discussion turned to some of the problems democracy faces as the twentieth century passes into the twenty-first. One, said Kohák, is the problem of cultural communication.

"Because democracy represents a commitment to non-coercive conflict resolution, it is critically dependent on the transmission of shared values that make such resolution possible. Democracy is basically discussion, substituting reasoned communication for confrontation as the means of conflict resolution. Discussion, though, requires a shared framework of understanding, a willingness and an ability to listen and understand, and a readiness to submit to a common cultural norm. The twentieth century has seen simultaneously a dramatic increase in global contact and a no less dramatic decrease in any sense of cultural community. In the affluent, high-technology segment of the human community, an overwhelming flood of information makes it ever more difficult to receive information critically and to process it in the form of a coherent world view.

"American higher education, surely the most privileged segment of humanity, provides a microcosmic example. Students find themselves bombarded with an electronic avalanche of sound bites that leaves them bewildered, with little sense of a cultural heritage or a cultural community. Even when it is not rejected as irrelevant, available information simply expands too rapidly to be absorbed. The discussion that is the life-blood of democracy degenerates into a meaningless barrage of sound bites. The problem of cultural communication in the West appears as technological, minds brainwashed by electronic sound reproduction. In the third world it appears as demographic. In the second half of the twentieth century, populations have expanded exponentially, far too rapidly for acculturation. In countries where the young account for a half or more of the total population, it is wholly illusory to suppose that their elders can effectively transmit any sense of cultural heritage to them. The feral children who live in roving packs in the margins of the great urban conglomerates of the third world share little of a common culture. It is more than likely that as they mature, primitive fanatic allegiance will be all that will provide them with a framework of orientation. Without a shared culture, both discussion and democracy become an unattainable ideal while coercion and conflict alone remain as the forms of social contact."

"It appears to many, and for some of the reasons you mention, that our world is becoming more divided and fragmented," I said.

"And that is another problem we face. The dominant trend of our time is polarization, not integration. The demands of the privileged on the finite resources of individual societies as well as of the globe as a whole have accelerated the pauperization of the underprivileged. Ours is one world but hardly one culture. In the days when populations appeared finite and resources infinite, the affluent north and west of the globe dismissed the problem with the consolation that increasing prosperity of the prosperous would marginally generate prosperity for the deprived. Popularly this came to be known as the 'trickle-down' theory which John Kenneth Galbraith is said to have described as feeding the birds by giving oats to the horse. Unfortunately, that theory has worked only to assuage the consciences of the privileged, not to alleviate the lot of the deprived. In the past fifty years, the gap between the haves and the have-nots has increased precipitously. The global south today is desperately poor and getting poorer, the affluent north is opulently affluent and becoming more so. The gap is increasing no less dramatically between the high-speed, high-tech segments of individual societies and the drudges of the earth, between the horses and the birds. We can't run a world polarized between incredible wealth and desperate poverty."

This brought us back to the subject of ecology, about which Kohák has written for so long and so eloquently. The need to save our land, he has said, is the one appeal that can still evoke a response in the young.

"That may well be our greatest problem," he told me in Prague. "Even with only one seventh of the world's population consuming—and producing waste—at Euro-American levels we are consuming resources faster than the earth can renew them and generating waste far, far faster than we can dispose of it. Were all six billion inhabitants of the globe to begin consuming and generating waste at that rate, the earth would become uninhabitable in a matter of hours, not days, buried beneath a mountain of trash. Here there are two scenarios; an optimistic one and a pessimistic one. The pessimistic is that if everyone consumed at the rate of the affluent the world would become uninhabitable in nine and one-half hours. The optimistic is twenty-one days."

The shadows were beginning to lengthen on a long day. I had a few more questions before we parted. The first had to do with how we might go about constructing a better democracy.

Kohák said: "Following from what we have just been talking about, the future of democracy depends on our ability to break free of the heritage of the cold war and address instead the means of building global balance and a sustainable economy. Our task now is no longer to fight for democracy but to rethink what democracy means, to rediscover all that was generous, all that was noble, all that was idealistic. Then democracy might have a future. Otherwise, I am not sure that it will and I am not sure that it should."

"Does this mean going back to origins, to roots?"

"I visualize from time to time those embattled American farmers at their rude bridge in Concord. What did democracy mean to them and their representatives in Congress assembled? It meant the conviction that all humans and not only a few are capable of assuming the full stature of free humanity, of accepting responsibility for themselves and for the commonweal without a tutor over them, benign or otherwise. Democracy was a vision of a voluntary cooperation, of a world without masters and serfs, a world of equals living together in freedom, in responsibility, and in mutual respect as citizens, not as subjects. The grand vision of the European Enlightenment was one of all humans as potentially capable of full humanity, regardless of race or creed, even the wretched of the earth, capable of making their own decisions and sharing in the care of the commonweal. Against the Hobbesian vision of humans as intrinsically egotistic, having to be restrained in their greed by a sovereign, it was the vision of humans as capable of voluntarily subordinating their private ends to a common good and the law of reason. It was and still is an audacious vision. And there are eloquent voices from your past that attest to it. The constitutional debates were about recognizing the common interests of the thirteen colonies. The Constitution speaks of liberty and justice for all. Abraham Lincoln urged malice toward none, charity and justice towards all. Martin Luther King Jr. dreamed his great dream of social justice. At its best this is what democracy has meant. We can find resources here to rethink the basic questions: What ought to be the goal of human striving? What is the *summum bonum*, the good we should seek to achieve?"

I asked Kohák what are the attitudes and habits that democracy presupposes in its citizens.

"Perhaps the basic is a certain moral maturity. Ralph Waldo Emerson spoke of 'self-reliance,' but that word has since acquired a whole range of rather unfortunate connotations. Other writers speak of accepting the responsibility of freedom, though that again is less than clear. Perhaps the most helpful distinction may be a Kantian one: the characteristic of adolescence is self-indulgence, that of maturity is self-respect, respect for humanity, whether in my own person or that of another. Democracy builds on respect and self-respect. Or again, we could say that a mature person is one who can act voluntarily, for good and sufficient reason, instead of merely reacting to stimulus. Democracy is about maturity, and democracy is about good will, about a certain generosity of spirit. Maturity means accepting responsibility for the common good, and that in turn means a willingness to subordinate momentary self-interest to a common interest. That, though, is something difficult to legislate and impossible to enforce without a massive repressive apparatus. A meanness of spirit makes such apparatus unavoidable; it takes a generosity of spirit to make it unnecessary. Democracy, finally, is about a good dose of idealism. Maturity, yes, and a generosity of spirit, but beyond that, democracy cannot get along without idealism. I stake my case on that high moral plane. I believe that if democracy is to survive we must learn that happiness is to be found not in acquiring but in giving, not in exploitation but in caring, not in self-gratification but in self-transcendence. That is a lesson we may learn in time."

I now asked a question I had on my mind throughout our conversation. The right moment had not seemed to present itself earlier. Kohák has from his youth been a man of the left, an embattled social democrat, indeed a socialist. I asked him what had been the appeal of socialism. To answer, he referred me to something he wrote earlier in his career: "[It] was the promise of freedom. Socialism promised to wipe out the privileges that gave economic aggregates their stranglehold on society. Social justice is not separable from economic justice. The core of the Czechoslovak socialist democracy I was introduced to as a youth was the determination to restore the rights of men without restoring the oppressive privileges of corporate entities. It was basically humanistic, concerned to propose an alternative to the impossible choice between democracy strangled by capitalism, or socialism strangled even more effectively by communist absolutism."

But those ideals were shattered in the great ideological battles of the cold war. Marxism did keep alive the dream that social justice is not separable from economic justice but early got bogged down in strategies and policies that belied that ideal. Kohák still wants to maintain that "traditional social philosophy has tended to treat human relations as autonomous from their economic context. It focused on human rights and obligations as if we were pure spirits. Socialism recognized that we are incarnate in our bodies and in our world. We become actual in our relations to the physical world, and our mutual relations are mediated by this embodiment. This has great consequences for economics. Practically, it means that property relations are not accidental but essential to any social ordering that all socialists have in common."

My next question was about the future of socialism after the collapse of communism. Kohák's answer is that "the outlook for socialism, certainly under that name, is absolutely nil, a snowball's chance in hell. Twenty five years ago, it was different, but the Brezhnev age of 'real socialism' managed to discredit anything that has the word 'social' in it. Even the idea of social justice or social welfare seems suspect: there is simply a powerful, gut level negative reaction to the word.

"Yet the need which social democrats sought to meet is very much there, and intensifying. The massive backlash against communism—locally called 'socialism'—creates conditions reminiscent of the age of the robber barons in the nineteenth century, now exploited by highly sophisticated international corporations with vast resources at their disposal. Though a new name has to be found for it, the old social democratic commitment to protecting the ordinary citizen from exploitation and assuring him or her the wherewithal of human decency, medical care, schooling, old age pensions, is once again highly relevant. Can the need, though, increasingly evident, overcome the powerful revulsion against anything 'socialist' after forty-two years of 'real socialism'? Or would we rather accept injustice and deprivation than risk return to what we have seen under the communists? Right now, that seems to be our tendency.

"There is another problem as well. Traditional socialism (or social democracy) was no less than 'capitalism' wedded to the idea of economic expansion and rising standards of individual consumption—or, in the terminology of a generation ago, to 'progress.' Given the twin realities of population explosion and ecological collapse, that is today a strategy for disaster, under socialist no less than under capitalist auspices. The urgent need facing any government in the coming century will be for population stabilization and leveling off of consumption to a globally sustainable level. Can socialism generate such a vision and such a strategy? Or will it remain constrained to what it was first designed to do, to compensating for the social failures of capitalism in its quest for ever expanding exploitation of nature?"

"Which way do you think it will go?"

"I do not know. I know that the capitalism which the postcommunist world is so painfully eager to create is already ecologically obsolete. Is socialism any less so? Or do we need to outgrow both sides of that cold-war opposition and look to a sustainable, green democracy? Time will tell . . . if we have time to find out."

I thought that was an answer well worth pondering. I ended the interview with some question about Kohák's new life in the Czech Republic. I asked him to compare teaching there and in America.

"Well," Kohák said, "we have a well noted problem of education in general in America. I estimate my students there have on the average an active working vocabulary of about 1,200 words. Teaching is contingent upon the student's capacity to receive, and we have produced a generation so incredibly impoverished. Many of them just blank out. Here the situation is very different. I sit on the admissions committee each year at Charles University and a big part of the admissions process is an interview in which we expect high school students to answer questions we could not expect juniors to answer here. Of course, the process is more selective. In this country well over 50 percent of high school graduates go on to some form of higher education. In Czechoslovakia only about twelve to fifteen percent do. That is partly because more can't afford to. But it is also a policy decision. We don't need more college graduates. So the end result is that Czech students are hungrier. In America when I assign a text the students say: 'Do I have to buy that?' In Czechoslovakia if I so much as mention a book students ask: 'Can I buy that?' And they will often sacrifice lunch money for books."

"What can Americans do for Czech educators?"

"I think first of all, following the point I just made, make grants available to translate textbooks. Second, establish a generous program of faculty exchanges, not just for college profs but for high school teachers as well. Czech teachers need to have their eyes open to the world. A third thing would be to establish contacts and exchanges at the departmental level with different schools. I emphasize the departmental level because when it is institution to institution the cream tends to get siphoned off by the administrators."

I asked Kohák what he liked most about America. The old socialist breathed in his answer.

"The working people. The honesty and down-to-earth-ness of working people. America is still largely a country of workers and peasants, far more than the Soviet Union ever dreamed of being. The Soviet Union was always an aristocracy, first of the czars, then of the Party. America is a genuinely democratic country."

"Would it be the same answer with respect to the Czech Republic?"

"No. What I like best about Czechoslovakia is the land—the land and its history. The land as a physical *presence*. I grew up in the city but I thought as though I were in the country."

"Was it hard for you to leave America?"

"Incredibly hard. I have a deep attachment to my homeland. But I have deep roots in New Hampshire as well where I built my own home and which I know better than my homeland. I don't know how it will all work out. I am very torn."

On my last day in Prague I went once again to stand in Wenceslas Square and watched people come by to lay flowers on the simple memorial to "The Victims of Communism." It was here on November 17, 1989, that one of the largest demonstrations in history for freedom from oppression took place and continued for ten days. When it was over, the face of Europe had changed.

Toward an Existential Politics

A most important conversation is going on today, both in this country and in the world generally, about the meaning of democracy. We seem to have come to one of those watersheds in history when our basic concepts stand in need of redefinition, our political concepts preeminent among them.

The outline of this conversation may be sketched in the image of a triangle. On one point we have an understanding of democracy that flows from its classical formulation. Democracy began in Greece as a response to problems that arose when states were ruled by oligarchies. The principal problem it sought to address was the arbitrary rule by self-serving elites or dictators. The remedies proposed included public deliberation to establish power, elections to select leaders, the diffusion of power, and the rule of law. Since in its original iteration democracy was direct, participation was a duty. Citizens had a high moral stake in their political community; they believed the polis was the premier means of achieving the good life, of maximally realizing human potential.

With the birth of modern democracy in the seventeenth and eighteenth centuries, what we now refer to as liberal democracy, the focus of political values shifted from the political community to the individual. What liberal democracy means to us today is that government is legitimized by the will of the people and its principal function is to protect the rights which inhere in each individual naturally. The Declaration of Independence stands as a noble testament to that ideal. With the hindsight of our twentieth century experience, however, the liberal notion of democracy is widely criticized because it has led, directly or indirectly, to intolerable social pathologies. It is charged that liberalism glorifies individual rights—often reduced to selfish rights—at the expense of common values, leads to egregious inequalities in the social order and gives an inadequate account of our social nature. Liberal democracy, we frequently hear, has no conception of community.

Socialism, the second point on our triangle, was the political response to the defects of liberal democracy. Socialism takes different forms—the conservative socialism of those who cling to tradition and the supposed holistic values of a Golden Age, Christian socialism which arose in Europe toward the middle of the nineteenth century to protest the excesses of the Industrial Revolution and shore up an eroding Christian faith, state socialism of the sort we found in communism, and more recently, welfare socialism which we associate with the mixed economies of Western European countries. Socialism in all of its expressions emphasizes community, equality, and increasingly, as its history has unfolded in the twentieth century, the authority of the state as the means of realizing these values. In socialism the community rather than the individual is the primary bearer of rights; the individual is subordinated to the social whole. Socialism runs into trouble when it appeals to authority to enforce its ideal of community and equality. At its worst this leads to totalitarianism and the repression of political rights. Thus through many cold wars, liberal democracy and socialism have battled to a standstill.

The socialist position has received support from what Christopher Lasch refers to as the communitarian point of view. Lasch uses the communitarian perspective to draw attention to two problems, one concerning the relationship between selfhood and tradition, the other concerning the relationship between civic virtue and social practices. Regarding the first he says: "Where liberals conceive of the self as essentially unencumbered and free to choose among a wide range of alternatives, communitarians insist that the self is situated in and constituted by tradition, membership in a historically rooted community." With respect to the second, he follows Alasdair MacIntyre, whose book *After Virtue* is an important contribution to communitarian literature, in emphasizing the character-forming discipline of social practices. Says Lasch: "It is specific practices, not civic life in general, that nourish virtue. We can define practices . . . as common projects in which the participants seek to conform to established standards of excellence."

The third point on our triangle is the development of postmodernism. Postmodernism is not so much an effort to reconcile the opposing elements of liberalism and communitarians as a repudiation of both. A pox on both of your houses, it seems to say, in rejecting universalistic claims of all colors. Postmodernism is iconoclastic, radically skeptical, and aggressively deconstructive in denying that there is any objective reality or any commonly acceptable knowledge of the good, the right, or the rational. One is reminded of the ancient sophist Gorgias who said: "Nothing exists. If anything did exist we could not know it; and if we knew it we could not communicate it." All the postmodernists seem to be left with is a constant power struggle of persons and groups to make their values prevail, an ever-shifting scene of signs and symbols we generate to give meaning to our lives. The resultant politics looks very Hobbesian: a war of all against all unto the death, a rhetoric of anarchy riding on the back of a Darwinian social ethic, the individual submerged in a sea of signifiers and hermetic views of reality.

All three of these positions lack something essential: they omit the category of the choosing individual that has been so richly explored in the existential tradition beginning in the mid-nineteenth century with Søren Kierkegaard. No one has so strenuously attempted to restore this dimension to our political discourse among younger scholars as Martin Matustik. In 1993 Guilford Press published his *Postnational Identity: Critical Theory and Existential Philosophy in Habermas, Kierkegaard, and Havel*. It was a large volume, large in both scope and vision. I talked to Matustik about his book when I met him in Prague in the spring of 1995 and more at length on a wind-swept day in the winter of 1996 at Purdue University where he teaches in the philosophy department.

"Why the focus on Kierkegaard?" I asked. "He is not normally thought of as a political thinker, far less a political activist."

"That is true," Matustik answered. "Quite the opposite. He is usually regarded as an antisocial and uncritical thinker if not downright irrational."

"How do you see him?"

"Well, I reject those received views. I read in Kierkegaard's critique of reason and society a critique of the truncated instrumental rationality and atomistic individualism found in modern politics and economics. Kierkegaard was much preoccupied with the demise of the human individual and argued that the leveling of the individual by the herd mentality of the present age cannot be resisted directly through social organizations like political parties or labor unions or revolutionary action or any other form of human association. He certainly didn't have much use for the nation-state or organized religion as instruments of individual transformation. In his 1846 critique of the present age he wrote: 'Not until the single individual has established an ethical stance despite the whole world, not until then can there be any question of genuine uniting.' And in his later essay, *The Individual,* he struck the same note: 'The individual is the category through which this age, all history, the human race as a whole must pass.'"

"Could this be called radical individualism?" I asked.

"It could if we give full force to the word radical," Matustik said. "This is not the possessive individual of liberalism nor the free-floating individual of postmodern thought. Kierkegaard's point is that unless individuals are capable of radical self-choice in the first place, social choices will be ungrounded. Deliberative democracy presupposes Kierkegaard's individual in order to sustain itself against cultural homogenizations.

"Kierkegaard's individual is already socialized (this defies individualist atomism) and yet is not commensurable with it, which runs against communitarians or any kind of social holism. His philosophy supports human rights (and therefore has something in common with liberalism) and community (thereby joining hands with communitarians) but always stops short of any universalist or regionalist forms of leveling. Liberalism risks making the individual too abstract; communitarians risks making her too thick. I believe that responsible citizenship begins with this individual dissent to totality. Human rights and deliberative democracy flourish only on the basis of well formed individual identities. This gives radical individualism a transgressive power that provides a check and balance on those totalitarian drives that always threaten human freedom. We can summarize Kierkegaard's position in this way: We are born situated in a social and linguistic world. The weight of this tradition comes to submerge the individual whence the necessity arises to open up some spaces of freedom so that individuals might flourish and, flourishing, become agents of effective social change. This is a leitmotif that runs from Kierkegaard to Václav Havel and his existential revolution."

I asked Matustik how he was introduced to this tradition. He said he came to it naturally growing up in Czechoslovakia as a member of a dissident community. There Kierkegaard's voice was reflected through the writings of thinkers like Franz Kafka, Milan Kundera, Havel and the great Czech philosopher, Jan Patočka, founder of Charta 77 and a martyr to the dissident cause.

"They did not read Kierkegaard as Germans and Americans usually do as a super-individualist. For them, questions of personal identity and authenticity are inherently political, not in any partisan sense but as a precondition of all practical politics, a non-political politics."

This was the philosophy that inspired the Velvet Revolution of 1989 which so caught the imagination of the West. In America we thought that here was democracy as it should be, breaking down the barricades of oppression and giving birth to freedom. It was a democracy, we thought, not unlike our own in the springtide of its conception. But in fact it was a quite different conception of democracy drawing upon philosophical sources quite different from those that inspired American democracy. When we begin to probe into those sources we discover a quite unfamiliar language and outlook on the world. Václav Havel told the American Congress in his famous speech there in 1991 that consciousness precedes being. Who knew what that meant?

Patočka speaks of "a life in truth"; "the care of the soul"; "the voice of conscience"; "the ethics of transcendence." American politicians simply don't speak that kind of language, and if they did we wouldn't understand it. The Velvet Revolution rode on a breaking wave of existential thought going all the way back to Plato, whose disciple Patočka was and to whose thought he returned all of his life. From Socrates he learned that self-knowledge is the beginning of social wisdom, the foundation stone of that strong humanism that makes democracy possible because it makes choices and responsibility for those choices possible. So while the Velvet Revolution may have looked like a latter-day American Revolution, it was in fact quite different. Democracy here meant something like the search for truth in a free community, the opportunity to live life in a humanly authentic way.

We digressed to talk about Matustik's youth in Czechoslovakia. He told me he was born in Bratislava but moved early to Prague where he went to high school and entered university. There he witnessed the Soviet invasion in 1968.

"Did you know Patočka?"

"Not well. But I was, so to speak, in his circle. I was part of the dissident community and I attended his flying university, seminars he gave in secret because he was barred from any official teaching post."

"When did you come to America?"

"In 1978. I was nineteen years old."

"Why did you leave Czechoslovakia?"

"One of Patočka's seminars I attended was raided. I was detained and interrogated by the secret police."

"What did they want to know?"

"What I knew about the dissident movement."

"What did you tell them?"

"What they already knew."

"Were you carrying big secrets?"

"I could have told them things that would have made me an informer."

"But they let you go?"

"Yes, but I was detained again at Patočka's funeral and again interrogated. By this time I knew that word would get back to the university and I would be expelled and sent to the military as a difficult case."

"How do you remember those years?"

"They were intense."

"How did you escape?"

"Some friends got me papers to go to India on what was called a work development program. When I got to Vienna I split and went to a refugee camp."

"And they sent you to America?"

"Well, there were some choices. I didn't want to go to Australia. Canada was too cold, although that probably would have been a more humane choice. So I was eventually placed with a family in California where I continued my studies, first in psychology, then in philosophy. I went to Fordham for graduate studies because there were some people there I wanted to work with and I was also able to study at the New School."

"I assume *Postnational Identity* came out of your work there?"

"In part. As a student at Fordham I went to the World Congress of Philosophers which met in 1988 in Brighton, England. There I met German philosopher Jürgen Habermas. He invited me to Frankfurt to work with him and as a result of a student Fulbright scholarship, I was able to go. That was in 1989—the year the Berlin Wall came down and the Velvet Revolution took place in Prague. I received a second Fulbright to teach at Charles University in Prague for the 1994-95 calendar year. Thus I returned to teach at the university where I had been a student eighteen years earlier."

At this point I wanted some clarity about key terms Matustik uses: "individual," "existential," "critical," and the like.

"Let's begin with 'critical,'" Matustik responded. "Traditionally theory has been detached from practice and action from concrete rooting. Kierkegaard, and the early Marx at about the same time, yoked the two and made the case that the purpose of thought is liberation. This was continued in the Frankfurt school which was concerned with the problem of totalitarianism as it manifested itself in Nazism and Communism.

"I define the existential as a form of praxis rooted in the attitude of a critical examination of those motives and presuppositions that influence the formations of identity, the parameters of communication, and theoretical ideals. My argument is that existential critique and social critique complement each other and overcome their respective limitations.

"A Kierkegaardian critic is explicitly focused on the attitudinal orientation that permeates a given sociopolitical critique, yet is only implicitly interested in shaping economic and political institutions. Honesty about motives does not deliver the critic into sufficient sobriety about what motivates any emancipatory theory and action. Thus the critic of the present age must learn to resist all abstraction from political and economic life, yet also embody radical honesty about critical theory and action. The 'existential' stands for a moment in emancipatory praxis that keeps the sociopolitical and economic reality (the 'what') of the theorist or activist pinned down to the reality motivated by the ways (the 'how') one engages material life."

"In your book you propose an alliance between critical social theory and existentialism. What is involved here?"

"Critical thought complements and carries on by other means the project of existentialism. The modern individual is a crisis individual—one no longer easily definable by the motives offered through the given traditions and cultures. She becomes a dissenting existential individual when she does not try to construct a new ideology in order to flee the anomie and fragmentation of modern life but views the identity crisis of the present age as an occasion for learning to live with an attitude of sobriety about the question of motive. The critical social theorist unmasks how systems of economy and political power, which govern the material reproduction of life, coopt the symbolic reproduction of life; the existential critic strives with honesty to resist any totalitarian closure of identity formation, communication, and community ideals. The critical theorist and the existential critic thus represent two forms of distinguishable though interrelated concretion."

I asked Matustik if he found fertile ground in America for his existential message. He said what he found in America was a predominantly liberal society that is balanced by communitarian elements.

"It is not enough," Matustik went on, "to be individualized as in liberalism, or socialized as in communitarianism. The point of the existential critique is that we must take up a critical stance toward both and ask the prior question: Which traditions will I permit myself to be socialized into and which will I jettison? What we can do as individuals is to take a certain distance from those forces that have formed us and that distance enables us to evaluate them. Kierkegaard is neither a communitarian nor a liberal. He is an individual of a nonliberal kind which is why I find him interesting. He makes it possible to have a critique of liberalism from the point of view of individualism. He invites us to ponder the question: What kind of sociality would we have if we took individualism as seriously as he did?"

I wanted to know if the kind of existential democracy Matustik was advocating was a necessary precondition for liberal democracy or, for that matter, communitarian democracy.

Matustik said that existential democracy was not intended to be merely a corrective for liberal democracy but a transformation of it. "We can see very well," he said, "that liberal liberty and existential freedom are not the same. We can have liberty or liberties, and not be free. We can be free but powerless. Freedom is more than freedom from constraints; it is an appropriation of one's self, a self that must become responsible for tradition, context, and socialization."

"What kind of sociality is implied in existential democracy?"

Matustik said the question points us to what the existential critique is centrally concerned with: problems of cultural identity, race, patriarchy, gender, and economic rights. These problems are very difficult to solve under liberal democratic majoritarianism. In fact they are often aggravated. We haven't made much headway in solving them.

"I argue for the need to attend to the distortions of communication in democratic procedures, what Sartre has called bad faith and what Kierkegaard calls motivated self-deception. It is these attitudes, these systematic forms of distortion, that I find responsible for the pervasiveness of racism, for example. Certain exclusions are built into liberal procedures due to unexamined preconceptions. In other words, our liberalism masks some fundamental choice we have already made to see the world in a racist way. A decision may appear to be free because we follow liberal principles and procedures but apply them in a systematically distorted way. I am trying to get to the bottom of these distortions."

"Where is the bottom?"

"Distortion stems from lack of a critical stance toward those very principles and procedures we take for granted."

"Perhaps," I said, "the problem is not in the principles and procedures but in human nature itself, such that any critical stance will always be foiled by a human propensity to mask our deepest intentions and motives. Could we say Kierkegaard was trying to reform human nature as a step toward reforming society?"

"But the question of human nature begs the question. Kierkegaard cuts beneath traditional conceptions of human nature as something already formed and given once and for all. There is no given essence. Human nature itself is shaped through our choices. We violate a certain personal integrity when we refuse to make these identity-forming choices. In this sense we can say that Kierkegaard argues not for an essentialist but a performative mode of identity."

"What, in summary, are those elements of Kierkegaard's thought that constituted a performative mode of identity and are relevant to deliberative democracy?"

"There is first of all his conception of the individual, a crisis individual who is capable of radical self-choice. Secondly, there is his theory of communication. Kierkegaard has an original theory of communication that no one else has, a unique sense of how language works to transform personality. Such communication for Kierkegaard is always indirect, involving large measures of irony, drama, humor, and storytelling. There is, thirdly, the transgressive power of self-choice and indirect communication, which discloses our inwardness and enables us to reconsider anew values which have great social importance such as honesty, responsibility, justice, action, and even love."

I asked Matustik to elaborate on Kierkegaard's theory of communication.

"Kierkegaard was concerned with the eclipse of the pronominal. 'I,' the tendency to cast all communication in abstract, objective terms; in newspapers, in churches, in bureaucracies, in the academy. Students, for example, are taught to eliminate the 'I' from their writing. Kierkegaard read in this fear of the self a dismaying effort to become something impersonal, anonymous, to make ourselves thing-like. One abdicates one's performative participation in communication for the third person perspective of the observer. This, Kierkegaard thought, was a wrong-headed, even comic, effort to maintain identity by not being discovered by anyone, least of all by oneself. Thus anonymous existence became a modern tyranny that establishes itself in mass communications and replaces traditional forms of oppression. Kierkegaard examined the question of why people refused to accept authorship for their own identity and for their own lives. He saw this as the root of the systematic distortions I spoke about earlier. For him the core of miscommunication lies in the impersonality that has been entrenched in modern life-forms by the anonymous public, the media, academia, and the churches."

"So Kierkegaard took it as his mission to reintroduce the 'I' into our discourses?"

"He did indeed. For him all concrete freedom is personal and all ethical behavior is rooted in communication from an I to an I. He said that the first prerequisite for the communication of truth is personality. The fear of self, on the other hand, was a most insidious form of tyranny that distorts human relations. He remarked ironically on the revolutionary period of 1848: What good is victorious nonpersonality? What good is storming the bourgeois castle in Paris if one does not have a clue as to how or who one is and wants to be? So Kierkegaard opted not for revolution but for a radical egalitarianism of communication. He found in nondoctrinaire Christianity crucial metaphors for open forms of communication and the radical equality of persons. For this reason he often wrote under pseudonyms to raise once again in the public's mind a voice, an 'I,' to reaccustom the public ear to hearing first-person discourse."

"Would it be true to say that Kierkegaard's responsibly communicating self is the key to your idea of existential democracy?"

"It would."

"In other words, Kierkegaard's radical individualism bespeaks a radical community ideal?"

"It does. I read Kierkegaard as the most unread modern sociopolitical thinker. He is the thinker par excellence who translates the dramatic authoring of one's existence into a moral imperative; one ought to act in such a way as to always meet as an individual the other as an individual. Kierkegaard dissents against all herd and fundamentalist religiosity and its technocratic cousin in politics and economics; he also subverts the nation-state by permanently opposing it."

"Whence the 'postnational' in the title of your book?"

"That is the source of it. I was thinking too of Havel who said that we are at the beginning of the global era, the era of the open society, the era in which ideologies give way to ideas."

"Let's pause for a moment on the religious dimension of Kierkegaard's thought. Religion seems ultimate for him, almost Bible-thumping in its stridency."

"We need not make any substantive commitments about Kierkegaard's Christianity. We need not interpret him through either theistic or atheistic glasses."

"How then are we to interpret Kierkegaard's frequent appeals to the religious?"

"The religious signifies that the individual is distinct from official production and from professional politics, and yet that one must positively resist any deification of the author and of social ethics. The religious signifies that the individual cannot appeal to canonical certitudes on metaphysical grounds, and yet that one must positively resist any self-assured, nonethical, fundamentalist confounding of religion with politics. Kierkegaard's religious view is political in the nonpolitical sense described by Havel. It claims the individual indirectly via the existential revolution of self-transformation, but it is directly embodied in nonpolitical resistance to any absolutization of the public sphere."

"Is it a straight step from Kierkegaard to Václav Havel?"

"Yes. I view Havel's literary and political posture as highly relevant for carrying through this new task of articulating a thoroughly sincere socio-politically and materially relevant critical theory. Havel envisions that deliberative democracy brings the experiences of dissent against totality into professional politics. His writings and activism, both before and after 1989, provide a fitting example for an examination of the proposed encounter between critical theory and existential philosophy. This examination is made in distinctly nondogmatic terms and is in contrast to both the conservative political existentialists of Nazi Germany and some left existentialists. Havel's opposition to totalitarian politics is in harmony with similar critiques by thinkers like Marcuse, Adorno, and Habermas.

"Havel's defense of human and civil rights in the context of resurgent hatred in Central-Eastern Europe is just as groundbreaking as was Kierkegaard's exposure of those who justified nationalism on the basis of the 'Christian' moral majority. Havel's personal style in politics embraces a vision of a democratic, multicultural community. We need not push him into a quietist, piously individualistic corner, where Kierkegaard's inwardness is so often placed. I find it more philosophically interesting and socially significant to examine the implications of Havel's Kierkegaardian politics for democratic multiculturalism after 1989."

"So communication is the common tie?"

"Yes. Havel critiques the leveling of words and strives to recover existential communication. For example, he gave up using the word socialism. It obfuscates more than it clarifies. But it is not just the 's' word. Our social relations are cluttered with unexamined language. Havel exposes the hollowness of that language: capitalism, liberalism, market, peace, race, religion, and so on. He argues that one should communicate what one means, not use slogans. By refusing to pledge allegiance to labels, Havel is annoying for anyone who communicates by using phrases good only for parades. Through unmasking the absurdity of slogans, existential drama occasions in the individual the recovery of a capacity for addressing one another as individuals. Therein lies Havel's egalitarian and anti-elitist project of existential revolution. Empty speech gives birth to a leveling culture; this in turn admits the possibility of a leveling politics of identity and difference. The recovery of genuine communication is the great bulwark against these leveling tendencies of our present age. Thus the circle comes full back to Kierkegaard."

"Well," I said, "this is all very rich. I am still having some difficulty seeing just how what you say bears on professional and institutional politics. How can these ideas of authoring, communication, and the like infiltrate the daily business of politics?"

"We have to bear in mind that none of this can be legislated or even imparted by the normal means of education. But these ideas should not be relegated to the private domain either. They must have a political impact. They came to life for me through my experience in a dissident community. I think the join is there, in the community of our civic forums, what Havel called the counter-institutions of democracy."

"Does that mean everyone ought to be a dissident?"

"In the sense that we are critical participants in our democracies, yes."

"What do you think is the greatest problem democracies face today?"

"How to coexist in a world that is becoming much more complex—in other words, global survival, which I define as local solutions to global problems. We can no longer rely on a presumed objective value structure to guide us in this. We have to draw on new sources."

"Human sources?"

"More specifically human creativity. Jan Patočka said that the human imagination is 'the trace of transcendence,' the means by which we move beyond limits and constraints. In early mythology, meaning and value were created through story telling; society was energized and held together by a shaping mythos. Today we have to decide what kind of stories we want to tell ourselves, what kind of imagination we need to have, how to reconfigure modern society in light of a compelling narrative now that the traditional narratives have lost much of their appeal."

"Meanwhile we have no answers?"

"Not many. But I am more concerned with laying the groundwork for possible answers than providing a blueprint. I look upon my work more as a project than an accomplishment."

"But let me assure you, as we conclude, that there is both help and hope in your project, in the way you have married critical theory and existentialism."

"Thank you. Let's hope there won't be a divorce."

As I drove home across the snowy plains of Indiana, I reflected on what Matustik had told me. I tried to imagine how his ideas might play out in a political campaign. But, of course, I could not. I wondered at what points they might impinge on our somewhat mealy culture, and not much came to mind. But when I pondered the pedagogical potential of Matustik's perspective, I was more heartened. To teach the young to be self-authoring individuals in a free society is not only an immensely attractive ideal but to some extent a doable one as well.

Jumping into History

When I first met Merab Mamardashvili, he was fretting about his medication. It was May 1990, and he was a visiting scholar at the Kettering Foundation in Dayton, Ohio, where I was a staff associate. I had gone to pick him up for lunch. "I've just run out of heart pills," he said, "and I'm worried that I won't be able to find the right prescription." I told him I imagined that wouldn't be too hard to do. With the help of some colleagues more knowledgeable about such matters than I, we soon had the problem solved. Merab was greatly relieved. I said he looked hale and hearty, as indeed he did, with clear blue eyes and a fair complexion that belied his age. "I have always enjoyed good health," he remarked. "But last year I had a heart attack that scared me a bit. The doctors told me it was a mild attack. But my definition of a mild attack is one you survive. So I don't credit the word 'mild' with much diagnostic power."

He wanted to go for a little walk before lunch. As we strolled about the grounds he began to talk about his native Georgia. "I was born a Georgian," he said. "And I love Georgia. It is a beautiful land. You must come visit sometime." He went on to complain that Americans very often assume that anyone living in the Soviet Union is a Russian. "I am not a Russian" he said with some emphasis. "In fact, I don't much like Russians." That would become clear as we got into our interview. He thought Americans in general were quite ignorant about this.

Then he asked me about philosophy in America. "It is quite doctrinaire in the Soviet Union," he said. I told him it was quite doctrinaire in this country as well, although in a different sense. Philosophy in America is the province of the academics. No one would ever think an ordinary person could be a philosopher. Few American philosophers would be caught dead mixing it up in the marketplace the way Socrates did. There is, of course, a certain plurality, but orthodoxies tend to prevail. The professors keep a tight rein on the flow of ideas. In that sense, I explained, philosophy in America is doctrinaire, too.

Merab Mamardashvili mused quite a long time on the point I had made. After lunch, in what turned out to be a prolonged interview, measured in days, I began by asking him about his career in philosophy. I was interested in what he thought philosophy was, his philosophy of philosophy, so to speak.

Merab Mamardashvili believes that all philosophy begins in the cave. Plato, he says, created the most powerful image in all of philosophical literature when he described the human condition as an underground chamber in which from birth men have been imprisoned, chained by their legs and necks in such a way that they cannot turn to see the light at the entrance of the cave but are forced always to watch the play of shadows on the wall before them. Philosophy begins when the prisoners desire to be released from their chains, to see the light, to be liberated.

Plato's parable is a parable of Mamardashvili's life.

"I came to philosophy," he recalls, "by way of life, by a sense of aloneness. I felt as a child as though I had come from another planet and found everything dark and strange." At some point quite early in life, he says, "I think we all have a sense of being wrenched out of the normal, of seeing ordinary things otherwise. Things that go by themselves for other people do not go by themselves for you. Life is full of signs to be interpreted. Most we let pass. Some, however, we think about. The shadows on the wall suggest another reality. Then we become philosophers. Then the signs begin to shed light on events."

As a philosopher Mamardashvili is primarily interested in the phenomenon of consciousness—how the active power of intelligence can shape reality, perceive reality, and be mistaken about reality. Plato helped him here, and Kant even more so. But it was Marx who first led him to the study of consciousness. "It is a great irony," Mamardashvili explains, "that Marx, who was a true philosopher of the Enlightenment, should have become the patron saint of one of the darkest societies in human history. This was partly Marx's own fault. He was wrong about many things; and even where he was right he was often so ambiguous and elliptical that he misled his readers. For example, he tended to glorify the power of the state as an instrument of human freedom, misunderstood the role of private property, favored violence, and dismissed the hard-earned rights of the liberal middle classes as mere ideological reflections of class interest."

When we add to the difficulties inherent in Marx's own thought the tortuous interpretations overlaid on it by Lenin and later Bolshevists, then the real Marx becomes exceedingly difficult to discover. "I am not a Marxist," Mamardashvili says, "because Marx was wrong or obscure about too many things. Nevertheless, it seems to me he was quite right about one thing, and I owe him an initial debt for my philosophical liberation—and that was what he said about consciousness, and especially false consciousness."

The first thing Marx did for Mamardashvili was disabuse him of the temptation to idealism, the notion that consciousness antecedes and remains autonomous of the material conditions that give rise to it. This is a time-honored tradition in philosophy, and most philosophers at one time or another have subscribed to it. There is a strand of Plato that reinforces this view; virtually the whole religious tradition of the West bought into it; and beginning with Descartes, a powerful European tradition of idealism commenced. Descartes' "I think, therefore I am" asserted the priority of ideas; the "I am I" of German philosophy assumed a pure consciousness; and Hegel's powerful logic gave the mind a status independent of concrete historical circumstances. Mamardashvili came to reject all of this. He came to understand that there is no such thing as a pure consciousness, a transcendental ego, or an autonomous soul. Marx showed that such idealistic constructs are mystifications, ideological ruses that cast a smoke screen over power structures, or as Marx called them, ideologies that bespeak a false consciousness.

Marx, Mamardashvili claims, brought philosophy back to earth and sought the ideal in the real. He was not the first to explore the subject of ideology but he explored it more thoroughly than anyone else and was the first to make the concept central to his analysis of consciousness. Marx showed that ideas are not merely products of the mind; they are even more the products of material activity and the language of real life. In a famous passage Marx wrote: "The mode of production in material life determines the general character of the social, political and spiritual processes of life. It is not consciousness of men that determines their existence but, on the contrary, their social existence determines their consciousness."

It was this meaty realism that attracted Mamardashvili, although he is quick to point out that Marx did not intend to substitute a simpleminded materialism for traditional idealism. What characterized Marx's realism—and this is Mamardashvili's second debt to Marx—was its dialectical nature. Material life does not determine consciousness univocally; it is a two-way street with consciousness also determining material life. To put it in other words, Marx was not a materialistic determinist, although he has sometimes been so interpreted. Consciousness cannot be totally determined by reality; otherwise it would make no sense to argue that history was a process toward human emancipation. And that is what Marx had primarily in mind. So the picture Mamardashvili holds of Marx seems to be something like this: Consciousness is determined by material reality but not totally determined; in a dialectical reaction it also determines that reality. Thus it retains a degree of autonomy and sovereignty over the reality it creates.

But Marx also argued—and this is a third, and perhaps the greatest, debt Mamardashvili owes him—that consciousness is very often trapped in its own creations, it becomes alienated in its own products. When consciousness is totally determined by its own creations, it becomes false consciousness, a form of human enslavement. This provided Mamardashvili with the perspective needed to get a philosophical handle on the reality of the Stalinist state. For the Stalinist state defined itself as the reality that determined the consciousness of its people. That is, by any other definition, slavery. Mamardashvili remembers an illustrative anecdote from the fifth grade. One day the class was studying the history of Egypt. In the text a slave complains about his life. He sees no good in it and wants to commit suicide in order to go to paradise. Says Mamardashvili: "I have always remembered the slave's complaint, and eventually I came to see reality as he saw it, and that raised questions of justice and rights in my mind. In due course, I judged that the slave was wrong in wanting to attain an ideal life through suicide. The ideal always has to be an aspect of the real if it is to be effective. The above is in the below. We can't take shortcuts through history. We can't jump out of history. Gradually it occurred to me that this is what Russia did: she jumped out of history and committed metaphysical suicide by trying to bypass the real for the ideal."

At this juncture, Marx's analysis of false consciousness and Plato's metaphor of the cave joined hands to give Mamardashvili the philosophical ammunition he needed to analyze the nature of social reality in the Soviet Union.

The problem presented itself to him in the form of a question: Could you have a social situation that so coopted consciousness that no philosophical question could ever arise, that no ideas could ever come into our heads which were not controlled by the social situation, which is to say by the state? It was clear to him that in the Soviet Union the state had complete control of the structures of consciousness. Moreover, as he thought about it, he became convinced that this had long been the case, that a long history of Russia had prepared the advent of Marxist-Leninism and Stalinism. It was not an accident that the Soviet Union had become in the twentieth century the kind of state it was.

Mamardashvili traces this history back at least to Ivan the Terrible in the sixteenth century. He finds there the substitution of what he calls anthropomorphic thought for historical thought, a characteristic common to all totalitarian states. According to Mamardashvili, Ivan destroyed Russian society. He left everything in ruins.

This is the way he tells the story: "You may recall that in his time the aristocracy was developing the idea that property was to be held in perpetuity. This posed a threat to the authority and power of Ivan. So he invented a police force whose role was to spy on the enemies of the czar. Not surprisingly, it turned out that there were quite a few such enemies and they were all property holders. In this way, Ivan substituted the reality of the czar as the central social and political reality. In time, that was to be the only social and political reality. Nothing was important if it didn't coincide with the will of the czar. All of society became the elongated shadow of the czar. But shadows aren't real. That is how unreality came to be the condition of social life in the Soviet Union."

That is why, too, the Enlightenment bypassed Russia. And it is clearly one of the reasons why the October 1917 Revolution succeeded. Russia was fertile soil for the Leninist interpretation of Marx and the apotheosis of the state. The revolution culminated a long a historical tradition, recreating the conditions that gave rise to it. It was unreality built on unreality. As a consequence, Soviet citizens are still shadowboxing, getting forty-eight kinds of permission to do simple things, not knowing ever who holds their destiny, finding every attempt at a rational action thwarted by the shadows. It was Kafka who described totalitarianism as a form of government in which the state envelops us everywhere but we can find it nowhere.

Mamardashvili illustrates the point with another story: "During Lenin's funeral there were banners everywhere proclaiming such things as 'Communism is the cradle of humanity'; 'We will lead humanity into paradise'; 'Let the little children come to us.' Lenin was buried in a position and in clothes reminiscent of Christ in the tomb. This deliberate parodying of religious symbolism in itself was indicative of ahistorical thinking; which is to say, a form of thought that postulates ideals in such a way that they can never effectively interact with the real." Mamardashvili goes on to draw the analogy with Marxist thinking. Marx, he says, "mystified the social process by appealing to the utopian thinking of the classless society, which is an updated version of the Golden Age myth. But where does the Golden Age exist? Nowhere. Utopia. To be meaningful, symbolic thinking has to illuminate reality. The myth of the Golden Age doesn't say that such an age once existed and we must recover it. It is not something material. It cannot be destroyed by a material event nor can it be realized by a material event. He thought that by getting rid of private property a classless society would come about. He converted a metaphysical entity into a material possibility. That is the mistake the alchemists made. They tried to turn material means into spiritual ends."

How do we know we are in history? The search for an answer to that question brings Mamardashvili's theory of consciousness to bear on political theory. Historical existence requires conscious human participation in the events of history. History begins with the ability to describe history reflectively, to give meaning to events. As he often does, Mamardashvili illustrates the point with an example. He asks us to imagine life as a journey through a forest. We can follow the rules to get from point A to point B. Or we can try to understand the nature of the forest and our relationship to it. Thus the philosophical question becomes: Why do some people see the forest and others only the trees? Mamardashvili thinks the best answer to this question was given by Plato: a spark in the soul ignites and produces the idea. In other words, we intuit it. He calls upon Kant to elaborate and emphasize the productive power of the mind. Where do we get the idea of eternal life? he asks. Or to take another example, no part of a machine nor all of its parts together can give us an idea of the machine. That has to come from the mind. There is no chain of empirical causes, there is nothing in our experience that can fully account for our ideas. In the three days of conversation I had with Mamardashvili he raised his voice only once, and it was to make this point.

It occurred to me that, in embracing Kant, Mamardashvili was abandoning the realism he had taken from Marx. We talked about this for some time, and while the point never became clear to me, Mamardashvili's position seemed to be something like this: Marx had attempted to maintain a healthy, which is to say a dialectical, relationship between the ideal and the real factors in experience. Social reality influences consciousness, and consciousness in turn reacts upon that reality. But what happened to Marx in the interpretation wars, and what particularly happened to him under the Bolshevists, was that the ideal element became submerged. And while one could go back to Marx to recover it, it would be a long and tortuous journey through the thickets of interpretation.

Moreover, in Stalinist Russia one could be, indeed would be, accused of subjectivist deviation. Mamardashvili took what he considered a safer as well as a clearer path and drew on Kant.

Kant helped him in two ways. In the first place, he vouchsafed unequivocally the creative, productive power of consciousness. Kant had first taken up cudgels against English empiricists like John Locke and David Hume, who argued that all knowledge is derived from the senses. The mind is, as Locke put it, a tabula rasa. But the mind, said Kant, is not a tabula rasa, a blank slate which passively records sensations. In the preface to his most important work, *The Critique of Pure Reason*, Kant wrote: "Experience is by no means the only field to which our understanding can be confined. Experience tells us what is, but not that it must be necessarily what it is and not otherwise. It, therefore, never gives us any really general truths, and our reason, which is particularly anxious for that class of knowledge, is roused by it rather than satisfied. General truths must be independent of experience—clear and certain in themselves." Later he put it more simply: "Perceptions without conceptions are blind."

What this meant to Mamardashvili was that ideas come from the inherent structure of consciousness; our minds are active organs that have designs on the world; they project intentions upon experience and transmute the deliverances of sensory experience into ideas. What is meant, even more concretely, was that consciousness always possesses the power to transcend its immediate circumstances. In the darkest days of Stalin's Russia, Mamardashvili sat in the library at Moscow State University reading Kant. Even then, he understood that consciousness gave him a measure of freedom not accorded by the state and a power of formulating his own designs on the world. He began to realize at that time what he was to state much more clearly later, in a lecture to the Institute of Philosophy of the Soviet Academy of Sciences: "The philosopher cannot but feel himself as occupying some kind of crossroads of social conditions and tendencies. They gather in his field of vision. And as a philosopher he must pull out from the wealth of mysterious impressions that fall upon him the truth by means of the laws of thought and language, the truth about his own state, which provides evidence of something. That is, the philosopher's primary responsibility is to his own individual consciousness; and focusing on this consciousness, he is obliged to state the truth of his condition." In plainer language, Mamardashvili was calling for intellectual freedom vis-à-vis a sclerotic Marxist dialectic.

I observed that Mamardashvili's philosophy of freedom and consciousness was similar to that of the French existentialist Jean-Paul Sartre. He said that didn't surprise him. Sartre began as a phenomenologist, a school that had deep roots in Kant's philosophy. For Sartre as for Kant—and of course as for Mamardashvili—because we have consciousness we can question being, we can deny being, and we can transcend being. Because of it we are always separated from the world of objective reality by a margin of freedom that keeps the future open. As Mamardashvili had put it in the same speech to the Soviet Academy: "The path before me is some kind of path arising out of my soul, and which I have no choice but to follow. And no one has the right to prevent me from following this path." As Sartre has Zeus say in his play, *The Flies:* "Once freedom lights its beacon in man's heart, the gods are powerless against him."

By reflecting upon history, consciousness, and freedom, Mamardashvili bit by bit formulated a theory of civil society. Here, too, Kant was of great help. Civil society is a term that took root with the rise of modern democratic theory to denote a sphere of associative activity on the part of citizens, not under the direct control of the state. By the time of the American Revolution this distinction was firmly in place. Thus Thomas Paine, in the *Rights of Man*, could speak of a society in which the nongovernmental sector functioned relatively independent of the state. He spoke of civil associations which "men promiscuously form" and which "invigorate the whole mass of civilized man." And Alexis de Tocqueville's *Democracy in America* is a veritable paean to civil society. Tocqueville wrote: "Americans of all ages, all conditions, and all dispositions constantly form associations" to perform vital public functions which would otherwise go undone or be taken over by government.

Marx's view of such voluntary associations was understandably dim. They were, he thought, pervaded by self-interest and corrupt economic relationships. In short, they were the result of capitalism and should be abolished. Marx's propensity to hypostatize economic activity, and further to see economic activity as the basis of all social interaction, set up a logic according to which the distinction between the state and civil society grew increasingly obscure. Carrying on that logic, Bolshevism suppressed civil society altogether. Independent associations of all sorts were outlawed. Of course, "dialectical" explanations were offered for such measures, but Mamardashvili early on saw through such specious reasoning; and his defense of civil society was in the first instance a criticism of a corrupt Marxism and the Soviet state.

Mamardashvili is on no point more eloquent. Hear him at some length:

"All my life I have lived in a compressed society. The distinction between the state and society was eliminated. Our public life was like a black hole in the universe, so dense that it collapsed in on itself. I will express my notion in an image. Think of a chess game. You cannot understand a chess game by examining the pawns; you cannot even understand a chess game by watching the moves; you can only understand a chess game by understanding the storm of psychic forces between the moves.

"Civic life is like that. It takes place in the pauses, in the intervals, in the spaces of public life. The poet Rilke spoke of *Leben in Figuren*—life as a play of symbols. I use spatial images to make the point that we need room to think, to find ourselves, to determine our common purposes. So the concept of civil society calls for some important distinctions: between public and private, between state and society, between the ideal and the real, between the inner and the outer worlds. Civil society is based on a belief that by trusting people to pursue their own interests a symmetry will develop between the private and the public worlds, that our free actions will converge for the common good.

"During World War II, it used to be said that Germans were well organized. But exactly the opposite was true. You cannot organize society by imposing everything from the outside, squashing and denigrating everything that arises spontaneously. That, of course, is what happened in the October Revolution. The state stepped in and tried to mediate everything. And that is the death of civil society. it condemns citizens to a death in life, to a minimal life that is guaranteed by the state but cannot grow."

Mamardashvili stresses the point with one of his frequent French quotations: *personne ne veut se vendre son âme*—no one wants to sell his soul. Now, Mamardashvili says, "We have to return to the foundations and think historically about how we got out of history. We have to lift up our heads and liberate independent social forces." And he calls Marx to the dock for a full share of blame:

"Marx was absolutely blind to the existence and the importance of privacy as a condition of politics. Private property and classes as independent social agents are necessary conditions for the civil society. When nobody is independent, no politics is possible. A state without citizens is a monstrosity. By denying private property Marx created an even worse form of it—what all totalitarian states know as privilege. That's devastating. It leads to the worst kind of political corruption; which is to say the arbitrary exercise of power."

Mamardashvili's critique is supported by Kant's theory of consciousness. But on the question of civil society he appeals more directly to Kant's little 1784 essay entitled "What Is Enlightenment?" The opening lines of this powerful (and often neglected) essay provided Mamardashvili with his gravamen against the Soviet state. Kant wrote:

"Enlightenment is man's release from his self-incurred tutelage. Tutelage is man's inability to make use of his understanding without direction from another. This tutelage is self-incurred when its cause lies not in lack of reason but in lack of resolution and courage to use it without direction from another. *Sapere aude*—Have the courage to think—that is the motto of enlightenment."

Nor could Mamardashvili fail to make a direct application of what Kant said about the self-appointed custodians of truth. The step to enlightenment "is held to be very dangerous by those guardians who have so kindly assumed superintendence over the people. After the guardians first have made their domestic cattle dumb and have made sure that these placid creatures will not dare to take a single step without the harness of the cart to which they are confined, the guardians then show them the danger which threatens if they go alone."

Kant, in effect, had issued a kind of magna carta for independent thought and political freedom. These are some of the characteristics of the enlightened mind as he outlined them in that essay: it is public ("not individualistic or idiosyncratic"), free ("the public use of one's reason must always be free"), universal ("a member of the whole community or of a society of world citizens"), self-governing ("what a people may not decree for itself can be decreed even less for them by a monarch"), tolerant ("each must be left free to make use of his reason in matters of conscience"). In his conclusion, Kant wrote: "Only one who is enlightened is not afraid of the shadows." The words left a lifelong impression on Mamardashvili.

Of the different characteristics Kant listed, Mamardashvili paid particular attention to the point about universalism. In his address to the Soviet Academy, mentioned above, Mamardashvili had said: "As far as I recall, my first steps into philosophy were conditioned not by some kind of empirical factors of a social character, and not by the problems of the society into which I was born; rather they were conditioned by my unconscious desire to unite with something that seemed to me to be a part of myself, but something which has somehow become lost, forgotten. As I judge this today, I sought to connect with some common human foundation of culture. In other words, I vaguely sought to stick to means of comprehension which Kant described as those of a citizen of the world.'"

Mamardashvili thinks that to be a citizen of the world is the highest political status we can aspire to, and the concept is central to his thought. He finds further support for it in Kant's later (1790) treatise, *Critique of Judgment*. Buried deep in that abstruse work are some brilliant pages in which Kant analyzes the mode of thought that enables us to think from the point of view of others or, as he puts it in one of his maxims, "to put ourselves in thought in the place of everyone else." Kant variously referred to this capacity as a common sense (*sensus communis*), representative thinking, taste, enlightenment, judgment, public thinking, enlarged thought. His idea of enlightenment is the same here as in the essay—that is, deliverance from superstition, ignorance, and abject independence.

What Kant is getting at is perhaps best conveyed by his treatment of common sense where he talks about "a sense common to all; i.e., a faculty of judgment which, in its reflection, takes account of the mode of representation of all other men in thought, in order, as it were, to compare its judgment with the collective reason of humanity and thus to escape the illusion arising from the private conditions that could so easily be taken for objective, which would injuriously affect the judgment." And on enlarged thought: "The man of *enlarged thought* disregards the subjective private condition of his own judgment, by which so many others are confined, and reflects upon it from a *universal standpoint*, which he can determine only by placing himself at the standpoint of others" (Kant's emphasis).

Reflecting on Kant's insights, Mamardashvili draws this conclusion about consciousness: "Consciousness is in the first instance consciousness of others. To be conscious of others is to be removed from the everyday world in which we live and begin to see another world that at first appears strange and unfamiliar." He uses a telling image to make his point. A squirrel, Mamardashvili says, is never so conscious of a tree as when it falls out of it. Only then does it see the tree as a whole. So, too, when we get beyond ourselves, our private experiences, the parochial world of our thoughts and relationships, we become conscious of the whole world, the world of the other. When we see the world that way, our objectives become clearer. We recognize better what we truly value—what we know and love and hate, what we need to do and what we should hope for.

Such thoughts kept Mamardashvili in hot water most of his life and, given the conditions of the Stalinist state, we can readily see why. If the type of consciousness Mamardashvili delineates can only be realized in individuals—that is, those who take the Kantian notion of enlightenment seriously—then the individual rather than the collective is at the center of things. Morever, if consciousness has to be realized by stepping back from the immediate, the given, from what we might call dictated reality, then there has to be space in which to do that. There have to be, in short, the spaces of a developed civil society which the state cannot penetrate, public spaces. These are not isolation booths or refuges from a tormenting world; they are places where we come together with others to compare perspectives, to make connections with another, to pool resources, to take action on what we have decided, together, is valuable and worth striving for.

In a totalitarian state, people are told what objects they should desire, what values they should embrace; there is no need to gather with others to decide what it really is they love and hate. So Mamardashvili lost a lot of jobs. And the authorities, from the point of view of their own interests, were quite right: he was truly a subversive man. The politics implied, indeed quite explicit, in his theory of consciousness undercut the assumptions of authoritarian regimes; they even undercut some of our own assumptions about democracy. Politics is more basic than advocating interests, more fundamental than voting. People themselves have to decide what is truly valuable to them as a public. Until they do so they are not truly conscious, and if not truly conscious then not truly political.

In stressing the cosmopolitan nature of enlightened thinking, Mamardashvili's thinking complements the work of such contemporary thinkers as Hannah Arendt and Ronald Beiner. A comparison with Hannah Arendt is particularly illuminating. She, too, set herself vigorously against much the same kind of totalitarianism as Mamardashvili did, and she, too, drew liberally upon Kant's philosophy to elaborate a theory of judgement, seeing it as the representative thinking of an enlarged mentality—an inherently social act because it depends on some degree of consensus for its validity and does not appeal to a timeless criterion of truth. Rather, judgment is forged in the process of dialogue, communication, and persuasion.

It struck Arendt with the force of revelation that Kant worked out his theory of judgment while discussing aesthetics and the problems of how we form our taste with respect to beauty. Arendt was struck by the analogy between how taste is formed and how social consensus is arrived at. In the one and in the other, there is a working through process, a thinking about particulars without reference to general rules which, Arendt said, "solves the problem of making oneself at home in an existence without fixed points of support." She sometimes spoke of judgment as "thinking without a bannister" to indicate that we are in life as on a staircase without conceptual guarantees. There is in such a remark some reflection of Arendt's own exilic wanderings; but it was also her way of making a philosophical statement to the effect that we do not deal best with experience when we approach it laden with theory. Much better to let the theory emerge from our deliberations about particulars.

Arendt first set forth her thinking about the political function of judgment in a 1952 article entitled "The Crisis of Culture." What at first appears to be a rambling lecture, on closer inspection, turns out to be a tightly reasoned argument establishing logical links between three distinct but interrelated concepts: those of art, politics, and the faculty of judgment. Arendt begins her essay with a critique of mass culture which, she thought, reduces true culture to mere entertainment and, in the process, strips citizens of the necessary public space in which political action can flourish. Mass culture privatizes. True culture, on the other hand, socializes. True culture, Arendt reminds us, is a Roman concept, *culture animi;* and it means the creation of and caring for spirit-enhancing objects. For this reason, she says, "any discussion of culture must take as its starting point the phenomenon of art." Why art? Precisely because art is a phenomenon; that is to say, an appearance. Art creates enduring objects of beauty in a public space which transcend any functional purpose they might otherwise have.

The cathedrals of the Middle Ages served religious needs. But their aesthetic qualities cannot be explained by those needs; they must be explained by the driving human impulse to fictionalize experience by creating suitable conditions of worldly existence. (In the same vein, Mamardashvili falls back upon art, particularly literature, to illuminate philosophical points. His favorite authors for this purpose are Marcel Proust, William Faulkner, Rilke, and the great Russian writers, particularly Chekhov.) Arendt's appropriation of Kant's analysis of taste brings out the analogy that our political sense develops much as our deliberation, communication, and eventually, some agreement. On a desert island, Kant said, "man would adorn neither his hut nor his person. In matters of taste we must renounce ourselves in favor of others." This is the way communities are formed. Arendt pushed the point further to say that this is the nature of all moral thinking. Both political and aesthetic judgments, then, are controlled by the objective reference to others, by the nature of the communities in which we have our social being, by the kind of world we wish to bring forth.

The specific nature of judgment is that it is the faculty of thinking about particulars—the sort of particulars that are encountered in our social and political lives. Kant distinguished between two kinds of judgment: one in which particulars are subsumed to a universal principle and another kind where no universal obtains but must, as it were, be generated from the particulars themselves. It is obviously this latter sort that Arendt and Mamardashvili stress. It is, in Kant's language, reflective rather than determinative judgment. Reflective judgment is what determines and reflects the four essential marks of the political process: choice, pluralism, communication, and consensus. What thinkers like Arendt and Mamardashvili are attempting to do, as I see it, is to rejoin public philosophy with the dialogic tradition. A healthy political philosophy is based on dialogue in much the same way as a healthy body is based on a good regimen. Because public philosophy is concerned with *res publicae*, with the public's business, we must learn to talk to one another in a common language about common interests. Until we learn to do this with a measure of success, we will not function adequately as citizens, and our public affairs will remain more or less in disarray.

This line of thought naturally prompts the question of how and how well Mamardashvili himself performs as a public philosopher. His own theory of consciousness and the Kantian legacy commit him to the spread of reason and the effort to illuminate social problems with the view to greater freedom and more civil liberties. Yet when he is pressed on the social role of the philosopher, or any thinker for that matter, Mamardashvili tends to hedge his bets. At the very least he wants certain distinctions borne clearly in mind. Philosophy works at two levels. It is the formal, often professional, activity of conceptual clarification. At this level it can be highly abstract, difficult, and remote. But there is a broad, shall we say, more generous conception of the philosophy according to which the philosopher is open to all streams of experience, to an existential richness of consciousness that assimilates art, literature, and politics, and is committed to a social agenda.

Mamardashvili finds the distinction in Plato, for whom philosophy was on the one hand a highly speculative venture and on the other a kind of salvation. Mamardashvili cherishes the first sense of philosophy and has done important work at that level. But he also appreciates the second sense. There are times when he seems to say it is superior, that indeed he is that kind of philosopher. But again he wants to qualify. "Speaking out and being socially committed," he says, "is not the only way of doing philosophy. Given my background I could make a case for the philosopher as spy. In any event, I will not be a martyr. I will speak to the leadership when it is ready to hear me. In my own ways, I will encourage and educate the leadership; within the confines of censorship that still operate in my country I will speak out, I will help the moment of liberation to come, and I will try to clarify that moment when it does come."

It is, of course, no longer literally censorship that inhibits Mamardashvili on this point. Principally it is what he calls the "very primitive social grammar" in the former Soviet Union, the result of long centuries of shadow existence. That is why Marxism struck so many Russians as a sophisticated political and economic philosophy. People didn't know the difference and were not equipped to examine it critically, in a historical perspective. There is still, says Mamardashvili, something woefully lacking in the average citizen's sense of reality, something broken in their relationship to the world around them. They lack drive, they lack a love of life, they lack the will to self-determination. They are what Arthur Koestler referred to in *Darkness at Noon* as people without consequence—that is, people who cannot understand social processes, who are unable to make social judgments, and who lack the ability every citizen must have to relate external events to their own internal convictions. In Marxist language, they are alienated.

"Some Westerners," says Mamardashvili, "say that what the Soviet Union needs is a good Constitution. But we have a good Constitution, perhaps the most democratic and forward looking of any in existence. The problem is that we have so few citizens who are capable of living according to it and realizing what is embodied in it. Recently, I was talking to some university students. They were complaining about the presence of so many policemen on their campus. I said, 'Why don't you organize and get rid of them?' These days that might have some chance of success. But they just gave me a blank look. That kind of self-determination hadn't occurred to them." Mamardashvili says his people must become eunuchs for the kingdom of heaven, using the biblical image as a metaphor to denounce anthropomorphic thinking. The kingdom of heaven is something that transcends particularity. As a Georgian, Mamardashvili says, "I love Georgia. But I must not be possessive about Georgia. As a citizen of the world and a thinker in history, I have the responsibility not to be egotistical in that way." (Mamardashvili often made biblical references in our conversation. At one point, I said he sounded like a religious fundamentalist. He laughed and said he found the Bible useful as a literary source. I suspected he found it more than that but I did not pursue the matter.)

Much cold war talk was an example of the primitive social grammar Mamardashvili speaks of, a deformity that afflicted partisans on both sides of the debate. Capitalism and socialism were spoken of as though they were two competing systems. But capitalism is not a system in the same way that socialism is a system. As Daniel Bell has pointed out, the Western democracies tend to be tripartite systems; they are at once an economic system, a political system, and a moral-cultural system. Each operates on a different vectorial axis, and although it may be true that in the recent past there is a convergence of these vectors, they still remain distinct—and capitalism denotes only the economic sector. It is one social phenomenon existing side by side with other social realities that are different in nature and account for a civil society in the Western democracies. Social energy is channeled through many social institutions and is driven by forces that are not necessarily related to capitalism. So a capitalist system, in the sense of a totalizing social force, does not exist.

But, says Mamardashvili, the same cannot be said about socialism. Socialism represents a system and a social structure that is totalizing; that is, one which by reason of its internal nature has penetrated all other social phenomena, including the moral and ideological strata. The problem for the Soviet Union, as Mamardashvili explains, is this: there is a socialist system but no developed civil society. "For us," he says, "the problem is to implement the socialist phenomenon, to convert what is so far the only system, into becoming only one phenomenon, along with other social forces, in a developed, articulated, and structured civil society in which socialism could really take its place."

And Mamardashvili insists that it should take a place. He stoutly defends socialism as an idea, "one of the great European ideas," as he puts it. He does not understand socialism as the welfare state. Quite the contrary. He deplores the welfare state as a nefarious instrument of enslavement, of making people dependent, of depriving people of a vital relationship with the sources of their existence which, Mamardashvili says, we develop through work and responsibility. The principle of welfare alienates people in precisely the sense Marx defined in his early writings. By socialism, Mamardashvili understands the principle of self-determination, a way of life and political structure in which citizens develop the degree of consciousness—the social judgment and the psychic muscles—for responsible, even risky, actions in a society where they cannot even imagine a life in which they would not recognize themselves or be "without consequence."

Mamardashvili puts it bluntly: "I do not want to live the kind of life in which I would not recognize myself. I could not consider that kind of life to be my life. Citizens are those who have not merely the right to take part in public affairs but are obligated to do so, are obligated to solve their own problems."

So our conversation turned finally, and inevitably, to *glasnost* and *perestroika* and the tumultuous events of late 1989 and 1990 that were unfolding in Eastern Europe. Again Mamardashvili was cautious. "The cat of reform is out of the bag and I do not think we can put it back in," he said. "Still, the outcome of the present efforts is far from certain. We are moving around in a kind of fog, and no one is quite sure about what is going on." He himself, of course, supports the reform movement and has since the 1950s, when a small band of rebel spirits, nourished on the writings of the early Marx, the great Russian writers of the nineteenth century (for whom already freedom was a central issue), and whatever other reading they could smuggle in from the West, would meet clandestinely to keep their thinking alive. "Some of our group went to concentration camps," Mamardashvili reflects ruefully, "some taught in obscure provincial schools, some went into exile, and some went my way of learning in the shadows, trying to keep out of trouble. And many died. In time, we came to have a certain influence."

Mamardashvili continued: "The idea of reform is solidly rooted in Russia and other republics of the Soviet Union today, not only among thinkers but among politicians and ordinary people as well. But it is by no means a guaranteed success. There is still the obstacle of a primitive social grammar; there is Gorbachev's precarious hold on political power; there is the problem of creating democratic structures (from scratch in most cases); there is the danger that whatever public spaces are created may be occupied by the wrong people."

Mamardashvili is unflinchingly realistic about this latter possibility. "There is no guarantee that civil society is always benign," he says. "Civil society corresponds to the historical possibilities of man; and history is a drama of good and evil. In this is the dignity of man: the choice of good and evil. There is no formula for human freedom or remedy for human idiocy. To think historically means to face this possibility squarely."

When I pointed out that we in the West tend to take a more pragmatic view of politics and resist dramatizing it in the bold colors of good and evil as historical drama, he gave me one of his rueful smiles and said nothing. But the smile said something, and I think I understood what it was. It said that when we strip politics of its historical and ethical underpinnings, when we reduce it to a zero-sum game of self-interest, when we substitute a concern for power and order for a concern with civic virtue (or conversely sink into a morass of utopian thinking), when the metaphor of the marketplace overrides a nobler ideal of excellence, then we are left with a very watery porridge. That is what I think the smile said. "In any case," Mamardashvili went on, "events have proved that the republican spirit still lives in the genetic memory of the Soviet Union. Reform is decidedly begun and in my own view it is now or never, the last chance for us to get on course. If this moment passes us by, another is not likely to come again soon."

I asked Mamardashvili what the most important piece of the puzzle is at this point. "Oh, education," he responded, as though he had rehearsed the answer. "Education. Definitely education." He again drew an image from his favorite poet, Rilke. Rilke said that the empty space through which a bird flies is changed by the bird's flight. It becomes, so to speak, full of bird meaning. Similarly, the spaces of our lives are changed by the meanings and values we impose upon them as we pass through. This, says Mamardashvili, is the work of education: to fill that which is empty, to animate that which is inanimate; to impose human meaning and name with a human voice what would otherwise be the impersonal passage of time. The job of education is the formation of the human: the ability to understand, to express ourselves in language and art, to celebrate and worship, to mourn and suffer, to enjoy and praise, and to die with dignity. In a word, to become conscious. If we do this well, we make a difference in the spaces we occupy, we make the world different. If we do this well, says Mamardashvili, then we can say with Rilke, "So after all we have not failed to make use of the spaces, these generous spaces, these our spaces."

It was a powerful metaphor. But it really comes from Plato, Mamardashvili pointed out. And so we concluded our conversation, as we had begun it, in the cave. "What attracted me to Plato," Mamardashvili said, "was his metaphor of the cave in which he depicts people struggling with the shadows. That was my problem, too. All my life I worked in the shadows. And Plato showed a way out; he showed that the shadows can be transcended by consciousness, by the ideal. In his great creation myth he shows how chaotic matter becomes a world, a human world, only after the infusion into it of intelligible, mind-governed ideas. That is where I think Rilke gets his image, and it is where I get my understanding of the function of education. And Plato showed further that there was not a complete rupture between the ideal and the reality. The *polis* can contain an ideal world as one element of its sociality. The body social is the carrier of rationality. Plato did not make the mistake of Marxist-Leninism: he did not let the ideal determine the real; rather he began with the real, with the shadows; and he reached the ideal in that way."

I carried three impressions away from my conversations with Mamardashvili. First, there was the strong sense of an encounter with a complex, ironic, and layered personality. Mamardashvili had lived all his life on the existential edge, in that lonely land between the permissible and the forbidden where his thinking was indeed "without bannisters," as Arendt so well put it. Much of the time he had been a knight fighting without armor. Perforce he developed strategies of indirect communication and paradox to parry the "either-ors" of existence. More than once he had felt the immediate threat of the gulag; and, although he was never imprisoned, he learned to think on the run. This kind of life has a way of toughening and maturing a person. Mamardashvili at sixty was a calm, collected, and considerate man. One is almost tempted to say that he had become at last a wise man, but for the certain knowledge that he would have rejected out of hand such a characterization. He remained, he would say, what he had always been: a seeker, still on the edge, with no final destination in sight.

Second, there was the clear articulation of a theory of consciousness at the core of his philosophy. Perhaps I shouldn't say clear, because it isn't always so; but it is surely central and clear enough in general outline. Certainly the basic message is clear: without consciousness the world is indeterminate; it is not a human world. Consciousness is awareness, insight, connectedness; and it is informed by all our experiences and all of our languages—the philosophical as well as the poetic, the religious, the aesthetic, and the political. At some point in the conversation Mamardashvili had said that it was through consciousness that we unite the dispersed elements of experience and take possession of ourselves. Plato claimed that is what philosophy will do in time; it is "like a blaze kindled by a leaping spark in the soul and at once becomes self-sustaining." One rarely meets anyone as deeply sustained by his philosophy as Mamardashvili, especially in America, where our commitment to ideas tends to be bland and instrumentalist. For Mamardashvili, philosophy was as much a way of life as a way of thought.

Finally, there was a lesson about politics, a profound lesson about civil society and deliberative democracy. As I thought about it after our conversation, it occurred to me that Mamardashvili might have found a better metaphor for his philosophy in Socrates than in Plato's cave: the Socrates who inhabited the sunlight spaces of a public world. One understands, of course, why Mamardashvili would be attracted to the cave image. After all, life in the Soviet Union was not unlike life in the cave as Plato described it. But Mamardashvili had wanted to get beyond the cave, and he did get beyond it; and where he got in his description of a civil society is much more comfortably accommodated and indeed explicated by Socrates.

Mamardashvili came to his notion of the civil society against the backdrop of a totalitarianism that denies plurality and closes off the forums of conversation. We do not have totalitarianism in America. But our reigning conception of politics, call it interest group politics for short, in its way does something of the same, if not to the same degree—which is to say, it impedes interactive conversation. We do not lack free speech; what we lack is deliberative speech. Americans are very good at talking past one another. We do not lack plurality; what we do lack is effective means of finding the *unum* in the *plurum*, of making our pluralism cohere. We are much better at focusing on what divides than on what unites us. Interest group politics is not adept at discovering common ground.

What interest group democracy leaves out is the whole area of shared values. Proponents of deliberative democracy deny there is some visible hand that will produce a common good out of aggregated interests. They deny that interest can be the cornerstone of a viable political system. What they hold to be more important is what concerns the totality of our political well-being, those larger interests that have been referred to us as "macromotives." When interests are thus broadly defined, deliberation becomes essential to the political process. It is the way we discover what our common interests are, the way we find the commonality in our most fundamental political motivations. When we learn how our individual or group self-interests tie to the common interests of the larger political community, we create the most potent of all our values—the political will to act.

Mamardashvili died ironically (as indeed he had lived) late in 1990 as the walls of totalitarianism were falling around him.

Democracy and Canada's Struggle for National Unity

This case study illustrates in the practical world of political give and take many of the issues that have been raised in the course of these conversations: liberalism and communitarianism, civil society and citizen participation, modernity and tradition, above all, the tensions and incompatibilities of democratic values.

Canada is either one of the world's most successful democracies or a country about to fall apart. In 1999, for the sixth consecutive year, the United Nations ranked Canada first among 174 nations in terms of human development, citing such criteria as earned income, life expectancy, education and political freedoms. "Canada can be described as on the human development efficiency frontier," the UN Human Development Report stated, "because it has translated its economic performance into the expansion of human capabilities with nearly maximal effectiveness."

But the United Nations assessment stands in marked contrast to the self-image many Canadians have of themselves and seems to gloss over some problems that are tearing at the fabric of the nation. Even the universal public health care system, which Canadians hold sacrosanct, is under fire. Over the past decade, the federal government has cut $22.2 billion (U.S.) from health care transfer payments to the provinces. These measures have quite severely affected health care services: hospitals are closing, merging, or reducing their bed capacity; doctors' incomes are capped; there are reductions in the number and type of medical procedures the government will pay for; waiting lists for surgery grow longer; and there is a shortage of medical technology. The inevitable result is the development of a two-tier system in which the government provides basic services and insurance companies provide the rest. And many wealthier Canadians buy medical insurance in the United States. As Robert Lewis, editor of *Maclean's* magazine, wrote in the February 24, 1997, issue: "Canadian health care, as we once knew it, no longer exists."

But by far the biggest problem in Canada is the threat to national unity brought about by the Quebec separatist movement. The referendum in October 1995, which the separatists came within a whisker of winning, had a traumatic effect on the whole country. Separatism is, of course, nothing new in Quebec. It has been an issue on and off since 1759 when the English defeated the French in the battle of the Plains of Abraham. Ever after the French Canadians have looked upon themselves as a conquered people, a subjugated culture in an alien English North America.

Their argument has a poignant simplicity: in the beginning the country was theirs; it is now time to take it back, at least that part of it which has been for centuries their home. The motto of Quebec is *je me souviens*—I remember. They remember, to be sure, the time when Canada was French. For some 150 years before the Pilgrims landed at Plymouth Rock they had been on the North American continent. By 1759, when the French army under Joseph Louis Montcalm was defeated by James Wolfe (both generals died in the battle), they had built durable elements of a cultural identity. They had a language, a religion, stable social institutions, a sound economy, and a concentrated population. But the Quebecois remember especially the long pain of defeat, the economic deprivations and the humiliation of being considered second rate in their own land. From the French Canadian point of view the Confederation of 1867 has always been an uneasy marriage of convenience, one in which the couple no longer sleeps in the same room.

This memory has served as the catacombs of their nationalistic spirit. It has been carefully preserved from generation to generation—handed on by the clergy, by writers and artists, by educators and politicians, and has now become an indivisible part of their folklore. In *Maria Chapdelaine,* one of the classics of French Canadian literature, a character sums up the Quebec mentality in these words: "Strangers have taken all the power and have acquired nearly all the wealth. But in the country of Quebec nothing has changed. Nothing will ever change for we are its witness. We have clearly understood what our duty is to ourselves and to our destiny: to hold fast, to ensure that, it may be, many centuries hence the world will look upon us and say: These people are of a race that knows not how to perish."

This almost mythic backdrop to the present separatist movement gives it a strong emotional undertow that few outsiders can grasp.

The story of the separatist movement since World War II is a fascinating piece of contemporary history and confronts Canada in a particularly dramatic fashion with the enduring democratic challenge of forging unity out of pluralism, of carrying on dialogue through conflict, and of combining aggressive economic policies with social justice. For our purposes here we can pick up the historical thread with Pierre Eliott Trudeau, one of the ablest and certainly the most colorful politician Canada has ever produced. Trudeau's interest—one might say passion—was constitutional reform, not separatism. But the two are so interwoven in recent Canadian history that we can't talk of one without talking about the other.

Trudeau was born in Montreal in 1918. His father was French Canadian and his mother of Anglo Scottish descent (whence his middle name). He received a classical education in his native city and eventually a law degree from the University of Montreal. He did graduate work at Harvard University and the London School of Economics and had been interested in the question of constitutional reform since the 1940s when it first began to be discussed seriously in Quebec. As a matter of fact, his first assignment on his first job in 1949 as a junior bureaucrat in Ottawa was to do research on replacing the British North American Act (BNA), a venerable piece of legislation that created the Canadian Federation in 1867 and remained virtually unchanged.

One reason the issue of constitutional reform arose in the 1940s is that the then prime minister Louis Saint-Laurent came to office trailing campaign promises to update the BNA. The not too subtle subtext was that any renewal would work in favor of the French Canadian population in Quebec. Saint-Laurent's successor, John Diefenbaker, also responded to Quebec pressure, and under his leadership the Fulton-Favreau proposal (as it came to be known) for constitutional amendment appeared. When Trudeau was elected a Member of Parliament in 1965 the constitutional debate heated up once again when John Robarts, the premier of Ontario, convened a First Ministers Conference to discuss the future of the Canadian Confederation.

By now the question of constitutional reform had become a veritable Pandora's box and Prime Minister Lester Pearson appointed Trudeau Minister of Justice in April of 1967 to find a ray of hope in the cacophony of voices that were beginning to emerge. At this time Trudeau was a constitutional conservative, arguing that the BNA was a worthy document and the best instrument for promoting federal interests and especially for stemming nationalist sentiment in Quebec.

Then one of those events that change history took place. The year 1967 was Canada's centennial year, and as part of the celebrations, French President Charles de Gaulle was invited to pay an official visit to Ottawa. Shortly afterward Daniel Johnson, then premier of Quebec, prevailed upon de Gaulle to visit his province before going on to the national capital. Whatever Johnson's reasons for this action were, the plan clearly fitted into de Gaulle's dream of a strong francophone presence on the international scene. So on July 23 he landed in Quebec City and was driven the next day to Montreal where he appeared before a large noonday crowd at city hall. There he pronounced his fateful words: *Vive le Québec libre!* The Quebec separatists were overjoyed, Ottawa canceled the visit, and Trudeau was outraged.

Six weeks later in a speech to the Canadian Bar Association, an occasion we may say marks his coming out as a constitutional activist, Trudeau proclaimed that a repatriated constitution with a charter of rights was the best way to make Canada a strong nation and deflect the rising separatist movement in Quebec. When he was elected Canada's thirteenth Prime Minister on June 25, 1968, he was ready for the constitutional task at hand. One could simplify, but not falsify, the accomplishments of Trudeau's tenure in two points: The Official Languages Act of 1968 and the Constitution Act of April 1982, whereby after years dogged effort and bone-numbing bargaining sessions with provincial premiers, Trudeau's dream of a national constitution was finally accomplished. Trudeau was widely criticized on both of these counts but I have always believed that his instincts were sound, at least in theory.

In practice they brought him much political grief and let yet more ills escape the Pandora's box of constitutional reform. Take the Official Languages Act. It stipulated that federal institutions must provide services in both English and French for all Canadian citizens. This meant, among other things, that bilingualism was a condition for advancement (or even for employment) not only in government agencies but as well in those companies like Air Canada and the Canadian Broadcasting Corporation that were operated by the federal government. All of a sudden everyone was enrolling in French immersion courses. But a backlash against bilingualism was not long in coming and remains strong to this day, particularly in the anglophone West. The question that continues to be asked, and not without reason, is: Why should the majority have to learn the language of the minority?

Trudeau moved quickly on the constitutional front. In June 1971 the First Ministers met in Victoria, British Columbia, and agreed on a formula for amending the constitution, an embryonic charter of rights and provincial approval for appointing Supreme Court judges. Robert Bourassa, now the premier of Quebec, signed the agreement but when he returned home he was so roundly criticized by the separatists that he withdrew his consent. After Victoria the gloves came off and the battle lines were drawn between Trudeau, staunch defender of federalism, and the growing separatist movement of Quebec which for the next decade would be led by the redoubtable René Lévesque.

Lévesque had formed the Parti Québécois (PQ) in 1968 with the avowed aim of taking Quebec out of the "creaky old double bed of Confederation." As he told a Toronto audience, "I sometimes find it hard to understand my French compatriots. But I understand the English damned well. They are poaching on our turf, a minority dominating a majority. The Confederation was created by the English for the English in order to head off an American invasion. Today the Confederation is seen in Quebec as a small sailor's suit on a growing child. We want to finish our quiet revolution." And he told the same audience: "I am a Quebecker first, a French Canadian second, and I really have . . . well, no sense at all of being a Canadian."

Lévesque's election was a blow to Trudeau's constitutional efforts because he was a fiery obstructionist in negotiation meetings and would have no truck with any constitutional arrangement that did not give Quebec, as he put it, "a guarantee that it will obtain all the powers it needs in order to ensure its development." Such a guarantee would minimally have to include distinct status for Quebec—to which Trudeau was opposed. In his vision of the new federalism all provinces would be equal and none distinct. Lévesque was also after more economic power for Quebec. Since the Conquest, the economic argument for separatism runs, Quebeckers have been treated like a colonial people, first by the English then by the English Canadians and most recently by the Americans. Quebec has supplied the resources and cheap labor, but the profits have gone elsewhere.

The PQ has steadfastly maintained that an independent Quebec would be economically viable, that the province has all the human and material resources necessary for independence. The economic argument for an independent Quebec is stronger today than ever before. Studies show that Quebec would have a Gross Domestic Product equivalent to that of countries like Austria and Belgium. Separatists are prepared for a difficult period of transition and are even resigned to suffering a lower standard of living for a time. But they view these short-run sacrifices in light of the long-run gain of controlling their own economic development. In Canada, they point out, the economic lines run as much north and south as east and west. While American investors would be jittery for the transitional period, it is not expected that they will turn their backs on profit-making opportunities in Quebec indefinitely. After eliminating the federal middle man, Quebec can deal with American and other investors on its own terms. "In a country that was supposedly founded on the dignity of the person," argued Lévesque, "it is no longer conceivable that the economy of Quebec should be geared to the advantage of outsiders."

High on Lévesque's agenda was a referendum on sovereignty-association which took place on May 20, 1980. Trudeau played a major role in the defeat of that referendum but at considerable political cost. Henceforward Lévesque would stonewall every move Trudeau made to create a constitution. Trudeau was by this time facing trouble on another front. Throughout the '70s he continued to meet with the provincial premiers to work towards agreement on constitutional reform. And throughout that decade the premiers became increasingly uncooperative. They were, as Trudeau put it, "catching the Quebec disease" and making demands of their own. Their game plan was to get as much power as possible transferred to the provinces with respect to regional economic resources, social programs, senate reform, Supreme Court appointments, and a host of other matters.

Trudeau played hedgehog to their fox. They wanted many things; he wanted one thing. Back and forth the battle raged. Trudeau threatened to proceed unilaterally on constitutional reform. The provinces demanded a supreme court ruling on the question. The court ruled that such an action would be legal but unconstitutional, an ambiguous decision that forced a final First Ministers meeting in November 1981, in which an agreement was reached. In April 1982, the most important date in Trudeau's career, the constitution was signed in the presence of Queen Elizabeth II. Predictably Quebec was not a signatory to the transaction. Thus a dark cloud hung over Trudeau's victory. Even as the new constitution was being signed into law—The Constitution Act of 1982—René Lévesque was telling an audience in Montreal: "This horror of a constitution was made against us and behind our backs." Efforts to bring Quebec back to the table dominated Canadian politics for the next decade, to the great dismay of many, probably the majority of Canadians, who were now fed up with constitution talk and were especially fed up with the incessant demands emanating from Quebec. A strong feeling began to build in English Canada that it would be perhaps best if Quebec separated. Trudeau for his part felt that no further discussion was necessary. The deed was done, the new constitution was binding on all of Canada, and the rantings of Lévesque and his cohorts were but the sour grapes of separatist losers.

But that is not the way the politics of the situation were destined to unfold. For one thing Trudeau's stand ignored a stubborn political fact: the Quebec problem, including the separatist movement, was not going away; nor could it be solved either by lofty rhetoric about national unity or legal devices like supreme court rulings. Quebec's aspirations are rooted in a long history; they are genuine and legitimate, although to be sure exasperating. At bottom they constitute a moral *cri de coeur* that ought to be and indeed can be accommodated by a creative political process. English Canada ought to recognize this if only for reasons of self-interest. It was clearly recognized by Brian Mulroney, elected prime minister in 1984. He committed his government to an all-out effort to secure Quebec's consent to the new Canadian constitution. The Quebec government, once again under the leadership of Liberal Robert Bourassa (who ousted Lévesque in 1983), thought they could do business with Mulroney and were encouraged to negotiate. Accordingly, in May 1986, they put forth a list of five demands as the condition of their agreement to the Constitution. They were:

1. recognition of Quebec as a distinct society;
2. a provincial role in appointments to the supreme court;
3. a greater provincial role in immigration;
4. limits on federal power in federal-provincial shared cost programs; and
5. a veto for Quebec on constitutional amendments.

On April 30, the First Ministers met at Meech Lake (a resort north of Ottawa) and agreed on a "Draft Statement of Principles" which addressed (some would say caved in to) the Quebec demands and a few weeks later signed the document called the Meech Lake Accord. It was ratified on June 20, 1988, by the Parliament of Canada and then sent to the provincial legislatures for their ratification by June 23, 1990. (Shrewd observers detected in so long a ratification period a political pitfall.) Throughout this process Mulroney had shown himself generously accommodating.

Quebec was delighted with the deal. As Premier Robert Bourassa put it: "We didn't expect after 20 years to reach an agreement. Then suddenly, without warning, there it is: an agreement. We could have waited until next year; we could have waited until after the next federal election. We were under no pressure. I was serene, but when I saw that it was falling to us piece by piece, I said to myself: *Bien voilà!* There it is." There were few enthusiastic voices in the rest of Canada. The Accord was immediately subject to a barrage of criticisms: it was said to be elitist, undemocratic, hastily drawn up, poorly drafted; there was no public debate; the veto clause was troublesome, making unanimity among the provinces a condition of any future change (as a joke at the time had it: Before Meech Lake there was fear that Canada would become two countries; after, the danger was that it would become ten countries); women, native Indians and multicultural groups protested they weren't given a fair shake. Indeed, there was no political necessity to revisit the constitutional question at that time. It came about, it was widely believed, as a result of Mulroney's opportunism in securing the Quebec vote.

When the June 30 deadline passed two provinces (Manitoba and Newfoundland) had failed to ratify the Accord. A patch-up effort called the Charlottetown Accord also failed in a national referendum on October 26, 1992. Thus a generation of intense constitutional debate and legislation ground to a halt. A document on which such high hopes had rested was dead in the water. The Meech Lake Accord failed for many reasons. Patrick Monahan, in his thorough *Meech Lake: The Inside Story*, argues quite plausibly that it was primarily the distinct society clause that did it in.

The Canadian experience underscores a central political debate of our time in a nutshell. Do individual rights take precedence over collective ends? Does autonomy trump substantive views of the good life? Must we settle for common procedures over agreed-upon ends precisely because we cannot agree upon what those ends would be? Charles Taylor, a prominent Canadian political philosopher (who incidentally ran against Trudeau for Member of Parliament in 1965), frames the debate in these words in his *Reconciling the Solitudes*.

"Two incompatible views of liberal society have come to square off against one another. The resistance to the distinct society which called for precedence to be given to the Charter came in part from a spreading procedural outlook in English Canada. From this point of view, attributing the goal of promoting Quebec's distinct society to a government was to acknowledge a collective goal, and this move had to be neutralized by being subordinated to the existing Charter. From the standpoint of Quebec, this attempt to impose a procedural model of liberalism not only would deprive the distinct society clause of some of its force but it bespoke a rejection of the [communitarian] model of liberalism on which Quebec society was founded."

Can these opposing views be mediated? We seem to be face to face with incompatible values à la Isaiah Berlin. But Taylor is not willing to throw in the towel. It is not likely that the differences can be settled on ideological grounds. Taylor advocates what he calls "deep diversity," a plurality of ways of belonging to the same polity, as the solution. "Procedural liberals in English Canada," he says, "just have to acknowledge first that there are other possible models of liberal society, and second that their francophone compatriots wish to live by one such alternative. The only way we can coexist is by allowing ourselves to differ on this. So let us recognize this now and take the road to deep diversity together."

Taylor has been writing on democracy and the problems of multiculturalism throughout a long career. In his 1991 book *The Politics of Recognition*, a title that calls attention to the fact that many political issues today are driven by the demand on the part of individuals and groups for recognition, he argues that our identities are dialogical, shaped by our interactions with other people, through language and culture. Part of who we are depends on how we are esteemed by others. This dialogical nature of our identities has implications for our understanding of equality. Equality in one sense, the most generally understood sense, means equality of rights. But another view of equality, what Taylor calls the "politics of difference," directs us to recognize the distinctness of others. This distinctness, says Taylor, "is precisely what has been ignored, glossed over, assimilated to a dominant or majority identity"—in other words, repressed by the universalist ideal of the Enlightenment.

Taylor's philosophy supports the Quebec claim for a distinct society, including the rather harsh language laws that have been enacted there. If the survival and flourishing of French culture in Quebec is a good, then the government there cannot be neutral between the collective goods of that culture and those who would favor a more individualistic politics. Nor can the Quebec model be written off as merely parochial. Taylor sees it as a guide for the multicultural world of the future. If democracy is going to work on a global scale it will have to be pluralistic in character. Taylor puts it this way: "If a uniform model of citizenship fits better the classical image of the Western liberal state, it is also true that this is a straightjacket for many political societies. The world needs other models to be legitimated in order to allow for more human and less constraining modes of political cohabitation. Instead of pushing ourselves to the point of breakup in the name of the uniform model, we would do our own and some other peoples a favor by exploring the space of deep diversity."

Taylor's position might be called strong multiculturalism. Whether it will work or not is not clear. But it is at least an intellectually rigorous attempt to deal with a political problem that strikes many as intractable.

Meanwhile, the separatist problem is in remission. Jean Chrétien called a premature election in June of 1997, and as expected his liberal government won. But it was hardly a cakewalk and left Canada, as *Maclean's* magazine reported, "a nation splintered as never before." A Quebec election was held on November 30, 1998. Again as expected the separatist party won, but by a very narrow margin. Lucien Bouchard, the PQ leader, says he will not call another referendum until what he calls the "winning conditions" for another referendum are present. He has also made it clear that his government remains committed to a sovereignty referendum during its current mandate, which would mean sometime before the year 2002. What then? Nobody knows.

As a precaution, the federal government continues to offer olive branches. Parliament passed a bill granting Quebec a veto over all future constitutional amendments. Parliament also passed a nonbinding resolution committing the federal government to a "distinct clause" in a revised Constitution. The rest of Canada (ROC) is little inclined to accepted either of these proposals. As well, the government is engaged in an ongoing (but painfully slow) process of devolving more power to the provinces. Such efforts are referred to as Plan A— an umbrella term covering the federal government's efforts to keep Quebec in the confederation. Plan B refers to a variety of what-if scenarios anticipating the eventual separation of Quebec.

Most recently, in December 1999, Prime Minister Chrétien tabled legislation which requires a "clear majority" voting on a "clear question" on secession. This was a response to an earlier Supreme Court decision authorizing the House of Commons in Ottawa to rule on the clarity of any secessionist question coming from a provincial legislature. This "Clarity Act" is intended to solve two problems: the deliberately vague language of the two earlier secession referendums (many didn't know what they were voting for); and second, to force discussion on many questions the separatists are not anxious to face—questions like the right of English-speaking parts of Quebec to secede if they choose, the rights of Indian and Inuit minorities, Quebec's share of Canada's $400 billion debt, defense questions, and so forth.

Quebecois were outraged by the federal initiative. Newspapers ran screaming headlines. PQ leaders fumed. A group of grass-roots, pro-secession organizations took out a fullpage ad in the December 20, 1999, edition of the *New York Times* protesting that Chrétien's bill "would put the people of Quebec in a political straitjacket, negating their fundamental right to self-determination." The people of Quebec, the ad proclaimed, "will never forfeit their right to freely decide their own future."

The separatist issue, which had been losing momentum, was now once again at the center of attention, strengthening Lucien Bouchard's resolve to call another referendum as promised. Can he win? He might. Michael Behiels, professor of Canadian history at the University of Ottawa, told me that if he does "all hell will break loose." ROC would be unprepared to deal with such a situation. Behiels, echoing Taylor, does not think that constitutional reform is the way to deal with problems "that are essentially matters of ethics and justice."

By the year 2002 a lot of things can happen. One of the things that could happen, according to James Reed, editor of *The American Canada Watch*, is that a deal will be struck. Canadians have struck many political deals in their history and are quite capable of doing so again. If they do not, one would have to ask some tough questions about the strength of democracy: Are our political options so pale and narrow? Has the tradition of dialogue, the life blood of all political life, so evaporated? Are the conditions of generating political will so fragile? Are human rights to be enshrined in charters but trammeled in reality? If one of the most successful democracies cannot hold the center, what kind of signal does that send?

It is not clear to me, or many others who stand on the edge of the debate, why attitudes have so hardened. One understands that a lot of history is in play, and a lot of emotion and symbolism. A major factor, as I see it, is the rise of the West as a dominant power on the Canadian scene; recent elections lend support to this opinion. In times past, Ontario spoke for English Canada. And Ontario is geographically closer to Quebec and traditionally politically sympathetic as well. The West, on the other hand, is far away and could care less about the problems of Quebec.

But the question persists: What does Quebec want that the rest of Canada won't give? And wouldn't they give a lot, and give generously, to keep Quebec in? It's hard to imagine Canada without Quebec. I wouldn't go so far as to say Quebec is the soul of Canada. But I agree with what Canadian writer Peter Newman told me: "Quebec has always set the cultural tone of Canada. Now it commands our political mood as well. Only in Quebec has there grown a spirit of self-determination, an interior kind of romantic mythology, which eventually translated itself into political power. The Quebec revolution proved that a vibrant politics requires a vibrant culture."

In 1945 Canadian novelist Hugh MacLennan published a widely read book on the French-English problem in Canada entitled *Two Solitudes*. One could get the impression today that the two solitudes are virtually unbridgeable. The difficulties of trying to communicate across so much history and such cultural difference are enormous. Anglophones say the French are demanding too much, that they dream of a Quebec that can never exist in the modern world. The French stress the accumulated injustices and rejection they have suffered at the hands of the English. And they remember, with a memory that winds back over their past to the time of their beginnings, isolating them from the common ground of dialogue.

Still and all, two solitudes is the wrong metaphor. It not only does not capture all that goes on between the two "founding nations" of Canada but it exacerbates their differences in politically unfruitful ways. I find a better metaphor in something Marshall McLuhan once said. In *The Global Village* he spoke of the borderline mentality of Canadians. Canadians, McLuhan said, are an "in between" kind of people which makes them adept in the roles of dialogue, forming liaisons, and making deals. Such a mentality is especially appropriate to the electronic age of decentralization and low profile identities, McLuhan wrote, and produces "great vortices" of political energy and power, a sense of "political ecumenism" lacking in larger and more sharply defined nations.

Political ecumenism! What a great metaphor! And how suited to the challenge of Canadian unity. And how exemplary for the larger world which itself seems so often to stand on the brink of dismemberment.

Afterword

It is now time for some concluding words.

These conversations were not conceived according to any grand plan or logical scheme, although they do have a certain logic as indicated by the table of contents.

My intention was to have some good conversation on the subject of democracy with some intelligent and interesting people, in a more or less spontaneous fashion and as in my travels and readings such people came to my attention.

I have been above all concerned to emphasize the dialogic character of democracy. Democracy was born in dialogue and dialogue remains its energizing principle. Dialogue, we may say, in all of its forums of debate and deliberation, of controversy and choice is the premier civic virtue of a democratic society. For this reason Charles Taylor's ideas struck a special chord with me and his analysis of the Canadian situation seems exemplary for wider application.

My own interest in the subject of democracy goes back to graduate school and my reading of the early Platonic dialogues. I was impressed by the fact that the dialogic method in philosophy emerged at a time when the Greeks were experiencing the first flush of their democracy. The conjunction between the two is not accidental but natural and necessary. The dialogic method is the democratic way of arriving at truth. Socrates went about talking with his fellow citizens. He wanted to know how the world looked to them and what they thought about things.

Political meaning is disclosed, as Hannah Arendt nicely puts it, when Socrates the citizen enters into dialogue with other citizens, not primarily to persuade them of anything but to find out what and how they think. The subtext here is that thinking is itself an important democratic virtue. What

Socratic inquiry revealed is that the world appears differently to different individuals. This sets both the political and philosophical problem: How can a public world be formed from the plural and the diverse? How can individual ideas lead to public truth? The means by which Socrates educed a public world was called midwifery; which is to say, the political art of determining the contours of our public spaces through conversation. This effort, to be sure, is always inconclusive, but without it no beginning is possible. We converse because we see things differently; we deliberate because we can find the common in the fleeting fragments of our political experience.

Overall, the conversations in this book reflect the main concerns and tensions in contemporary political theory. In America virtually all of our debates fall between the liberal and communitarian, or what some would call the republican, poles of political thought. The liberal strand can be traced from Locke and Kant, through the utilitarian axis to rational choice theory. The communitarian strand originates with classical republicanism and comes down through Rousseau to Marx and present-day varieties of socialism. To simplify somewhat (but not overly), we can say the core value of the liberal tradition is autonomy, with an emphasis on individual freedoms and rights. Conversely, the core value of the republican tradition is civic virtue and the responsibilities of an active citizenry for the common good. Republicanism gives primacy to the public over the private. Liberalism reverses that primacy. Liberal thinkers like Adam Smith and David Hume claimed that the private, that is, economic activity, was the essential realm of life. Hume famously said that given a choice between a despotism under the rule of law which would protect property and his economic rights, and democracy, which wouldn't, he would choose the former. In the liberal paradigm the public fades to secondary importance and the ideal of rights-bearing individuals comes to the fore. The state is ancillary to the pursuits of private interests, and the virtues of citizenship give place to the efficacy of checking and balancing mechanisms.

These polar values generate endless discussion about private morality and public issues. They underlie our entire civic culture. And indeed they are often incompatible. But when we say values are incompatible we aren't saying anything very politically significant. At this point Berlin's thesis must be highly qualified. It is obvious that values conflict. But we can't leave it there. Democracy from the time of the Greeks embodies the notion of public reason which enables us to deliberate across differences. The genius of democracy is to find common ground in polar opposites. This is the wellspring of democracy's vitality, the badge of its superiority to other political regimes.

This course was set early in the history of America, in the Federalist-Antifederalist debates that preceded the signing of the Constitution and in the debates about the Constitution itself. The Antifederalists drew upon the long tradition of republicanism to put forth a view of human nature and a set of values which they enunciated with great clarity and adhered to with great passion. They stood for equality, fear of big government, local roots, participation, the public good, agrarianism, citizen virtue, and populism. The Federalists for their part had a different view and embraced different values. They argued that the values urged by the Antifederalists, values which largely sustained the American Revolution, were inadequate for the new nation they had in mind. The failure of the Articles of Confederation supported their position. As George Washington put it, "We have probably had too good an opinion of human nature in forming our confederation."

The Federalists were convinced that no political system could be built on the basis of citizen virtue or any other such "soft" values. They assumed that human beings on the whole were little prone to virtuous action in the public sphere, much more likely to pursue their selfish interests at the expense of the common good. The Federalists had a relatively high tolerance for human vice and were willing to accept the risks of freedom, even the risk of frequent social chaos. The passions and interests that drove human action could not be stemmed, only harnessed. Thus the Federalists emphasized individual rights and freedoms, commerce, weak citizenship, and strong government with effective checks and balances: in a word, what we now recognize as the liberal strand of political values.

These early debates put at the center of our political dialogue a long list of hyphenations: individual-community, organic-mechanistic, democracy-elitism, unitary-plural, federal-state, empiricism-rationalism, private-public, belief-unbelief, country-city, virtue-luxury, rights-responsibilities, idealism-materialism, and a particularly grievous hyphenation, what Gordon Wood has called "the beginning of a hiatus in American politics between ideology and motives that was never again closed."

The list of such hyphenations is virtually endless and, as noted, the source of great social tensions. There are always extremists who opt strongly for one side of the spectrum against the other. They are certainly heard in the land today, and indeed across the globe. The struggle of the Quebec separatists, reported in this book, is a case in point.

But nothing is really new here. The democratic dynamic remains what it has always been: an abiding challenge to reconcile the opposites, to engage in a pragmatic search for balance. Hyphenation implies unity as much as it implies separation, the joining together of the dissimilar. The distinctions we introduce into our political language are rarely as sharp as they first appear. All contemporary political theories, as Will Kymlicka reminds us, work on the "egalitarian plateau" and assume all human beings are of equal moral worth and are equal bearers of basic rights. We paint ourselves into a corner by reifying distinctions that are otherwise helpful. Look, for example, at how readily we pit the values of liberalism against those of communitarianism, perhaps a legacy from Tocqueville. But as Richard Dagger quite rightly says in an article in the fall 1990 *Civic Arts Review*, these are not incompatible values but "two sides of the same conception of the relationship between individuals and the political order." Or again, Kymlicka in the winter 1997 *Review of Politics:* "Liberalism has consistently held that individuals are free to choose their own life plans and their own conceptions of the good. It follows that they are free to choose membership in ethnic or multicultural groups."

The constitutional debates, long held to be exemplary of political discourse, were an amalgam of different views and values, a matchless example of finding common ground. Thus James Madison argued for a strong, central government yet firmly believed in popular sovereignty; he held to a realistic view of human nature but also advocated the necessity of civic virtue; he favored commerce but also shared some of Jefferson's agrarian sentiments. Liberal and republican elements were quite thoroughly mixed in his thinking.

This we may say is the democratic paradigm. It is not easy. The examined life is painful. At times it seems impossible, especially since democracy seems to be undergoing one of its periodic legitimation crises. But it is a crisis of a peculiar sort, not so much a disbelief in the idea of democracy which is everywhere triumphant as a vexing puzzlement about why it doesn't work better in practice. As a Czech friend told me when I asked him how democracy was progressing in his country: "It is working as badly here as everywhere else." This discontent is everywhere in evidence and is exacerbated by the new economic and global conditions that are emerging. We all at one time or another pine for an easier politics.

Democracy may not be for the ages. But at this time in history, for good and sound reasons, there is no persuasive alternative.

Selected Bibliography

Arendt, Hannah. *The Human Condition*. New York: Doubleday, 1955.

Barber, Benjamin. *Strong Democracy: Participatory Politics for a New Age*. Berkeley: University of California Press, 1984.

———. *Jihad vs. McWorld*. New York: Times Books, 1995.

Berlin, Isaiah. *Four Essays on Liberty*. London and New York: Oxford University Press, 1969.

Bryce, James. *Modern Democracies*. New York: Macmillan, 1921.

Connolly, William. *Political Theory and Modernity*. London and New York: Oxford University Press, 1988.

———. *Identity / Difference: Democratic Negotiations of Political Paradox*. Ithaca: Cornell University Press, 1991.

Crozier, Michael, Samuel P. Huntington and Joji Watanuki. *The Crisis of Democracy: Report on the Governability of Democracies to the Trilateral Commission*. New York: New York University Press, 1975.

Boorstin, Daniel. *Democracy and Its Discontents: Reflections on Everyday America*. New York: Random House, 1974.

Dahl, Robert Alan. *Democracy and Its Critics*. New Haven: Yale University Press, 1989.

Dionne, E. J., ed. *Community Works: The Revival of Civil Society in America*. Washington, D.C.: Brookings Institution, 1998.

Dunn, John, ed. *Democracy: The Unfinished Journey 508 B.C. to A.D. 1993*. New York: Oxford University Press, 1992.

Elshtain, Jean Bethke. *Democracy on Trial*. New York: Basic Books, 1995.

Fishkin, James S. *The Voice of the People: Public Opinion and Democracy*. New Haven: Yale University Press, 1992.

Fullenwider, Robert K., ed. *Civil Society, Democracy, and Civic Renewal*. Lanham, Md.: Rowman & Littlefield, 1999.

Habermas, Jürgen. *Legitimation Crisis*. Trans. by Thomas McCarthy. Boston: Beacon Press, 1975.

Held, David, ed. *Prospects for Democracy: North, South, East, West.* Stanford, Calif.: Stanford University Press, 1993.

Kemmis, Daniel. *Community and the Politics of Place.* Norman: University of Oklahoma Press, 1990.

―――. *The Good City and the Good Life.* Boston: Houghton Mifflin Co., 1995.

Kennon, Patrick. *The Twilight of Democracy.* New York: Doubleday, 1995.

Kingwell, Mark. *Better Living: In Pursuit of Happiness from Plato to Prozac.* Toronto: Penguin, 1998.

Kroker, Arthur and David Cook. *The Postmodern Scene: Excremental Culture and Hyper-Aesthetics.* New York: St. Martin's Press, 1986.

Kroker, Arthur and Michael A. Weinstein. *Data Trash: The Theory of the Virtual Class.* New York: St. Martin's Press, 1994.

Lakoff, Sanford. *Democracy: History, Theory, Practice.* Boulder, Colo.: Westview Press, 1996.

Lasch, Christopher. *The Culture of Narcissism: American Life in an Age of Diminishing Expectations.* New York: W. W. Norton, 1978.

―――. *True and Only Heaven: Progress and Its Critics.* New York: W. W. Norton, 1991.

―――. *The Revolt of the Elites: And the Betrayal of Democracy.* New York: W. W. Norton, 1995.

MacIntyre, Alasdair C. *After Virtue: A Study in Moral Virtue.* Notre Dame, Ind.: University of Notre Dame Press, 1981.

Marcus, George E. and Russell L. Hanson, eds. *Reconsidering the Democratic Public.* University Park, Pa.: Pennsylvania State University Press, 1993.

Mathews, David. *Politics for People.* Urbana-Champaign: University of Illinois Press, 1999.

Matustik, Martin. *Postnational Identity: Critical Theory and Existential Philosophy in Habermas, Kierkegaard, and Havel.* New York: Guilford Press, 1993.

Mueller, John E. *Capitalism, Democracy, and Ralph's Pretty Good Grocery.* Princeton, N.J.: Princeton University Press, 1999.

Murchland, Bernard. *Voices in America: Bicentennial Conversations.* Ann Arbor, Mich.: Prakken Publications, 1987.

―――. *Higher Education and the Practice of Democratic Politics: A Political Education Reader.* Dayton, Ohio: The Kettering Foundation, 1991.

Pateman, Carole. *Participation and Democratic Theory.* Cambridge, England: Cambridge University Press, 1970.

Popper, Karl R. *The Open Society and Its Enemies.* London: G. Routledge, 1945.

Putnam, Robert D. with Robert Leonardi and Raffaella Nanetti. *Making Democracy Work: Civic Traditions in Modern Italy.* Princeton, N.J.: Princeton University Press, 1993.

Riker, William H. *Democracy in the United States.* 2d ed. New York: Macmillan, 1965.

Sandel, Michael. *Democracy's Discontent: America in Search of a Public Philosophy.* Cambridge, Mass.: Harvard University Press, 1996.

Saul, John Ralston. *The Unconscious Civilization.* West Concord, Ontario: Anansi, 1995.

Skocpol, Theda and Morris P. Fiorina, eds. *Civic Engagement in American Democracy.* Washington, D.C.: Brookings Institution, 1999.

Taylor, Charles. *Multiculturalism and "The Politics of Recognition": An Essay.* Princeton, N.J.: Princeton University Press, 1992.

———. *Reconciling the Solitudes: Essays on Canadian Federalism and Nationalism.* Edited by Guy Laforest. Montreal: McGill-Queen's University Press, 1993.

Tocqueville, Alexis de. *Democracy in America.* New York: Vintage, 1990.

Yankelovich, Daniel. *Coming to Public Judgment: Making Democracy Work in a Complex World.* Syracuse, N.Y.: Syracuse University Press, 1991.

———. *The Magic of Dialogue: Transforming Conflict into Cooperation.* New York: Simon and Schuster, 1999.

Index